The Heinemann
Accountancy and Ad

General
J. BATTY, DCom.(SA), M
MInst.AM, MIPM

THEORY
AND PRACTICE
OF INVESTMENT

THEORY
AND PRACTICE
OF INVESTMENT

T. G. GOFF FIB (SCOT)

HEINEMANN : LONDON

William Heinemann Ltd
10 Upper Grosvenor Street, London W1X 9PA
LONDON MELBOURNE
JOHANNESBURG AUCKLAND

First published 1971
Second edition 1975
Revised reprint 1978
Third edition 1980
Reprinted 1980, 1981
Fourth edition 1982
Fifth edition 1986

British Library Cataloguing in Publication Data

Goff, T. G.
  Theory and practice of investment. –
  5th ed.
  1. Investments
  I. Title
  332.6   HG4521

ISBN 0 434 90663 8

Phototypeset by Wilmaset, Birkenhead, Wirral
Printed in Great Britain by
Redwood Burn Ltd, Trowbridge

Contents

Foreword

The *Heinemann Accountancy and Administration Series* is intended to fill a gap in the literature that caters for accountants, company secretaries, and similar professional people who are engaged in giving a vital information service to management. As far as possible, due recognition is given to the fact that there are two distinct bodies of readers: those who aspire to professional status – the students – and others who are already managing and/or serving management.

This book covers the theory and practice of investment. The latter includes all expenditure incurred with the object of obtaining income, capital gains or other benefit. The motives of the investor may be to receive a high rate of income; alternatively, the main concern may be to transfer money to an asset which will be secure without any appreciable reduction in its real value. Some investments are primarily of a short-term nature, whereas others favour a longer period. There are many other different characteristics each of which is possessed to a smaller or larger degree by each type of investment.

Because of the multitude of possible investments and their many differences in terms of income, risk, stability of value or other factor, *expert advice* becomes essential. An adviser should possess all the theoretical knowledge and, at the same time, be experienced in the capacity of investment management. Fortunately, Mr T. G. Goff possesses these qualities and is also an experienced lecturer.

In this book Mr Goff has encompassed the whole field of investment in a very concise and readable fashion. Being a book primarily for students the main emphasis is given to the *basic* facts and principles. I am sure these students will find the book of great value in their studies. At the same time, *all* who are interested in investing funds whether as bankers, accountants, stockbrokers, solicitors, company secretaries or investment managers will find this practical manual a very useful work of reference.

J. Batty, Editor

Preface

The impetus for the writing of this book arose from the examinations on investment set by the Institute of Bankers and the Institute of Bankers in Scotland. These examinations are based on wide-ranging syllabuses covering the types of investment available to United Kingdom residents, stock exchange practice, the structure of the joint stock company, share assessment, portfolio management, etc.

Some of these subjects require a thoroughly detailed study while others demand only a more general understanding. For example, a student must be completely familiar with the distinction between fixed interest and equity investment but is not expected to be the master of, say, all the facets of corporation tax.

Many excellent publications are available on investment and allied subjects. It is, however, felt that no single book or combination of books is entirely satisfactory for the student. There is, therefore, a gap to be filled and in an endeavour to do so this book has been written giving, it is hoped, the proper degree of emphasis as and where required.

While the Institutes of Bankers' syllabuses gave rise to the book the requirements of all students of investment have been kept in mind. Basically the subject remains very much the same no matter who is studying it. Teachers of commercial education who may not themselves have had the opportunity of practical experience in financial affairs may also find the book to be of some value.

As far as the more general reader is concerned this is obviously not a 'get rich quick' book, nor is it presented in a racy style. It is quite frankly for someone who for professional reasons must, or for personal reasons desires, to understand the fundamentals in the world of investment. These mastered then he/she is the better equipped to cope with the problems of looking after money, either in the capacity of adviser to others or on his/her own behalf.

A difficulty when writing a book of this nature is the using of tax rates in examples. Ideally one would wish to use current rates but as these are constantly changing it would be a matter of pure chance if the rates applicable at the time of writing remained the same for any lengthy period after publication. Accordingly it has been decided, except where indicated otherwise, to work examples with corporation tax at 50%, advance corporation tax and basic rate income tax at 30%, and the flat rate of capital gains tax at 30%. Readers will, when tackling practical problems, require to use the appropriate current rates which are, of course, readily available in order to obtain the information which they require.

The author wishes to thank the Institute of Bankers, the Institute of Bankers in Scotland, the Savings Bank Institute, and the Chartered Institute of Secretaries, who have granted permission for the publication of their examination questions, also the Stock Exchange for its prompt response to requests for information. Specimen answers, where given, are provided solely by the author. He also wishes to thank his colleague, Mr Iain H. Muir, for carefully reading most of the typescript and making several useful suggestions.

T. G. G.

1 Preliminary look-round

People vary considerably in their attitude towards money. Some regard it as something to be spent and enjoyed as and when it is received. They soon acquire, if it is not already inbred, a high degree of expertise in developing their spending propensities and even huge sums can be disposed of in an amazingly short space of time. Clearly such people can remain blissfully ignorant of the problems attaching to investment.

Others, when they come into possession of a sum of money over and above what is required for their everyday requirements will wish to employ it in some dynamic manner with a view to rapidly producing from it a vastly greater sum. This will almost certainly lead them along the paths of some venturesome although not necessarily unworthy enterprise. They will rely either on their exceptional ability or good fortune and must be prepared to suffer substantial loss should their plans go awry. By temperament the cautious approach to investment which sets great store on the avoidance of loss of capital will have little appeal to them.

A large number of people, however, will be content to invest their cash surplus in such a way that it will maintain its real value while at the same time earning for them a reasonable return. Superficially it might appear that the relatively modest requirements of this latter group might easily be met. In the heyday of 'Soames Forsyte' this might have been so but in the present era of inflation and high taxation it is far from being the case. What might appear to be safe investments may, because of these two factors, be actually yielding an overall negative return to their owners. In other words, the annual rate of inflation may be depreciating the value of their capital by more than the net income which they receive from this capital. This is a far from satisfactory state of affairs which, obviously, the successful investor must avoid.

Over the years many ways, some of them highly sophisticated, of saving and investing money have been developed. It is essential that anyone who wishes to look after money prudently should be aware of all the possibilities open to him/her and appreciate such advantages and disadvantages attaching to each in the light of his/her particular circumstances and investment objectives.

In this first chapter it is proposed to make a brief survey of several non-Stock Exchange investments. Some of these are of interest not only to the small saver who cannot afford to take any of the risks associated with Stock Exchange investment but also to richer investors as they provide them with remunerative repositories for their liquid funds.

1.1 National savings

All forms of national savings are in effect loans to the Government and can, therefore, be regarded as being absolutely safe in money values. The terms given for each category are those current at the time of writing. They do in many cases vary considerably over the years but the general characteristics of each remain relatively constant.

1.11 *National Savings Bank Accounts*

These accounts, which are operated through the medium of the Post Office, fall into two main categories, ordinary accounts and investment accounts.

An ordinary account may be opened with as little as £1 and there is normally a limit of £10,000 on the amount that may be deposited. Up to £100 may be withdrawn on demand at a Post Office but where the amount involved is more than £50 the bank book is retained for checking at the National Savings Bank. When larger withdrawals are required an application form must be completed and payment is made within the course of a few days. However if an account has been designated as a Regular Customer Account £250 can be withdrawn on demand at a specified Post Office without the bank book being retained. Before applying for a Regular Customer Account a depositor must have used an ordinary account at the chosen Post Office for at least six months.

Two rates of interest are paid on ordinary accounts and for 1986 these are guaranteed at 3% and 6%. In order to obtain the higher rate it is in the first place necessary to keep £100 or more in the account for the whole of the calendar year. If this requirement is met interest will be paid at 6% for each complete calendar month in which £500 or more is kept in the account. Otherwise the 3% rate obtains.

The interest on sums deposited in ordinary accounts commences to accrue from the first day of the month following deposit and ceases on the first day of the month in which withdrawals are made. This means that no interest is paid on any amount not deposited for a full calendar month. An attraction of this type of account is that the first £70 of interest in any one year is tax free and both husbands and wives may take advantage of this concession. To the extent that it applies these rates of interest are equivalent to 4.29% and 8.57% for a basic rate (30%) taxpayer.

A much higher rate of interest is paid on investment accounts, 11.5% at the time of writing, where the minimum and maximum amounts of deposit are £5 and £50,000 respectively, and the rate current at any particular time can be ascertained at a Post Office. Interest is calculated on a daily basis and is earned on each whole pound for each day it is held on deposit up to the date on which a withdrawal warrant is dated. Withdrawals require one month's notice from the day the application is received by the National Savings Bank.

The tax concession does not apply to the interest on investment accounts but it is paid gross without deduction of tax at source as is also the case with interest on ordinary accounts. On both types of account interest is credited annually on 31 December.

1.12 Save As You Earn (Third Issue) Index-Linked

Save As You Earn (SAYE) schemes were introduced to encourage regular saving and the Third Issue was available between July 1975 and May 1984 after which it was, like the earlier SAYE issues, withdrawn from sale. However existing contracts will run their course.

The Third Issue is a five-year contract under which regular fixed amounts of between £4 and £50 (in round pounds) may be saved each month. No interest is paid during the period of the contract but after five years the saver is entitled to repayment of the total amount of his/her revalued contributions, each contribution being revalued to reflect the difference between the UK General Index of Retail Prices figure applicable to the month beginning with the day following the due date of that contribution or, in the case of the first contribution, between the Index figure applicable to the month in which the starting date falls and the Index figure applicable to the month in which the fifth anniversary of the starting date falls.

The starting date of the contract is the first day of the month following the month in which the first monthly contribution is paid. The due date for the payment of the second monthly contribution is the last day of the month in which the starting date falls, and the due date for payment of each succeeding contribution shall be the last day of each succeeding month.

After five years the saver can without making any further contributions leave them for two more years whereupon the repayment to which he/she is entitled is related to the Index figure applicable to the month in which the seventh anniversay of the starting date falls due together with a fixed bonus equal to two monthly contributions.

It should be noted that even if the Index should fall the repayment will never be less than the total amount of the contributions plus in the case of payment after seven years the fixed bonus.

When a scheme is discontinued during its currency and the money is withdrawn it will earn interest at the rate of 6%. If a saver dies no further payment should be made after the date of death and repayment of a deceased saver's contract will attract Index-linking on repayment at any time between the 1st and 7th anniversaries of the start date.

During the period of the contract up to six payments may be missed and on each occasion that this happens all payments made previously are deemed to have been paid one month later, thereby attracting the Index figure applicable to that later month.

Should the saver not take repayment after the seven-year term ends the benefits of Index-linking are still available but to encourage holders both of current (only if repaid with Index-linking) and completed contracts not to withdraw their funds during a phase of falling inflation annual supplements are being added. Supplements already granted were 2.4%, 2.4%, and 3% on 1 December 1983, 1 December 1984, and 1 December 1985 on the respective contract values on 30 November of the previous years. It has been stated that at least three further annual supplements will follow the first of these being 3% on contracts outstanding on 1 September 1986 on the contract value on 30 November 1985.

No UK income tax or capital gains tax is payable on any interest or capital accretions under the scheme. It is attractive compared to other forms of saving during periods of high inflation.

1.13 Yearly Plan

This scheme was introduced on 2 July 1984 for regular savers following the withdrawal of Index-linked Save As You Earn. Amounts of between £20 and £200 in multiples of £5 may be invested each month by standing order and after twelve months a Yearly Plan Certificate will be issued to the value of such payments plus interest.

The rates of interest offered on a Yearly Plan agreement, which are all tax free, are those in force when the saver's application is received at the Savings Certificate Office. The rates when offered are fixed and guaranteed for five years, not being affected by rates which may vary from time to time for new agreements. At the beginning of 1986 the five year average overall return on the investment where all twelve monthly payments are made was 8.19% made up of 6% for the first year and 8.5% for the next four years.

Certificates can be cashed at any time subject to reduced interest but the monthly payments do not earn any interest at all if they are cashed in the first year. The corresponding rates of interest for early encashment relative to the average five year return of 8.19% were 6.75% for each whole month for Certificates held for less than two years and 7.5% for Certificates held for at least two years but less than four years.

After the Certificate has been held for four years it will earn interest at the General Extension Rate (see 1.142) which varies from time to time.

In the event that not all but at least seven of the twelve monthly payments are made the rate of interest applicable after the Certificate is issued is not affected but the interest for year one is based on the timing of such payments. If six or fewer monthly payments are made a low rate of interest is applied to the scheme making it wholly unattractive.

The Yearly Plan can at the saver's option be extended by a year at a time provided seven or more payments have been made under a current agreement. The interest rates at which this may be accomplished will at the appropriate time be notified to the saver by the Savings Certificate Office.

The tax free interest guaranteed in the Plan certainly has an appeal to high rate taxpayers but also to be taken into account by savers are the outlook for inflation, the anticipated trend of interest rates over the five year period, and the likelihood or otherwise of being able to hold the Certificates for the full term.

1.14 National Savings Certificates

1.141 31st Issue

Since they were introduced in 1916 there have been many issues of National Savings Certificates, the current issue being the thirty-first. Certificates of this issue are purchased in units of £25 and after five years they are worth £36.48, no interest having been paid on them in the meantime. The accretion in value from £25 to £36.48 is not spread evenly over the five years but builds up as follows:

Year 1   At end of year   £1.44 added
Year 2   At end of each three months £0.44 added
Year 3   At end of each three months £0.55 added
Year 4   At end of each three months £0.68 added
Year 5   At end of each three months £0.84 added

This is the equivalent of 7.85% (11.21% grossed at 30%) per annum compound interest over the whole period of five years and again is completely free of tax. It will be observed, however, that nothing is added until the first anniversary of purchase and that over the remainder of the life of the certificate the accruals become progressively greater. National Savings Certificates should not be purchased on a very short-term basis but rather with the intention of holding for the full five years.

The maximum number of thirty-first issue certificates which can be held by any one person at present is 200 (cost £5,000) although this limit may be exceeded as the result of certificates inherited from a deceased holder. Certificates, together with increments already added thereto, can be cashed at any time subject to at least eight working days' notice being given.

Over the five year period the return on NSCs is slightly inferior to that on the Yearly Plan. They can, however, be purchased in lump sums, at irregular intervals, and there is no obligation to keep buying them.

1.142 General Extension Rate

This is a variable rate of interest for matured certificates when they have completed their fixed terms. The rate is changed periodically in order to keep it competitive to the extent of discouraging savers from cashing their certificates and reinvesting elsewhere.

Interest is calculated separately for each completed month, but only increases the repayment value of certificates after each completed period of three months. The interest for each month is one-twelfth of the annual rate and at each anniversary of purchase it is capitalized thus increasing the amount on which future interest is calculated.

At the beginning of 1986 the General Extension Rate was 8.52%.

1.143 Index-Linked

The First Issue Index-Linked National Savings Certificate, originally nick-named 'the granny bond' and the Second Issue Index-Linked National Savings Certificate are no longer on sale but continue to earn accretions which like SAYE (Third Issue) are linked to increases in the UK General Index of Retail Prices. Also as with SAYE (Third Issue) supplements are being added to encourage savers not to withdraw their funds. These so far have been 2.4%, 2.4%, and 3% payable on 1 November 1983, 1 November 1984, and 1 November 1985 of the indexed value of certificates held on 31 October 1982, 31 October 1983, and 31 October 1984 respectively. It has been stated that there will be at least another three annual supplements, the first of these being 3% on 1 August 1986 on the value of certificates on 31 October 1985.

On 1 July 1985 Third Issue Index-Linked National Savings Certificates became available issued in units of £25 with a maximum holding for any individual of £5,000. They have an initial life of five years during which they will grow by the annual rate of inflation as measured by the Retail Price Index plus an extra interest rate for each year as follows:

Year 1   2.50%
Year 2   2.75%
Year 3   3.25%
Year 4   4.00%
Year 5   5.25%

This totals an overall return of 3.54% a year compound in addition to the inflation proofing. The index-linked return and the guaranteed extra interest, both of which are earned monthly, are capitalized annually and the total sum index-linked over the following year thus maintaining the real value of the interest. It has been stated that the Certificates may be held beyond the five years when they will earn extra interest at a competitive variable rate as well as inflation proofing.

Third Issue Index-Linked Certificates can, like their conventional brethren, be cashed at any time but if this occurs within the first year no inflation proofing or extra interest are earned. If inflation over the five year period exceeds 4.31% (7.85%–3.54%) per annum they provide a better return than National Savings Certificates thirty-first Issue.

The accretion in value of all index – linked certificates is free of all UK taxes, providing them with considerable appeal to taxpayers, although of vital importance to all investors is the extent to which the rate of inflation rises or falls during the period for which they are held.

1.15 National Savings Bonds

1.151 Income Bonds

This is a Bond for lump sum investment the minimum being £2,000 with additions then being allowed in units of £1,000 up to a maximum holding of

£50,000. Interest is paid gross on the fifth day of each month and is at a competitive rate which may be varied from time to time on six weeks' notice being given. In early 1986 the rate was 12% per annum. Each Bond may be held for an initial period of ten years which term may be extended by the Treasury.

Repayment requires three months' notice and if this occurs after the first year interest is paid in full. Should repayment take place within the first year interest is at half rate from the date of purchase to the date of repayment on the amount repaid. Part encashment of holdings must be in multiples of £1,000 and the amount left must not fall below £2,000. On the death of a bondholder withdrawal is allowed without notice or loss of interest.

The payment of interest gross without deduction of income tax at source makes them attractive to individuals or organizations not liable for UK income tax.

1.152 Indexed-Income Bonds (1st Issue)
As indicated by the title these are Bonds designed to protect the investor incomewise from inflation. The Bonds which have a life of ten years are subject to a minimum investment of £5,000 which may be increased in multiples of £1,000 to a maximum of £50,000.

Interest on the Bonds is paid gross without deduction of tax at source on the twentieth of each month and for the first year is at the 'start rate' of 8% per annum. On the first anniversary the monthly income is increased to match the increase in prices over the previous year (as measured by the Retail Price Index) and so on at each subsequent anniversary until the end of ten years.

Repayment requires three months' notice and if this occurs after the first year interest is paid in full. Should it take place within the first year interest is at half rate from the date of purchase to the date of repayment. Part encashment of holdings must be in multiples of £1,000 and the amount left must not fall below £5,000.

The Bonds may have some attraction for non-taxpayers but investors worried by the possibility of high rates of inflation will take into account that there is no inflation proofing of capital. While obviously the course of inflation is important in the assessment of the Bonds it should also be remembered that the interest rates are guaranteed whereas in many other competing products they can be varied.

1.153 Deposit Bonds
This is another Bond for lump sum investment but unlike Income Bonds interest is not paid out monthly being instead added to the capital value of the Bond on the anniversary of the purchase date. The Bonds are available in multiples of £50 subject to a minimum purchase of £100 and a maximum holding of £50,000 although this figure may be exceeded by interest credited.

The rate of interest, which can be varied from time to time on six weeks' notice, was 12% in early 1986. Although the interest is capitalized gross it is still liable for UK income tax and must be entered in the investor's tax return. Another point to keep in mind is that interest paid annually is not quite so rewarding a return as the same nominal amount of interest paid at shorter intervals (see 1.21). Bonds may be held for an initial period of ten years which term may be extended by the Treasury.

Repayment requires three months' notice and if this occurs after the first year interest is at the full rate. Should repayment take place within the first year interest is at half rate except in the case of the death of the bondholder when no such penalty arises. Part of a Bond may be repaid providing the amount is not less than the minimum limit of £50 and the remaining balance does not fall below £100.

1.154 Premium Savings Bonds

Premium Savings differ from other savings media in that they introduce an element of gambling. The bondholder's capital is absolutely safe and he/she can obtain repayment in full at any time. However no interest is payable on the Bonds, and whether or not the holder receives any prizes depends on the random number selections of an electronic device known as ERNIE. The holder is in effect gambling with his/her interest.

Bonds are issued in multiples of £5 with a minimum purchase of £10 and a maximum holding allowed of £10,000 worth. Each £1 unit gives the holder one chance of a prize in every draw, a Bond becoming eligible to participate in the prize draws after it has been held for a clear three calendar months following the month in which it is purchased.

The amount available for providing prizes is calculated at a given rate of interest, currently $7\frac{3}{4}$%, on each Bond available for draws each month. From this prize fund there is first of all set aside an amount to provide single prizes of £100,000, £50,000, and £25,000 each week. The remainder of the fund is allocated for monthly prizes as follows:

```
 1 prize of    £250,000
 5 prizes of    £10,000
25 prizes of     £5,000
```
Over 155,000 prizes from £1,000 to £50.

The number of £1,000, £500, £100, and £50 prizes varies according to the total value of eligible Bonds in each draw.

Even though a Bond has won a prize it still participates in all future draws until it is repaid. On the death of a holder a Bond remains eligible for all draws held in the month of death and in the following twelve calendar months unless it is repaid earlier. Premium Bond prizes are exempt from all UK taxes. The chance of a single £1 Bond unit winning a prize in a monthly draw is 1 in 11,000.

1.2 Banks, buildings societies, licensed deposit takers

Historically there existed clearly established demarcation lines which distinguished joint stock banks, Trustee Savings Banks, building societies, and finance houses but over a relatively short span of years these are becoming progressively blurred, certainly so far as the saver and investor are concerned. While the competition arising from this benefits the depositor, he is obliged to look more closely at the various products offered if he is to obtain the best return on his money. He should also compare them with what is available from the National Savings Movement.

An example of this converging of the main deposit taking institutions is that as from April 1985 they all (in contrast to the National Savings Bank) pay interest to UK resident depositors net of composite rate tax (CRT) which means that the depositor is not liable for basic rate income tax on the interest received. The composite rate tax, at present 25.25%, is based on an estimate of what depositors would pay if they were assessed directly and is paid by the institutions to the Inland Revenue. Previously this method of taxation was peculiar only to the building societies. A drawback is that the non-taxpayer is unable to reclaim the tax deducted.

Accounts providing the facility of payments being made by cheque were once available only at the banks but are now to be found at certain building societies and licensed deposit takers. Worthwhile rates of interest may even also be paid although conditions not to the depositor's liking may exist such as a high minimum balance or charges on withdrawals.

Traditionally an account from which withdrawals could be made on demand paid a lower rate of interest than where a period of notice was required. This is now not necessarily so as a higher rate of interest may still be paid if a substantial balance remains in the account.

A point to be kept in mind is that interest rates on most types of account are sensitive to market conditions and are liable to vary markedly within a short space of time. As a possible counter to this there are usually term deposits, sometimes described as bonds, available from some of the institutions where a fixed rate of interest is guaranteed for a specific period of time. If a depositor takes the view that interest rates may fall and he will not require his money during the period involved this may be a suitable repository for part of his funds. More commonly as a variation of this theme an institution may offer on special types of account high rates of, say, 2% over its basic deposit rate for a number of years. It is important to remember that if the basic rate moves in either direction the high rate moves by the same amount.

For the saver plans can usually be found at relatively high rates of interest if he is prepared to enter into a commitment to make deposits on a regular basis.

The protection of depositors dealing with these institutions is dealt with in

Chapter 16 but it is, nevertheless, a wise precaution for a depositor to take heed of the financial status of the party to whom he is entrusting his funds. However normally a major UK joint stock bank or building society would, for example, not require the same degree of investigation from a security angle as would the branch of a small overseas institution. The offering of an exceptionally high rate of interest should as a general proposition prompt a prospective depositor to pause and make an appraisal of all the aspects involved.

Clearly the depositor if he hopes to get the best return on his available cash must not only check out the wide array of sources now open but also be prepared to keep watching the savings market and switch his funds among the various institutions when this is to his advantage. He must of course be wary of not losing by precipitate action the main benefit of any scheme just prior to its maturity or of falling into the trap of tying up funds which he will require in the short term.

1.21 The rate of interest

As the interest on deposits with the various institutions is paid at different intervals it is necessary to apply a common standard in order that a fair comparison may be made one with the other. The method used is to calculate the compounded annual rate (CAR) which is the effective return if interest at the nominal rate of interest is reinvested when received.

For example if bank A pays interest of 8% per annum annually on its deposits the CAR is 8% but if bank B pays 8% per annum quarterly the CAR is:

$$2\% + 2.04\% + 2.0808\% + 2.1224\% = 8.2432\%$$

In other words if £100 was the original deposit after one year it would have grown to £108 in bank A and £108.24 in bank B, the balances in the latter after the four quarters being £102, £104.04, £106.12, and £108.24 respectively.

Obviously the more frequently the interest is paid the greater the excess of CAR over the given nominal rate.

1.3 Local authority mortgage loans

Most local authorities of any size have loans quoted on the Stock Exchange and these are dealt with in Chapter 2. However, some local authorities from time to time invite the public to lend money to them directly at a fixed rate of interest over a certain period of time. The interest is usually paid half yearly and as from April 1986 it has been subject to cumulative rate tax so that basic rate taxpayers are not liable for any further tax.

The terms offered by local authorities show considerable variation, particularly as to the minimum sum which they are prepared to accept – although £500 is now fairly common – and the period of time which will elapse before it will be repaid. This may be on a few days' notice by either side or it may be fixed for several years ahead.

As a type of investment it is risk free and provides a good return of income, the yield being slightly above that obtainable from similar quoted local authority stocks. A snag is that the money is to some extent locked up for the full period of the loan, which could be for, say, two, five, or ten years. Although there is a limited market in the loans and there are often arrangements whereby money can be repaid should an emergency arise, some penalty may be incurred, and it is wise only to invest in such loans when the money can be left for the full period. A point in favour is that the investor is involved in no expense either initially or on repayment of the loan.

1.4 Real property

This is the investment in land and buildings. The buildings may be freehold which means that the ownership may include the land on which they are situated, or leasehold in which case the ownership of the buildings is separate from the land. In the latter event the ownership of the buildings will, in due course, revert to the owner of the land, frequently ninety-nine years from the beginning of the lease. The attractions of leasehold property are therefore limited, particularly as the term nears its conclusion. In Scotland real property is known as heritable property and the system is different, there being no equivalent of leasehold property.

While the ownership of property can be very profitable as values rise over the years, especially during periods of inflation, it presents certain problems. In the first place no acquisition should be made without the advice of a qualified surveyor well acquainted with the type of property involved. To the initial cost of the property there will, therefore, fall to be added the surveyor's fees together with the solicitor's fees and outlays, including stamp duty.

Then there is the question of administering property occupied by others. In such cases arrangements must be made for:

(a) Letting the property.
(b) The collection of rents.
(c) Attending to repairs.
(d) Adequate insurance of the property, the value of which may increase rapidly in times of inflation.
(e) Watching the dates of break clauses in any lease with a view to considering a possible increase in rents.
(f) Paying the ground rent in the case of leasehold property.

In addition it is necessary to keep abreast with legislation affecting the various categories of property, such as rent restriction.

Apart from house owner occuriership which has much to commend it, the private individual should think twice before involving himself in the somewhat onerous responsibilities of owning real property.

1.41 Mortgages

Another way in which investment may be made in property is by mortgage (bond* and disposition in security in Scotland). This is a different type of investment from ownership of property, there being no question of capital profit being obtained. Only the amount lent on the mortgage will be repayable when it is called up. The mortgage should, however, make provision for its being repaid at six months' notice, or at the latest after five years, in order that the rate of interest may be raised if rates have gone up in the meantime.

It is also essential to make sure that the property over which the mortgage is granted would, in the event of a forced sale, have a realizable value sufficient to pay off the mortgage. As a precaution the loan should only be for a proportion of the estimated realizable value of the property, leaving a margin to take care of possible fluctuations. Here again expert advice is necessary before the investment is made. Most important, too, is to ensure that the property is always adequately insured. The premiums will be the responsibility of the borrower, but the lender for self-protection should satisfy him/herself that they have been paid.

Investment in mortgages is more complicated than many other forms of fixed interest investment. For them to be worthwhile the lender must be able to obtain an appreciably higher return on his money in compensation.

1.5 Annuities

A person at some stage in his life, usually on retirement, might feel that the income which he can obtain from his capital each year is not sufficient for his requirements and he may wish to augment it by spending part of his capital. One of the difficulties of this situation is that no one knows just for how long he is going to live and, accordingly, it is impossible to decide the appropriate proportion of capital to be spent each year.

The answer to this problem is to purchase an annuity by paying a lump sum to an assurance company which then pays a fixed amount each year, frequently in six monthly instalments, to the annuitant. The amount payable is based on the average life expectancy at the age on which the annuity payments commence. If the annuitant dies earlier than the 'average life' the assurance company makes a profit, but if he/she survives for a longer period the assurance company loses. As women are expected to live longer than men the annuity rates offered to them are less attractive.

There are various types of annuity, although the basic principle – that of converting capital into income – remains the same. For example, some may provide for the annuity to continue for, say, ten years even although the

---

* Now by means of 'standard security' in Scotland.

annuitant dies before this time has elapsed in which event the remaining payments will be made to his/her heirs. A common practice is for a husband to take out a joint annuity so that the payments continue until the death of the survivor of himself and his wife. These deviations from the straightforward annuity for one life mean that the annual payments relative to the purchase cost are for a lesser amount, as the assurance company must take into its calculations the additional obligations which it is assuming. Obviously, the older the annuitant at the commencement of the payments the higher they will be for any given capital sum.

One of the attractions of annuities is the manner in which they are treated for tax purposes. A proportion of the annuity is regarded as being a return of capital and is not taxable. For example, a man of sixty-five might pay £10,000 in order that he might receive an annuity for the remainder of his life. The actual amount of the annuity depends on interest rates at the time of purchase. At the beginning of 1986 it would have been around £1550 of which about £700 would be tax free. There are, however, exceptions to this treatment tax-wise, such as when the annuity is purchased under the terms of a will. The total amount of each payment is then liable to tax.

A drawback of annuities is that the capital used for their purchase is out of the control of the purchaser and he cannot get it back again, nor can he leave it to his heirs. It may well, therefore, be prudent for only part of one's capital to be committed to the purchase of an annuity, thereby retaining some flexibility in one's financial arrangements.

A further snag is that if the annuitant lives for a long time the purchasing power of his/her payments will decline with rising prices. Schemes are, however, now available to counteract this by linking the annuity payments in some measure to the performance of a portfolio of ordinary shares or of real property.

1.6 Guaranteed bonds

These bonds are offered to investors by life assurance companies on terms which are guaranteed by the company issuing them. The value of this guarantee depends on the financial strength of the life office concerned. With well-established companies and those with sound backing it can be regarded as undoubted. New companies which have not had time to build up reserves should be regarded with some caution. Investors should consult with insurance brokers on this and on the other aspects of bonds before a purchase is effected.*

---

* The Policyholders Protection Act 1975 now ensures, except where benefits offered are excessive, that holders will in the event of a company's failure receive at least 90% of the value of their policies. The Act is administered by the Policyholders Protection Board which when funds are required may impose a levy on insurance companies not exceeding 1% of net premium income and also on 'accountable intermediaries' to the extent of a proportion of their commission from the failed insurer.

Attractive returns are available to investors because of the favourable tax treatment afforded to the annuity funds of life offices. Briefly the investment income of a fund is tax free so far as it does not exceed the annuity payments out of the fund. Where the situation arises that the investment income falls short of the annuity payments there is scope for the issue of further bonds. Once the imbalance is corrected the life office will cease to be in a position to issue more bonds and this is why the offer of growth bonds by a life office is restricted to a maximum amount and individual offices are only able to make such offers from time to time.

Guaranteed bonds are purchased by the payment of a lump sum (sometimes described as a 'single premium' as technically they are 'non-qualifying policies' as defined by the 1968 Finance Act) and are available in two different forms – growth bonds and income bonds.

1.61 Guaranteed growth bonds

These offer to the purchaser after a fixed period of years either a deferred annuity or a lump sum in cash. Except where a non-taxpayer is involved it will usually be beneficial on maturity to take the cash option rather than the guaranteed annuity as the tax free capital element relates only to the original purchase price. If at the end of the term the investor wishes an annuity he/she will probably find it more advantageous to take the cash and then make an annuity purchase in a separate transaction.

Bonds are only issued for relatively large sums and are seldom available in amounts of under £500. The terms vary with interest rates and even at any given time quite appreciable differences arise between offerings from life offices of comparable standing. A typical bond in the earlier part of 1974 offered the following returns for each £1,000 of purchase money.

Term of bond	Guaranteed cash option on maturity
5 years	£1,591
10 years	£2,533
15 years	£3,916

Apart from reservations as to the effects of a possible acceleration in the rate of inflation this is a worry free method of obtaining useful capital appreciation over a period of years.

When applying for bonds it is necessary to state the number of years ahead when the proceeds are to be taken. This is in order that the life office may ensure that its investment portfolio is arranged in such a way that cash becomes available at the appropriate time.

No income tax at basic rate (see 1.63 for bonds issued after 1974 Budget) or capital gains tax is payable when the bonds are cashed. There may, however, be a liability for higher rates of tax on the gain between the purchase price and the proceeds (for calculation see Section 13.51).

To derive full advantage from bonds it is essential that they are left until maturity. The 'penalties' for early surrender or death during the term of the bonds vary. Typically 95% of the original purchase money might be paid together with interest at the compound rate of 5% per annum.

Restrictions often apply as to the age of the purchaser who may require to be between, say, thirty-five or eighty on maturity of the bond. It is however, usually possible to select from the bonds available one that satisfactorily caters for the requirements of investors in most age groups.

1.62 Guaranteed income bonds

Many investors' circumstances are such that they do not wish to set aside part of their capital so that it shows substantial appreciation over a period of years. What they require is that it produces a high current income for them right away. The life offices provide guaranteed income bonds for this purpose.

In return for a lump sum the bonds provide a guaranteed income for a fixed period of years after which the lump sum will be paid back in full unless the holder then elects to receive instead an annuity for life. As with growth bonds the cash option will normally prove to be the more advantageous.

Although income bonds are marketed as one package they are usually treated by the insurance companies as consisting of two separate constituents. On receipt of the purchase money the insurers accordingly divide it up, one part to provide an immediate temporary annuity and the other to provide the alternative benefits of cash or deferred annuity at the end of the term.

The income received from the bond arising as it does from the temporary immediate annuity is partly regarded as a return of capital and to this extent is not liable to tax. The precise portion so treated depends on the age and sex of the purchaser. The balance which will be relatively small will be paid under deduction of basic rate tax and will be liable to tax as normal investment income. At the end of the term if the cash option is taken there will be no liability to basic rate income tax (see 1.63 for bonds issued after 1974 Budget) or capital gains tax but there may be a liability for higher rates of tax on the 'profit' between the cash proceeds and the part of the original purchase price allocated to provide the alternative benefits.

Example

A man aged sixty could, by investing £5,000 some years ago, perhaps have obtained the following:

Payable for ten years		£485
(in half-yearly instalments of £242.50)		
Taxable portion	£125	
Tax thereon at 30%		37.50
Net annuity		£447.50 (a net yield of 8.9% to

the basic rate taxpayer and equivalent to a gross yield of 12.7%)

After ten years

Annuity for life of £625 gross (payable for five years in event of death within this period)

or cash sum of £5,000.

If the original purchase money had been split as to £2,800 to provide the temporary annuity and £2,200 for the alternative benefits, then should cash be taken there could be a liability to higher rates of tax on £5,000 less £2,200, i.e. on profit of £2,800 (see 1.63 for bonds purchased after 1974 Budget).

The capital invested in bonds can be withdrawn during the term on conditions varying considerably from one contract to another. Frequently there is a graduated scale of withdrawal of, perhaps, 92½% to 100% of the purchase money according to the length of time which has elapsed before the withdrawal is made. If death should occur during the term of the bond the majority of contracts provide for a complete return of capital to the deceased's estate.

The bonds provide a high safe income and so far as this type of investment is concerned have much to commend them, particularly to those taxpayers not looking for capital growth. The return of capital intact at the end of the term is also an attractive feature.

Should it be considered that inflation will continue unabated and that interest rates will rise it is advisable that the term of a bond should be for as short a period as possible in order that the capital can be recovered fairly soon and reinvested to take advantage of the higher rates then prevailing. On the other hand, if rates were to fall the holder of a bond stretching over a longer period would score. The minimum amount required to purchase an income bond is frequently £1,000 and although varying age restrictions apply they are generally available to most investors apart from the very young and extremely old.

1.63 Bonds issued after 1974 Budget

As a result of a change in legislation 'old style' growth and income bonds purchased after the Budget on 26 March 1974 have been made less attractive in that the profit on encashment of a deferred annuity is now liable to tax at basic rate as well as at the higher rates if applicable.

For instance, if such a growth bond purchased for £1,000 is cashed after fifteen years for £3,916 the gain of £2,916 will be liable for basic rate tax. Similarly in the Example in 1.62 if after the ten years had elapsed the investor took back his £5,000 capital he would be liable to basic rate tax on the gain of £2,800.

However it must be emphasized that bonds issued on or before 26 March 1974 are not affected by the new law.

Bonds are still being issued and while a few continue to make use of deferred annuities most are based on a different structure. Growth bonds usually consist of a single premium endowment policy and income bonds may also consist of such a policy with guaranteed bonus additions being cashed to provide the income which is free of any further tax to the basic rate taxpayer. (For taxation of single premium policies see 13.51 and 13.53.)

Alternatively an income bond may be structured on a series of single premium endowment policies, the number of these policies exceeding by one the years during which the income is to be paid. Each year a policy is cashed at its purchase price and as no profit therefore arises the proceeds are not taxable although technically a chargeable event has occurred. At maturity the remaining policy provides the return of capital on which higher rates of tax may be payable but which remains intact in the hands of a basic rate taxpayer.

It should be noted that guaranteed early surrender terms, if available at all, are now substantially less generous than was previously the case. Generally the bonds are attractive mainly to the basic rate taxpayer (however, see 13.52) but before making a purchase he/she should compare the current terms with other forms of fixed interest investment.

Typical question

Explain what an annuity is and discuss the advantages and disadvantages of this type of investment.   (The Institute of Bankers, *Investment*)

Suggested answer

An annuity is the entitlement to receive an annual payment, this usually being acquired by the handing over of a lump sum to an assurance company. The amount of the annuity to be obtained from any given lump sum depends largely on the age of the person at the time the payments are to commence, together with various other factors such as whether the joint lives of husband and wife are involved or whether there is a guaranteed period of, say, ten years during which the payments must be made to the annuitant's heirs should he die before the period has elapsed. As women have a longer life expectancy than men they receive lower annuity payments in return for the same lump sum.

The purchase of an annuity is a good method of obtaining a guaranteed income for the rest of one's life and where elderly people are concerned a very high income indeed can be obtained relative to the purchase cost. It also means that they can in effect spend their capital without the fear of using it up too soon, i.e. if they live longer than might be anticipated. In this connection it is worth noting that as part of the annual payments is really the return of capital, what is deemed to be his capital portion is, in a straightforward purchase, free of tax in the hands of the annuitant.

A disadvantage of an annuity is that once the lump sum is paid to the assurance company all further control over it is lost. It is therefore not suitable for someone who wishes to leave money to his/her heirs or who may wish to invest his/her money in some other way at a later date. A wise compromise may often be to commit only part of one's capital in the purchase of an annuity.

Another snag is that should the annuitant live for a long time the purchasing power of his/her annuity, which is usually a fixed amount, will fall as prices rise with inflation. Some efforts are however being made to counteract this by linking the payments to the performance of a portfolio of ordinary shares or of real property.

Additional questions

1 What categories of National Savings are currently available in this country for lump sum investment to provide (a) high income, (b) capital growth? Detail the salient features of each.
2 Explain the relative attractions of (a) the Yearly Plan, (b) Premium Bonds.
3 Distinguish between the manner in which interest is paid by the National Savings Department and other deposit-taking institutions. What do you understand by 'the compounded annual rate of interest'?
4 Do you consider that real property is a suitable investment for a private individual? Give reasons for your answer.
5 Distinguish guaranteed growth bonds from guaranteed income bonds. In what various ways might they be structured?

2 Public authority quoted stocks

Having explored some of the avenues in which an individual can invest his/her money by dealing direct with the party to whom he/she is lending it, what further range of investments are there available through the medium of the Stock Exchange? First of all there are a wide variety of what are known as fixed interest stocks issued by the Governments, public boards, and local authorities of Great Britain and the Commonwealth.

2.1 Some basic features

The importance of the words 'fixed interest' is self-evident. If an investor owns, say, £100 nominal of a stock whose rate of interest (known as the coupon rate) is stated to be 5% per annum, each year during his/her ownership of the stock he/she is entitled to £5 gross interest, no more and no less.

The prices quoted for these stocks are for £100 nominal although much smaller quantities can be purchased. In fact British Government stocks can be dealt in to the nearest penny. The nominal amount of stock held and its value may, however, differ widely depending fundamentally upon what investors are prepared to pay for the rights they acquire when they purchase the stock. Put in simple terms, if the general body of investors consider that a fair rate of interest for lending money indefinitely to the Government is 7% per annum then they will be prepared to pay £50 for £100 nominal of 3½% War Loan. For each £50 paid they would receive £3.50 interest each year. If they were willing to accept 3½% for such a loan then £100 nominal of 3½% War Loan would cost £100.

2.11 Payment of interest

The interest on these public authority stocks is normally paid at half-yearly intervals, although in one or two cases, for instance 2½% Consols, it is paid quarterly. It is the usual procedure for tax to be deducted at source by the paying agent and handed over to the Inland Revenue, the investor only actually receiving the net amount. For example, a holder of £400 3% British Transport Stock 1978/88 would each half-year receive an interest warrant for £4.20 calculated as follows:

Gross interest	£6.00
Less tax at basic rate (30%)	£1.80
	£4.20

The holder would also receive a tax certificate covering this deduction of tax and if he is not liable to tax at the basic rate, depending upon his personal circumstances, he can submit this certificate in due course to his Inspector of Taxes and obtain a refund of the tax overpaid.

2.12 Interest gross

There are exceptions to this rule of tax deduction at source, the most notable being the interest on $3\frac{1}{2}$% War Loan which is paid gross. Other exceptions are the interest on British Government stocks when held on the National Savings Bank Stock Register and interest payable out of public revenue not exceeding £2.50 per half-year. As far as overseas holders are concerned interest is paid free of tax on many British Government stocks issued for the first time in recent years. Stocks coming within this category are indicated by a denoting symbol in the 'British Funds' section of the Financial Times Share Information Service.

2.2 Significance of dates

As well as having a rate of interest attached to their description, most public authority stocks have a date or dates as part of their title. This is in connection with the provision for their redemption which in all cases is at par* or, in other words, their nominal value. For instance, 9% Treasury Loan 1994 must be repaid at par by the Government on 17 November 1994.

Many stocks, however, do not have just one date but two; for example $5\frac{3}{4}$% Funding Loan 1987/91 which must be redeemed not later than 5 April 1991 but may be redeemed at the Government's option any time after 5 April 1987 on three months' notice. The Government has the advantage of having a period of four years within which to choose its time of repayment, and repayment in fact very often means fresh borrowing at a new rate of interest. With interest rates at the time of writing at the high levels of 1986 it appears most unlikely that the Government could issue a new stock at par at a lower coupon rate than $5\frac{3}{4}$% before 1991, so that most investors will assume that this Stock will not be redeemed until the last possible occasion. However, theoretically at least, it might always be possible for a fall in interest rates to take place to such an extent that the Government could issue a loan with a coupon of, say, 5% in 1987. It would therefore redeem the Stock at the earliest opportunity. From the authorities' point of view obviously the further apart the two redemption dates are, the better, as they then have more scope for choosing a suitable time for repayment.

While it is possible to anticipate the likely redemption dates for stocks with reasonably short lives it is a different matter when one comes to consider the long dated stocks. It would be a rash person, indeed, who would attempt to

---

* Except index-linked stocks.

predict with any certainty exactly when repayment of 5½% Treasury Stock 2008/12 will take place. Much can happen to interest rates in the meantime.

2.21 Protection of capital

One factor which should now be apparent is that as a stock approaches its redemption date its market value will not fluctuate very much from par. This is a very useful protection to anyone holding these stocks as he/she knows that there is a stabilizing influence in money terms in the value of his/her investment. There is, however, no safeguard against depreciation in the purchasing power of money owing to inflation. The further away the redemption dates the less effective they are as stabilizing forces and the prices of long dated stocks are liable to much wider fluctuation than their short dated brethren.

2.22 The irredeemables

There are, unfortunately for many investors, a few stocks which have no definite redemption dates, the best known of which is 3½% War Loan. This is technically what is known as a one-way option stock as the Government had the option to redeem it at par in 1952 and since then has had the right to redeem it at par at any time on giving three months' notice. The holder, however, has no rights as regards forcing the Government to effect repayment and therefore in the present era of high interest rates the price of 3½% War Loan has dropped to a pitiful fraction of its nominal value. In January 1986, for instance, £100 nominal could be purchased for as little as £35. It is now regarded by investors as being virtually irredeemable.

Other British Government stocks coming into this "irredeemable' category are 2½% Consols, 4% Consols, 3% Treasury Stock (1966 or after), 2½% Treasury Stock (1975 or after), and 3½% Conversion Loan (1961 or after). The low prices of these stocks are eloquent testimony to their irredeemable status in the eyes of investors. Nevertheless all these British Government stocks are not true irredeemables in view of their one-way option. A few out and out irredeemables such as Manchester Corporation 4% Consolidated Irredeemable Stock can, however, be found in the corporation market.

2.23 Recovery potential

An advantage of irredeemable stocks is that when purchased at times of high interest rates they offer the possibility of greater capital appreciation than can be obtained from dated stocks carrying the same coupon rate, should interest rates fall. Similarly, long dated stocks can rise in price more dramatically than short dated stocks. For example, as at 7 January 1986 consider the scope for capital appreciation of the following three stocks.

	Price
3% Treasury 1987	92×d
3% British Gas 1990/95	69½
3% Treasury Stock 1966 or after	30½

A dramatic drop in interest rates could not benefit 3% Treasury 1987 to anything like the extent to which it could the other two. A rise of 9 points would take it over 100 and its impending redemption at par would be a powerful deterrent to purchases above that level. On the other hand the 3% British Gas and 3% Treasury Stock 1966 or after could rise approximately by 30 and 70 points respectively before the redemption provisions could act as a limiting factor to price increases. The 3% British Gas could, of course, in any event not be redeemed before 1990.

In the middle 1980s it would have appeared to be approaching fantasy to talk of the irredeemables in terms of substantial capital appreciation. However, times change, and with them the rates of interest. It is perhaps worth recalling that during the cheap money drive by the Chancellor of the Exchequer in 1946/47 investors actually rushed to lend money to the Government by subscribing for 3% Savings Bonds 1965/75 at par when they thought that this 'high' rate of interest would not be obtainable for much longer. However, the unnaturally low rates of interest which the authorities at that time sought to sustain by exploiting to the full extent the mechanisms at their disposal failed fundamentally, because it was in conflict with basic economic forces and the objective of a $2\frac{1}{2}$% long-term rate of interest was only momentarily achieved. It is also of interest to note that $3\frac{1}{2}$% War Loan having been as low as $22\frac{1}{4}$ in 1976 had staged a substantial percentage recovery to over 35 in the early part of 1979.

2.24 Price movements and yield

One vital feature of fixed interest stocks must be emphasized. Their prices vary inversely to changes in the rate of interest. If new borrowers require to pay a higher rate of interest for their money the prices of stocks already issued fall to come into line with the new rate. On the other hand if new borrowers pay a lower rate then prices rise.

As well as affecting the size of the fluctuation in the price of a stock the redemption date also has an influence on the yield or the return of income which an investor receives on purchasing a stock. The arithmetic of yield calculation is a little involved and will be dealt with more fully in a later chapter. As a general proposition, however, it can be stated that the longer the time to redemption the higher will be the yield to be obtained.

In practice conditions frequently diverge from the normal. A very powerful factor is public opinion regarding the future trend in interest rates. Should it be considered that rates are going to rise there will be a movement of money from long- to short-term stocks to avoid the loss of capital which will follow the drop in prices of long-term stocks. This will increase the yield differential in favour of long-term stocks. Conversely, if interest rates are high, but this is believed to be temporary and that there will soon be a fall, a higher yield may be obtained from short-dated than from long-dated stocks. This is because there has been a movement of funds from the short to the long-term in order that the relatively high rates to be obtained should be secured for as long a time as possible.

2.3 Gilts

Mention has been made of short-dated, long-dated, and irredeemable stocks. The gilt-edged market which is comprised of British Government stocks includes issues by the nationalized industries, the local authorities, and most public board stocks of Great Britain and Northern Ireland, and the stocks of the majority of Commonwealth governments and corporations is divided into the following categories according to the length of time to redemption:

(a) Shorts with a life of not more than five years.
(b) Mediums with a life of five to fifteen years (five to ten years in some classifications).
(c) Longs with a life of over fifteen years (over ten years in some classifications).
(d) Undated or irredeemables where there is no definite date for redemption.

A point to note about 'gilts' is that a purchaser pays the market price plus the gross accrued interest since the last date of payment. For instance, the interest on $10\frac{1}{2}\%$ Treasury Stock 1989 is paid on 14 June and 14 December. If £1,000 of the Stock was bought on 7 January at $96\frac{3}{4}$ the wording on the contract would read:

£1,000 $96\frac{3}{4}$ £967.50

Plus accrued interest at $10\frac{1}{2}\%$ from:

14.12 to 8.1   25 days   7.21

The reason why the interest is calculated to 8 January is that payment is made for gilt-edged stocks on the day after the date of the transaction.

However, if the stock is quoted 'ex dividend' then interest between the date of purchase and the next payment date is deducted. Prior to 10 February 1986 this only applied to 'shorts' and with other gilt-edged stocks the market price included the accrued interest (see 2.5).

The term gilt-edged has perhaps in recent years become rather tainted, but its significance is that it is applied to those stocks that are backed by public authority. Holders of these stocks have, therefore, the highest possible security that the terms under which they are issued will be complied with (see 2.33). That is, interest payments will be received at regular intervals and in the case of dated stocks capital will be repaid at par no later than at a predetermined time. Their misfortune is that they have no protection against the ravages of inflation.

2.31 British Government Stocks

The gilt-edged market is made up of various types of securities of which by far the largest is British Government stocks. Because of the size of these stocks on issue – for example there is approximately £1,909 million 3½% War Loan – and their wide distribution they are very much easier to buy in large amounts than any other class of security. It is possible at most times to buy or sell hundreds of thousands of pounds of government stock without moving the price by more than a fraction of a pound if at all. This could not happen to a security of any other organization or authority as, say, £500,000 stock would represent a relatively large proportion of the total issue outstanding instead of a small fraction as in the case of a government stock. The largest corporation issue at present is £46,250,000 Birmingham DC 13½% Stock 1989, and most are for sums much smaller than this. As British Government stocks are regarded the safest of all stocks the income from such stocks which a buyer is willing to accept will be lower than that from any other fixed interest issue with similar characteristics.

2.311 Index-Linked Stocks

The first gilt-edged index-linked stock was introduced by the Government in March 1981 and originally such stocks could only be held by pension funds. A series of index-linked stocks has now become available and the restriction limiting holders to pension funds was removed as from March 1982.

The purpose of these stocks is to provide investors with inflation proofing both as regards income which is paid half yearly and the eventual repayment of capital. This is achieved by adjusting each income payment and in due course the capital repaid on redemption by reference to the Retail Price Index. For example a stock issued with a nominal annual coupon of 2½% would have each half yearly income payment adjusted as follows:

$$\frac{2\tfrac{1}{2}\%}{2} \times \frac{\text{Index figure applicable to the month in which income paid}}{\text{Index figure applicable to the month in which stock issued}}$$

The index figure for any month is defined as the Retail Price Index for eight months earlier which is, in fact, the figure announced seven months earlier.

A feature of these stocks is that because the inflation proofing provides a real return they can be issued with very low nominal coupons. A further distinguishing attribute is that, as they will be redeemed at their inflation adjusted values, there is no question of their prices falling to par when this date approaches. In fact until redemption is near their current 'real par value' will normally be above their market price. For instance, the first stock to be issued 2% Index-Linked Treasury Stock 1996 was trading around 112 in December 1985 when its current 'real par value' was 139.57 (100 × 373.9/267.9). The reason for this is that because of their low coupon, albeit index-linked, the stocks must hold out the prospect of an adequate measure of capital appreciation to enable them to compete with other forms of investment (see 11.23).

As during their lives the prices of index-linked stocks fluctuate in the market like other stocks the protection against inflation may only be fulfilled if they are held to redemption.

2.312 *National Savings Stock Register*

Mention has already been made of British Government stocks on the National Savings Stock Register in connection with the interest being paid gross. This is useful for the small investor in that he/she does not have the trouble of reclaiming the tax. The commission charged is usually less than that for the equivalent transaction carried out by a stockbroker (see Appendix A).

There are one or two snags. First of all the Department for National Savings will not accept instructions at any specified price nor undertake to deal on any particular day. Also the Department will not buy more than £10,000 nominal of any stock for any one investor in any one day. Instructions for the purchase and sale of stocks are sent on forms obtainable from Post Offices to the Bonds and Stock Office, Blackpool, Lancashire, and are carried out as soon as practical after receipt. There is therefore a little delay in the execution of orders as compared with instructions telephoned to a stockbroker which are carried out immediately. This could result in a transaction being carried out at a price which had moved slightly to the investor's disadvantage.

Approximately fifty British Government stocks are held on the National Savings Stock Register as well as the Bank of England Register. They are transferable from one to the other free of charge, although there is a limit of £5,000 of any one stock from the Bank of England Register to the National Savings Stock Register in any one calendar year.

2.313 *The Funded Debt*

In discussion of government borrowing reference may be made to the Funded Debt. This is debt which the Government has no obligation ultimately to redeem. Examples are 2½% Consols, 3½% War Loan, etc. It now consists of a relatively small proportion of the total government borrowing most of which has a definite date when repayment must be made. The latter, the Unfunded Debt, includes quoted securities, National Savings Certificates, Premium Bonds, Deposit and Income Bonds, SAYE, Treasury Bills, etc.

2.32 *Local authority stocks*

Much smaller in total value are the stocks of the local authorities which are dealt in on the Stock Exchange. The range and variety of these can best be envisaged by reference to a copy of the Stock Exchange Official Daily List. Theoretically the security for these stocks, which is a charge on the local rates, is ranked a little lower than that for British Government securities. However, in practice they can be regarded as being just as safe and there is no case of any British local authority defaulting in its obligations. Not surprisingly a stock of a well-known authority such as the Corporation of London may command a slightly higher market rating than the stock of a lesser known body. They are a useful medium, particularly for the private investor who does not wish to acquire a huge amount of stock, for obtaining a higher income than can be obtained from government stocks.

Like all government stocks most local authority stocks can be purchased without the buyer paying transfer stamp duty which is at present £1% (see Appendix B). Duty in the majority of cases is paid by the local authority under a compounding arrangement with the Inland Revenue.

Closely akin to the local authority stocks are the issues of the public boards, many of whom are concerned with the supply of water to their respective areas, such as the Metropolitan Water Board and the North Devon Water Board. Although many of these approach the corporation stocks in quality, the nature of the underlying security for a board's obligations should always be ascertained and assessed by a potential investor.

2.321 Yearling Bonds

Every week on a Tuesday local authorities issue a batch of bonds and as most have a life of only one year they have come to be known as 'yearling bonds'. Some do have lives stretching up to five years and as would be expected the longer dated bonds offer higher rates of interest. The rate of interest payable on the bonds varies with each issue in the light of market conditions and the total on offer each week is regulated by the Bank of England. Variable rate bonds are now by no means uncommon.

An investor wishing to receive an allocation from the weekly issue may apply through his/her stockbroker or bank manager. Thereafter the bonds are dealt in in the normal way on the Stock Exchange although only in denominations of £1,000 and multiples thereof.

Prices of yearling bonds fluctuate like other marketable securities but owing to the proximity of the repayment date they are a safe medium for securing a high rate of interest on funds available for short-term investment.

2.33 The Commonwealth

A sector of the market which has seen considerable shrinkage in recent years is that of the issues of Commonwealth governments and provincial and local authorities. While technically most of these stocks are included in the gilt-edged market it is impossible nowadays to appraise them in general terms. The creditworthiness of some of the governments concerned is of a very high standard and accordingly their issues are rated perhaps just slightly below the home corporations. Unfortunately, owing to political upheavals or instability in many of the former colonial territories, there cannot be complete confidence that all the present or future governments of some of these countries will meet their obligations as and when they arise. The fate of the United Kingdom holders of the Southern Rhodesian Stocks who for many years following UDI received no capital redemption of, or interest on, their holdings emphasizes the risks involved. Although in 1980 the Zimbabwe Government offered terms to settle the debts of the previous regime, these were hardly generous.

Before investing in Commonwealth Stocks in order to take advantage of such higher yields as may be obtainable, the only course is for a thorough assessment to be made of the possible risks involved. As always, the higher the yield the greater the risk.

2.4 Foreign bonds

Distinct from the gilt-edged market there is an extensive list of foreign government and institutional bonds quoted on the Stock Exchange (London). Although the credit standing of many of these borrowers is good unfortunately a number of these foreign issues have at some time or another been in default in that the borrowers concerned have failed to meet interest payments or redeem capital as and when the terms of issue demanded. Such stocks vary in quality and when offering far more attractive yields than British securities must be regarded as speculative.

Sometimes these issues are described as being 'assented' or 'unassented'. This arises when a government, after being in default for some time, offers new terms to the holders under which it will be willing to service the loan again. These terms are invariably poorer than the old ones being replaced, but most bondholders accept them on the grounds that it is better to salvage some of their losses. When they do so their bonds are marked to show that they have agreed to the new terms. They are therefore described as 'assented' or 'enfaced' to distinguish them from those of holders who have not acquiesced to the new terms.

2.5 Accrued interest

Over the years the practice developed with high tax paying investors of buying high coupon fixed interest stocks after they went 'ex div' and selling them when they were full of interest, the price being thus inflated, just before a subsequent 'ex div' date. This procedure, known as bond-washing, resulted in interest being capitalized and not being subject to income tax.

To counter this on transactions of fixed interest securities on or after 28 February 1986 the accrued interest is identified on a day to day basis and subject to income tax or corporation tax in the hands of the seller. In order to prevent double taxation the purchaser will be allowed relief of the same amount to set against the interest which he/she eventually receives.

For example, an investor sells £10,000 12% Treasury Stock 1995 on 26 November 1986 (for settlement on 27 November 1986). Interest on this stock is paid on 25 January and 25 July.

$$\text{Accrued interest to 27 November 1986} = £600 \times 125/184$$
$$= £407.61$$

Accordingly, the seller would be taxed on £407.61 and the purchaser would have this amount of relief to set against the interest of £600 which he/she would receive on 25 January 1987.

In the case of 'ex div' transactions the interest accruing will be charged to tax on the purchaser and the seller will be entitled to corresponding relief.

For the purpose of this treatment securities include any loan stock issued by any government, local authority or company whether secured or unsecured.

Individuals are exempt from this procedure if the nominal value of their securities when aggregated does not exceed £5,000 at any time in the relevant or immediately preceding tax year. Other exceptions include bodies exempt from taxation, persons not resident or ordinarily resident in the UK, and financial concerns whose profits from the sale of securities are charged to tax as income rather than as capital gains.

Typical question

Outline fully the characteristics of the following British Government stocks explaining the reason for the difference in their prices.

	Price 7/1/86
3% Treasury Stock 1990	80⅝
3% Treasury Stock 1966 (after)	30½

Suggested answer

There is no doubt that the terms under which both stocks have been issued will be complied with as they are backed by the British Government. In both cases for every £100 nominal amount of stock held the holder is entitled to £3.00 interest per annum payable in half-yearly instalments.

The reason for the large divergence in the prices of the stocks is that the 3% Treasury Stock 1990 is dated and must be repaid by the Government not later than 1990. This results in the stock having a strong pull upwards as the final redemption date approaches.

The 3% Treasury Stock 1966 (after) is a one-way option stock, i.e. the Government has had, since 1966, the right to redeem it at par if it chooses but is under no obligation to do so. As interest rates are very high and do not appear likely to fall substantially in the foreseeable future, the 3% Treasury Stock 1966 (after) is regarded as being virtually irredeemable and therefore there is no redemption date to support the price which is subject to the full effects of high interest rates and inflation.

Additional questions

1 Of what stocks is the gilt-edged market comprised? In what respects do they differ?
2 What do you understand by the Funded and Unfunded Debt? Give examples of each.

3 Explain how interest payments are usually made to holders of fixed interest stocks. Give exceptions to the normal procedure.

4 How do index-linked stocks protect the investor against inflation? Mention any other characteristics of these stocks.

5 Outline the advantages and disadvantages of acquiring a holding of British Government stock on the National Savings Bank Register.

6 What possible advantages might there be in purchasing long-dated as opposed to short dated stocks?

3 Company stocks and shares

Although the largest amount by value of Stock Exchange business is accounted for by public authority stocks, largely due to institutional activity in the 'shorts', when it comes to the actual number of deals transacted it is the stocks and shares of joint stock companies which are predominant. Before examining these in detail it is important to appreciate a fundamental difference between the two broad categories. Failing anarchy the public authority has always in the last resort someone to fall back on in order to provide the funds to meet its obligations, for example the tax payer and the rate payer. On the other hand the joint stock company has no such support and must, by and large, stand entirely on its own feet. The vital factors are its assets and its profitability.

A point which sometimes gives rise to a little bewilderment is the distinction between stocks and shares. Some companies' capital consists of stock which is transferable in units of, say, £1.00, 50p, or 25p. In this case a stockholder might have a certificate stating that he/she is a holder of £100 stock transferable in units of 25p each. An alternative way of describing the holding would be '400 stock units of 25p each'. On the other hand another company might have share capital, each share having a nominal value of, say, £1.00, 50p, or 25p. For practical purposes there is now no significant difference between stock units and shares and the terms tend to be used interchangeably.

The nominal value of a company's stock or shares is, of course, quite a different thing from its market value. For instance, a £1.00 share may be worth perhaps £2.50 or 50p according to the company's worth in the minds of investors.

3.1 Loan capital

This is capital provided not by the company's 'members', or in other words its shareholders, but by outside parties who are in effect creditors of the company. It may be issued at par, at a discount, or at a premium, i.e. each £100 nominal might be issued for subscription at a cost of £100 (par), say £98 (at a discount), or say £102.50 (at a premium). The actual terms of an issue depend on current market conditions at the time it is made.

The total amount which a company may borrow by way of loan capital is laid down in its Memorandum or Articles of Association. These however may be altered, and to protect themselves against this the holders of loan capital would normally have a restriction on further borrowing written into the terms of their loan. For example, it may be laid down that no prior ranking loan capital may be issued and that the total loan capital must not exceed three-quarters of the paid-up share capital and reserves of the company. In addition to the capital limitation it may also be stipulated that no further charges may be created to the effect that the gross amount of one year's interest payable on all loan capital would exceed an amount equal to, say, one quarter of the average profits for the three years previous to the time the additional loan capital is raised. The inherent weakness of this income provision is that there is no guarantee that future profits will be maintained at the same level.

Holders of loan capital are entitled to interest at a fixed rate, normally payable at half-yearly intervals. This interest constitutes a debt against the company, and if there are not sufficient profits available it can be paid out of capital.

The terms for repayment of loan capital are varied and, although basically similar, tend to be more complicated than those for public authority stocks. For example, a well-known company has on issue a $7\frac{1}{4}\%$ Unsecured Loan Stock 1988/93. The Stock must be redeemed by the company at par not later than 6 May 1993. It has, however, the option to redeem at par the whole or any part of the Stock on, or at any time after, 6 May 1988. Should part only be redeemed in this way the holders to be repaid will be selected by drawings. Furthermore, the company is entitled at any time to purchase the Stock on the market at any price, or to purchase Stock by tender or private treaty at premiums not exceeding 5%.

When a company raises cash by way of loan capital it does not remain liquid as the funds are employed either for the repayment of temporary loans or utilized in the purchase of buildings, plant, machinery, etc., required for the conduct of the company's business. Practically all loan capital is redeemable not later than on a specified date and therefore consideration must be given as to how it will be repaid.

Sometimes this can be done by a new issue of loan capital, but this could be expensive if interest rates were high at the vital period and, say, a stock with a 5% coupon could only be replaced by one carrying a 10% rate. Accordingly, when issuing loan capital a company often makes definite provisions for its redemption by allocating annually a fixed sum for that purpose. This is the procedure known as setting up a 'sinking fund'. The fund may be operated by making annual repayments of capital by drawings, usually but not always at par, or alternatively by purchase in the market. When a stock is standing below par it is the latter method that will be employed.

The holders of loan capital are not entitled to vote at company meetings and have no say in the running of its affairs so long as the company is complying with the obligations under which the capital was issued. Loan capital is raised in a variety of different names and it is necessary to examine the terms of issue to determine what exactly is involved in the debt contract. There are, however, two main classifications – debenture stocks and loan stocks.

3.11 Debenture stocks

The essential feature about a debenture stock is that the holders have security for the debt due to them by the company. Where public quoted companies are concerned, invariably a 'trust deed' is executed pledging the security to a trustee, usually a body corporate, i.e. an insurance company, a bank, or a trust company, on behalf of the stockholders. This has a twofold benefit. It is much simpler for the company to deal with the trustee rather than with a multitude of individual stockholders, and the trustee who must be completely independent from the company can, if the occasion arises, act more effectively on behalf of the stockholders than they could themselves.

The security may be a charge on specific assets, such as land, buildings, plant, machinery, etc., or it may be in the form of a floating charge over the company's assets as a whole. In practice it is not unusual for the debentures or debenture stock to be secured by a fixed charge on specific assets plus a floating charge on the remainder.

Where specific assets are mortgaged the company is not able to deal with them by way of sale or the creation of another charge except subject to the terms of the trust deed. On the other hand, where the security is by way of a floating charge the company may deal without restriction in the ordinary course of business with the assets involved. It follows, therefore, that with the fixed charge the stockholder knows exactly what assets comprise his/her security. Their market value in the event of a forced sale may, of course, be a completely unknown quantity, particularly if they are of use only in a very specialized capacity. The floating charge provides a wider security, but there is the risk that during a period of difficulty assets may be disposed of in order to try and ward off disaster before the debenture holders or their trustee have realized the seriousness of the situation.

There may also be debentures ranking first, second, and even third over the same assets. A further variant is that two debentures with otherwise differing conditions may rank *pari passu* (on an equal footing). For example, a company might have the following stocks:

$3\frac{1}{2}$ per cent First Debenture Stock 1970/92
$4\frac{1}{2}$ per cent Second Debenture Stock 1982/92
$6\frac{3}{4}$ per cent Second Debenture Stock 1995/2000

The first debenture stockholders would be entitled to full satisfaction of their rights in priority to the second debenture stockholders. After these were met, if there were not sufficient assets to satisfy both classes of second debenture stockholders in full they would both suffer proportionately.

3.12 Loan stocks

Increasingly common in recent years have been the issues of unsecured loan stocks. These differ from debenture stocks in that the holders do not have the right to take over assets should the company default in its obligations. They have the company's promise to pay in accordance with the terms of issue, and in a liquidation rank along with the general body of creditors. They may, however, have an order of priority among themselves. The loan stock's position of strength is that it must be serviced before the shareholders can get anything out of the company.

3.13 Purchase considerations

Before buying debenture or loan stocks the terms and conditions of issue should be checked by the prospective investor to find out, for instance, whether further debenture stock may be created ranking *pari passu* with existing stock and, if so, subject to what limitation; or to what extent the position of unsecured loan stockholders is protected by restrictions on further borrowing.

For practical reasons it is, however, highly desirable that it should never be necessary for the holders of loan capital to have to take the extreme step of forcing their rights. Should a company get into difficulties it may in fact be to the advantage in the long run of stockholders not to put it into liquidation but to try and keep it as a going concern in the hope that it will get on its feet again. Quite commonly when difficulties arise a scheme of arrangement is agreed upon providing perhaps for a moratorium, which is a complete suspension of interest for a period, or for the postponement of maturity or of sinking fund payments.

It is, therefore, prudent only to purchase debenture or loan stocks in those companies whose profit record and future prospects suggest that the possibility of their ever having difficulty in meeting their obligations is so remote as to be virtually non-existent.

In recognition, however, that there is a greater risk of default than with the stocks of public authorities it is accordingly necessary to compensate for this by paying the investor in loan capital a higher return on his/her money. The exact amount of this varies according to the status of the company. In the case of a first class company the differential between it and a similar British Government stock might well be in the region of 1% although in times of lower interest rates $\frac{1}{2}$% would be a more likely approximation. Should investment be made in companies of inferior ratings a progressively higher return will be demanded. Also, in the same company the stocks with the greater measure of security will yield less than the stocks ranking after them.

When comparing company stocks and shares with public authority stocks it should be remembered that higher commission is charged when purchasing the former. Debenture and loan stocks (including index-linked issues), but not convertibles, are now exempt from the £1.00% (see Appendix B) stamp duty payable on the purchase of company stocks and shares.

3.14 Deep discount securities

In times of inflation and high interest rates companies requiring additional finance have to consider how this can be achieved most economically. One approach to solving their fund raising needs is to issue securities well below but redeemable at par and paying a very low or a nil rate of interest. For example, a company in 1985 issued a stock at £47.30 paying no interest and redeemable at par in 1992.

Such deep discount securities are subject to rules set out in the Finance Act 1984 in which they are defined as any redeemable security issued at a discount which either represents more than 15% of the amount payable on redemption or exceeds 0.5% per annum over the number of complete years between the date of issue of the security and the redemption date. For the purpose of determining whether or not a security has been issued at a deep discount the amount payable on redemption excludes any interest payable. A deep discount stock could also be redeemable at above par.

The new rules which apply only to deep discount securities issued after 13 March 1984 effectively treat the discount as income accruing over the life of the security and when a deep discount security is sold or redeemed the investor is regarded as receiving all the accrued income to date in that year and so liable to tax thereon.

The accrued income element is calculated for every income period this being the period for which income is paid, normally half yearly, or in the case of a zero coupon stock the income period is yearly commencing on the anniversary of the issue of the stock. The calculation of this income element involves compound interest and to assist the investor a company with deep discount securities must issue a certificate showing the income element for each income period between the date of issue of the security and the redemption date.

Although the investor is only subjected to tax when his/her holding is sold or redeemed the company obtains tax relief annually by being able to reduce its profits by the accruing income element.

The 1984 Finance Act rules for taxing as income the capital appreciation on deep discount securities make them less attractive than they would otherwise be for high taxpayers seeking capital growth rather than income. However they retain an appeal for investors who for reasons such as retirement will be in a lower income bracket when redemption takes place.

3.2 Share capital

While a joint stock company may or may not have loan capital it is essential that it has share capital, the owners of which are the members or proprietors of the company. There are two main categories – preference share capital and ordinary share capital. The exact rights pertaining to the holders of a company's different types of share capital are usually laid down in its Articles of Association, although occasionally they may be specified in its Memorandum of Association. Certain characteristics are commonly associated with each type of share capital but the descriptive wording may be misleading and the position should always be checked.

3.21 Preference capital

This has an important similarity with loan capital in that a fixed rate is involved. It is, however, not a rate of interest but a dividend. There is no charge or debt against the company as the shareholder is him/herself a proprietor and the dividend when paid must be declared by the directors out of profits.

Even if there are profits available after the interest on the loan capital has been paid, the directors are not compelled to pay a dividend on the preference shares, but they must do so before any dividend is paid on lower ranking capital such as ordinary shares. For example, the directors after making allocations to reserves, etc., decide they have £160,000* available for the dividends on £1,000,000 7% Preference Stock and £1,000,000 Ordinary Stock. This sum will be allocated as follows:

£1,000,000 Preference Stock at 7%	£70,000
£1,000,000 Ordinary Stock at 9%	90,000
	£160,000

In the event of profits falling to £70,000 the directors, if they wished, could still pay the preference dividend in full, but whether or not they did so there would be no dividend on the ordinary shares.

Frequently a company has more than one class of preference share capital and these may rank in order of priority, i.e. the dividend on the prior ranking classes must be paid in full before anything is paid on the lower ranking stocks. Usually it is possible to tell the order of ranking from the titles, a first preference stock ranking before a second preference stock, etc. It is also quite common for companies to have preference stocks ranking *pari passu* although different rates of dividend are payable. For example, a company might have a 6% Preference Stock and an 8% Preference Stock. Should these rank *pari passu*, if the full dividend is paid on the 6% Stock the full rate must be paid on the 8% Stock. However, if the directors for one reason or another are unable to declare the full dividend on both Stocks they must both abate proportionately. If $4\frac{1}{2}$% is paid on the 6% Stock, 6% must be paid on the 8% Stock.

3.211 Cumulative preference

Preference stocks may be either cumulative or non-cumulative. If cumulative the right to the preference dividend, if unpaid in any year or years, accumulates. For example, should the dividend on a first preference share be cumulative, if it falls into arrears all such arrears must be met before any

---

* To simplify the illustration tax implications are ignored.

further dividends can be paid on lower ranking stocks, such as second or third preference shares and ordinary shares. On the other hand, if a preference dividend is not cumulative the preferential rights exist for each year in isolation and are not carried forward. Thus if the dividend is passed in any one year it is lost and no more than the current rate of preference dividend is paid when distributions are resumed.

3.212 *Participating preference*

A few companies have participating preference shares which means that holders are entitled to a preferential dividend and also in certain circumstances to a further participation in profits. The conditions attaching to such shares vary widely, but the following example will serve to indicate the general pattern.

A company has an issue of $7\frac{1}{2}$% Cumulative Participating Preference Shares which are entitled first of all to a cumulative $7\frac{1}{2}$%. After payment of a non-cumulative $7\frac{1}{2}$% on the Ordinary Shares they rank *pari passu* with the Ordinary for a further non-cumulative $2\frac{1}{2}$%.

If in year 1 the Ordinary get 5% the Cumulative Participating Preference get $7\frac{1}{2}$%
If in year 2 the Ordinary get $7\frac{1}{2}$% the Cumulative Participating Preference get $7\frac{1}{2}$%
If in year 3 the Ordinary get 8% the Cumulative Participating Preference get 8%
If in year 4 the Ordinary get 10% the Cumulative Participating Preference get 10%
If in year 5 the Ordinary get 11% the Cumulative Participating Preference get 10%
(maximum entitlement)

3.213 *Redeemable preference*

As the description suggests there are provisions for the redemption of these preference shares at a predetermined time, or times, subject to the statutory conditions that such redemption may only be made from accumulated profits otherwise available for dividend, or from the proceeds of a new issue of shares. The reason for these conditions is that the security of creditors might otherwise be seriously impaired should repayment be made from, say, the realization of assets used in the conduct of the business.

In some ways redeemable preference shares are similar to redeemable loan capital, but from the security point of view they are inferior. Should the redemption dates arrive and the company is not in a position to effect repayment, the preference shareholders cannot take legal action against the company and can only look to the Articles to obtain satisfaction of their rights as against the other classes of shareholders.

It is also worthy of note that even if preference share capital does not have specific redemption provisions it may still be possible, following a House of Lords ruling, for it to be redeemed if the company has the appropriate funds available. However, the terms of preference shares issued in recent years usually provide safeguards against holders being repaid at a disadvantageous time, for instance when they could only reinvest at a lower rate.

3.214 *Preferred and preferred ordinary*

Some companies have preferred shares instead of preference shares and usually it can be assumed that the only difference is in the choice of the descriptive word. More uncertainty, however, surrounds the status of the preferred ordinary share. Sometimes it has merely the characteristics of a preference share whereas, on the other hand, it may have attaching to it in a greater or lesser degree some of the attributes of ordinary shares. As always the exact position may be ascertained by reference to the Articles or Memorandum.

3.215 *Voting*

Preference shareholders do not usually have the right to vote at company meetings. This is not universally the case as occasionally they have some restricted voting rights but with control of the company remaining with the ordinary shareholders. However, should the dividend fall into arrears effective voting powers are normally accorded under the Articles to the preference shareholders.

On some matters affecting them directly, such as the issue of further preference shares ranking *pari passu* or in priority to those already in existence, preference shareholders are entitled to a separate class meeting at which the proposals can, if necessary, be thwarted if they are considered to be damaging to the preference shareholders' interests.

3.216 *Investment merits*

From the investor's point of view, prior to the introduction of corporation tax, he/she would have expected to obtain a higher return from preference shares than from unsecured loan stocks. Both have a fixed rate of payment but unsecured loan stocks rank before preference shares and therefore have the greater security. As, however, preference share dividends are now 'franked' income for corporation tax purposes (see Section 9.24), this enhances their value to many of the institutions and they may now be found to yield less than both debenture and loan stocks. They have, therefore, little attraction for the private investor.

3.22 *Equity capital*

The holders of this type of capital – usually the ordinary shareholders – are broadly entitled to what is left over after the rights of the holders of the prior charge capital have been satisfied. They also normally have the voting power at company general meetings.

The greater attraction of ordinary shares is that, barring government intervention which has so far only been on a limited scale, there is no restriction on the amount which might be paid out by way of dividend should the company's profits keep on increasing. Thus, if the investor has chosen his companies well his dividend income will rise with the passing years although not probably at a regular rate. Along with this increase in dividends, or perhaps partly in anticipation of it, the market value of his shares will rise and, accordingly, both from the income and capital point of view he has at least some protection against the fall in value of money.

Not all the profits available are paid out to the ordinary shareholders, as according to the requirements of the company the directors plough back a certain proportion into the business. However, on the assumption that this in turn increases future profitability and dividends, such retentions are to the ultimate benefit of the equity holder. The risk attaching to ordinary shares is that should a company run into hard times it is the ordinary dividend which will be reduced or passed before any cut will be made in the preference dividends.

3.221 *Not always ordinary*

A point to watch is that the ordinary share capital is not always the equity of the company. The equity may occasionally rest with the deferred shareholders* and if the same company also has ordinary shares these may in fact be more akin to preference shares. It is also possible for the equity to be owned in varying degrees by ordinary, preferred ordinary, and participating preference shareholders.

3.222 *'A' ordinary*

Anyone who is concerned with investment will from time to time come across 'A' ordinary shares. This is a class of capital which usually ranks equally with the ordinary shares of the same company in all respects except that it has no voting power. The number of 'A' shares in existence has been reduced owing to strong opposition to them from the Stock Exchange and other influential bodies on the grounds that shareholders who bear the same risks as the ordinary shareholders should have an equal say in the running of the company. It is likely that the issue of further non-voting shares will soon be effectively banned.

The attraction of 'A' shares is to directors who have been able to issue more equity capital, for example in connection with takeover bids, without exposing themselves to loss of control of the company. Shareholders will, of course, not grumble so long as the company is prospering and their shares rise in value.

The market price of the 'A' shares may, however, be lower than that of the ordinary although the wide disparity which sometimes formerly arose when a

---

* Deferred shares have varying rights and it is necessary to check each individual issue to ascertain what these are.

struggle developed for control of a company has now been eliminated (see Section 16.42).

3.23 Ranking for capital

In discussing the rights of the holders of share capital the emphasis has been mainly on income rights. Although it is seldom anticipated that a company will be wound-up, it must be borne in mind that while ranking for repayment of capital may be in the same order as for the payment of dividends it is not necessarily so.

Usually, after all outside interests have been satisfied, the preference shareholders have the nominal amount of their capital repaid to them. They may perhaps be paid out at a premium, for example every preference share of £1.00 may be repaid at £1.25. Thereafter the ordinary shareholders will be entitled to what is left. On the other hand it is quite possible that a preference share might rank on an equal footing with the ordinary in a winding-up.

3.3 Convertibles

There are nowadays many issues of loan capital* which carry the right to convert into a stated number of ordinary shares at a definite time or times in the future. The features of such stocks can best be illustrated by using an example.

Suppose in May 1983 a company issued a $7\frac{3}{4}$% Convertible Loan Stock 1995/98 at par and in exchange for every £100 nominal holders have the right to convert into:

34 Ordinary Shares in January   1988, or
33 Ordinary Shares in January   1989, or
32 Ordinary Shares in January   1990

and at the time when the convertible was issued the ordinary shares were worth £2.87$\frac{1}{2}$.

Any subscriber for the convertible who exercised his/her right to convert in 1988 would in effect be acquiring his/her ordinary shares at a cost of £2.95 (£100/34). The conversion premium, i.e. the cost of the right to convert, would therefore be £0.07$\frac{1}{2}$/2.87$\frac{1}{2}$ × 100 = 2.6%. Similarly, conversion in 1989 or 1990 would be at a cost of £3.03 or £3.12$\frac{1}{2}$ and premiums of 5.4% and 8.7% respectively.

It will be observed that the later conversion takes place the fewer ordinary shares received. Some years ago this was a very common condition but recently the tendency has been for the same terms of conversion to be available over a period of years.

---

* There are also a number of convertible preference issues giving holders the right in due course to convert to ordinary shares. Investors should keep in mind the inferior security accorded to preference shares as opposed to loan capital.

Convertible issues are almost invariably made to the company equity shareholders on a 'rights' basis. For instance, in this particular issue the ordinary shareholders may well have been entitled to subscribe for £1 Stock for every two shares held. The reason why convertibles are offered to existing shareholders and not direct to the public is that they create a potential increase in the company's equity. If this passed into the hands of outsiders it would reduce the equity shareholders' proportionate share of the ownership of the company and they could justifiably feel aggrieved. Should a shareholder not wish to subscribe for the new issue there is no obligation for him to do so. He can sell his subscription rights for whatever they will fetch in the market.

There are several variations in convertibles and the conditions of each issue must be studied carefully to determine the precise rights available to the stockholder. Sometimes perhaps only half the loan stock may be convertible, or the company may have the option of repaying all the unconverted stock once the last occasion for conversion has passed instead of it remaining in existence with the status of a normal loan stock. In order to maintain the value of the convertible terms it is necessary that provision should be made for their adjustment should the company make further issues of equity capital while the convertible is still outstanding. For instance, should a company make a one for one scrip issue (see Section 8.11) the number of ordinary shares to be received on each occasion of conversion thereafter would require to be doubled.

3.31 Attraction of the convertible

The reason why a company issues a convertible is, briefly, that at certain times it is the easiest method of obtaining the required finance. Investors may not be willing at that particular time to subscribe for a straight fixed interest stock without the bait of a potential equity interest attached. Alternatively, the market price of the company's ordinary shares may not be sufficiently above their par value to permit of a satisfactory rights issue (see Section 8.12) being made, or such an issue might be less desirable than a loan capital issue because of the incidence of corporation tax.

The appeal of convertibles to investors is that they offer, if not the best of both worlds, at least some of the advantages. The income to be obtained from the convertible is invariably higher than that from the ordinary shares, sometimes substantially so. Should the company not make the progress in profitability that might be desired, the value of the convertible holders' capital is afforded some protection by its fixed interest status. On the other hand, if the company does well and the ordinary share price rises the convertible will move up in anticipation of the increase in capital value which will crystallize on conversion. It must be appreciated, however, that the higher the convertible rises the further will it be removed from its fixed interest support level.

Consider the 7¾% Convertible Unsecured Loan Stock to which reference has already been made. Suppose in September 1984 it is standing at a price of 112 and a closely parallel loan stock but without conversion terms is standing at 74. Thus, should the conversion terms cease to be attractive as the result of a drop in the ordinary share price the convertible could fall to 74 – a substantial capital loss indeed – before its fixed interest status is effective as a support. Looked at another way, because the convertible is standing 38 points above its value as a straight fixed interest stock it could be said that to a buyer at 112 the cost of the option to convert is 38/74 × 100 = 51%.

The cost of ultimately obtaining the ordinary via the convertible would be:

In 1988 112/34 £3.29½.
In 1989 112/33 £3.39½.
In 1990 112/32 £3.50.

If at the same time the price of the ordinary shares is £3.22½ a buyer of the loan stock at 112 who converts in 1988 will in effect have paid a premium of 2.1% over the current price of the ordinary. Should conversion take place in 1989 or 1990 the premium will be 5.2% and 8.5% respectively. The price of the convertible is in fact tied closely to that of the ordinary shares and the buyer of the convertible at this price is exposed to the same risks as the ordinary shareholder but with a 'safety net' at around 74. The price on a fixed interest basis would also be vulnerable if the company's fortunes really took a severe turn for the worse.

3.32 Whether to convert

When the time comes for a holder to decide whether to convert there are various factors to be taken into the reckoning. These may be summarized as follows:

1 The company's prospects from an equity holder's point of view.
2 Future opportunities, if any, to convert and their terms.
3 Will the price drop when the last conversion date passes and the convertible becomes a straight fixed interest stock?
4 Can the loss of income arising on conversion be accepted?

If the answer to 3 is affirmative but 4 is negative the action required is a sale of the convertible while its conversion terms are still available, and the investment of the proceeds in another stock with a suitable yield.

A different problem will arise when the conversion premium is large and the value of the convertible in its fixed interest form is greater than the equivalent number of ordinary shares. There will be no question of conversion taking place and the holder will have to make up his mind whether he wishes the stock to remain in his portfolio on its fixed interest merits.

Should he still be desirous of acquiring an equity interest in the company he could sell the convertible in the market and use the proceeds to purchase the ordinary shares.

3.4 Warrants to subscribe

A company may require to raise additional finance but as an alternative to a convertible loan stock may decide to issue a loan stock along with warrants carrying the right to subscribe at some time in the future for ordinary shares at a fixed price. As soon as they are issued or shortly afterwards the loan stock and the warrants are dealt in as separate entities.

The life of a warrant is specified when it is issued and may be for a shorter or longer period of years or, rather exceptionally, of unlimited duration. Warrants become valueless if not exercised before the end of their lifespan. Some warrants are exercisable on any day of their life, while others can only be exercised during certain periods or on certain days.

Warrants do not form part of a company's issued capital and do not confer on their owners the right to attend or vote at ordinary meetings of the company. However usually they have inwritten provisions for preservation or adjustment of their terms in the event of capitalization or rights issues being made by the company. Where quoted on the Stock Exchange they are dealt in like shares and are similarly treated for capital gains tax purposes.

The advantage to the company is that it can obtain its finance more cheaply as the rate of interest payable on the loan stock will be less than would have been the case if it had been issued entirely on its own. No interest or dividend is payable on the warrants but in due course if the rights contained in the warrants are exercised this will result in a dilution of the equity.

While some warrant issues have arisen from a package offering on a 'rights' basis to a company's equity shareholders others have been created to form part consideration when one company is making an offer to the shareholders of another company which it wishes to take over. In several cases where the warrants have been issued with loan stock there is the option, when the time comes, to subscribe for ordinary shares by the surrender of this loan stock at par as an alternative to cash subscription.

3.41 Value of a warrant

The value of a warrant depends on a number of factors of which the price of the ordinary shares and the subscription price are the most obvious. However this is not all that is involved.

Consider the situation where a company has on issue warrants which may be exchanged for ordinary shares on the basis of one ordinary share per warrant at 160p exercisable on 30 April each year over a period of the next six years. The current price of the warrant is 43p and the ordinary shares 172p. The reader may ask why an investor would be willing to pay 43p for the right to subscribe for a share at 160p – a total cost of 203p – when he could purchase the shares for 172p now. The reason is, of course, that before the end of the lifetime of the warrant he hopes the share price will have risen above his capital break even price of 203p. If, for instance, an annual growth rate of 5% is anticipated this would indicate a price of 230p in six years' time. Until he subscribes for whatever number of shares he holds warrants for he will have committed less of his capital to the company than if he had made an outright purchase of the shares.

It will be observed that the current price of the ordinary shares 172p is 12p more than the subscription price of 160p. This gives the warrant an 'intrinsic value' of 12p. As the warrant has a market value of 43p it is standing at a conversion premium of 18% (31/172 × 100) over the ordinary price.

Warrants normally stand at a premium but frequently they may be found to have no intrinsic value. This occurs where the subscription price is the same as or is in excess of the market price, i.e. in the above example if the market price fell to 160p or under. When the subscription price is above the market price this does not mean that the warrants will be of no value unless the final subscription date is close at hand and there is little likelihood of the market price rising to above the subscription price in the short period remaining. When the warrant has several years to run investors, as stated above, may expect the ordinary share to rise in price during the interval and this is why they are prepared to purchase the warrant at a premium. Thus the life of a warrant has a considerable bearing on its price.

When considering the attraction of warrants compared with the ordinary shares weight must be given to the dividends which are paid on the ordinary shares and also the interest which could be earned by the saving in capital achieved by the purchase of warrants. If an investor had £1,720 available for investment in the company he could buy 1,000 shares. Alternatively he could purchase 1,000 warrants for £430 leaving him with £1,290 capital. If the ordinary shares at their current price and rate of dividend were yielding (see Section 11.1) 4% they would produce an annual income of £68.80. On the other hand, in a period of high interest rates he might be able to purchase a safe fixed interest stock (preferably maturing at around the final subscription date) with £1,290 to yield 10%, i.e. producing £129. This difference in the return produced when compounded over the lifetime of the warrant is a significant factor in the assessment of its value. The rate of dividend paid by the company would in all probability vary, hopefully upwards, as the result of which calculations must be made on an estimated dividend basis. Taxation and dealing expenses would in practice also require to be taken into account.

3.42 Gearing

To many investors the main attraction of warrants lies in their 'gearing' which means that price movements in the ordinary shares are magnified in the corresponding price movements in the warrants. If the share price in the above example rose from 172p to 215p it would not be unlikely for the warrant price to rise from 43p to somewhere in the region of 86p. However the appreciation in the ordinary share would have only been 25% whereas that of the warrant is 100%. This 'gearing factor' is measured by dividing the ordinary share price by the price of the warrant. Thus with prices respectively of 172p and 43p it would be four times. As price levels rise the gearing is reduced and at levels of 215p and 86p it is down to two and a half times.

Gearing is unfortunately a two-edged weapon so that a relatively minor fall in the share price can be reflected in a severe percentage drop in the price of the warrant. In any event prices are constantly fluctuating and this inherent high volatility of warrants makes them an obvious medium for short-term speculation.

3.43 Shares per warrant

For simplicity in the example used for illustration it has been assumed that one warrant provides the right to subscribe for one share. This often is the case but it is not unusual to come across warrant/share relationships which are not on a one for one basis. In order to make the required calculations it is first of all necessary to establish the warrant price per share and then relate this instead of the warrant price to the other relevant data. For instance, in the example if the warrant had entitled the holder to subscribe for two ordinary shares the warrant price per share used for the calculations would have been 21.5p.

Typical questions

Distinguish between the following:
1 A cumulative preference share.
2 A non-cumulative preference share.
3 A non-cumulative participating preference share.
4 A redeemable cumulative preference share
   with particular reference to their respective rights to participate in profits. What rights to participation in assets would you normally expect to find in these classes of shares?
   (The Institute of Bankers, *Principles and Practice of Investment*)

Suggested answers

1 A cumulative preference share gives its holder the right to receive a dividend at a fixed rate per annum payable from profits before any dividend is paid on lower ranking capital such as second cumulative preference shares or ordinary shares. If the dividend is not paid in full in any one year the arrears must be paid in full, together with the current year's dividend, before any distribution may be made on the lower ranking capital.
2 A non-cumulative preference share differs from a cumulative preference share in that if the dividend is passed in any one year it is not made good

in subsequent years but is lost to the holder for ever. In other words the preferential right to a dividend over lower ranking capital only exists in respect of each year's profits in isolation.

3 A non-cumulative participating preference share has the usual non-cumulative preference rights for each year at a fixed rate over lower ranking capital, usually in this case ordinary shares. However, when the dividend on the ordinary shares in any one year exceeds a certain percentage the non-cumulative participating preference shares will rank *pari passu* with the ordinary, subject normally to an upper limit. For instance, they may be entitled to a preferential 5% and once the ordinary dividend has reached 5% to rank *pari passu* with the ordinary for any distribution in excess of this up to a further 3%, i.e. the maximum distribution on the participating preference in any year could be 8%.

4 A redeemable cumulative preference share has the same rights to profits as a cumulative preference share. There are, however, definite provisions for the repayment of capital to the shareholders during the lifetime of the company. Such redemption may only be made from profits otherwise available for dividend or from the proceeds of a new issue of shares.

Normally in a winding-up the holders of preference shares have their capital repaid to them in full before the ordinary shareholders get anything. The preference shareholders may be repaid at par or at a premium. After that they cannot participate further in the assets of the company which are then divided among the ordinary shareholders. However, this is not always necessarily the case as the preferential rights may only extend to dividends and the preference shares could rank *pari passu* with the ordinary as far as participation in assets are concerned. In order to find out the exact position of any particular preference share it is necessary to examine the company's Articles of Association together, perhaps, with its Memorandum.

Additional questions

1 Examine the differences between holding debenture stock and ordinary shares and consider their relative attractions as forms of investment.
   Explain also the respective voting powers of the holders and their rights in the event of a winding-up of the company.
   (The Institute of Bankers in Scotland, *Theory and Practice of Investment*)

2 By what methods do companies provide for the redemption of loan capital? Differentiate between debenture and loan stocks.

3 Explain what you understand by:
   (a) Ranking in priority
   (b) Ranking *pari passu*
   and exemplify your answers.

4 How has the introduction of corporation tax affected preference shares?

5 Discuss the merits and demerits of non-voting ordinary shares to the investor and to the company.

(The Institute of Bankers, *Principles and Practice of Investment*)

6 You have in your portfolio a holding of Convertible Loan Stock which may be converted into Ordinary Shares within the next thirty days. What factors would you take into account on coming to a decision to convert, sell or do nothing?

(The Savings Bank Institute, *Personal Savings and Investment*)

7 A number of UK companies have issued, in the past few years, a new form of investment called subscription warrants.

(a) What are these warrants?

(b) To whom are they most likely to appeal as an investment and why?

(c) What advantages are to be gained by the company making such an issue of warrants?

(d) How would you evaluate a warrant?

(The Institute of Bankers, *Investment*)

4 Companies and their shareholders

Chapter 3 was concerned with the range of securities of joint stock companies available to investors. It is now necessary to examine the structure of companies and the company/shareholder relationship. The latter is periodically under attack from those who in the interests of industrial democracy wish workers to have a greater say in the running of a company. At the time of writing no specific legislation to this end has been proposed.

4.1 Limited liability

All the companies quoted on the Stock Exchange are public joint stock limited liability companies. Before going any further it may be that the important words 'limited liability' require some explanation. What they mean is that once a shareholder has purchased shares which are fully paid-up he has no further liability. If the company fails and goes into liquidation all he loses is the money he paid for the shares. He cannot be held liable for the debts of the company and his other personal assets made available to satisfy the company's creditors, as can happen in the case of a partnership.

This was not always so, as originally the personal liability of shareholders for their company's debts was unlimited. The result of this was that many innocent shareholders were ruined by company failures and not surprisingly it became difficult to induce people to subscribe money for shares in joint stock companies. In order to ensure the survival of the joint stock company system limited liability was eventually, after some opposition, introduced in 1855.

Apart from new issues which are sometimes only partly paid during the first few months of their lives, it is normal for the shares quoted on the Stock Exchange to be fully paid. However, in the event that shares are partly paid a further but limited liability may devolve on the holders. For example, if a company has £10 shares which are £2.50 paid-up, each holder of one of these shares may be liable to meet a maximum of another £7.50 per share should circumstances arise which necessitate the company making such a call.

4.2 Company formation

4.21 Purpose

It may be asked why companies have come into being and what function they serve. The short answer is that they enable people with ideas and organizing ability to obtain the use of the capital without which they would be unable to develop and expand their businesses. They do this by forming a company and issuing shares to people with spare capital available. This capital may arise from large amounts of inherited wealth or it may be the hard earned savings of a manual worker. However, through the medium of the company it can be put to work to increase the wealth of the community whatever the source.

Before proceeding further it should be mentioned that very many companies are small affairs – known as private companies – and the shareholders may all even be in the one family. Investors in general are not concerned with companies at this stage in their development. They may frequently have certain disadvantages for the investor, such as the right of directors to restrict transfers, and lack of marketability of the shares.

However, many of these companies prosper and expand with the result that they become public and seek a quotation for their shares on the Stock Exchange. This is the time when the general body of investors become interested as once the shares are quoted on the Stock Exchange they can be bought and sold freely. The Stock Exchange's function in this is to provide a market place.

4.22 Legislation

With the company providing a method whereby an individual or a group can control large sums of money and assets belonging to other people it has been necessary to introduce legislation to prevent abuse of the position of trust which this entails. The principal source of company regulation in this country is the Companies Act 1985. This consolidated all previous Acts including the Companies Act 1948 which was the previous consolidating Act.

4.23 Memorandum and articles

When a company is formed those responsible must lodge with the Registrar of Companies two basic documents, the Memorandum of Association and the Articles of Association.

The matters covered in the Memorandum are:

1 The name of the company which must end with the word 'limited' if it is a private company or 'public limited company' (alternatively some form of abbreviation e.g. 'plc') if it is a public company.
2 The location of the registered office, e.g. England or Scotland.
3 The objects for which the company has been established. These are often extremely wide and may even border on the fantastic. The reason for this is that at one time it was very difficult to alter a company's Memorandum and a company has no power to do anything not authorized by its objects clause. Nowadays, however, the objects of a company may be altered by special resolution, sanction of the Court only being required if holders representing not less than 15% of the capital object. Should such

objection be made the Court may confirm the alteration either wholly or in part and on such terms as it thinks fit. If necessary it may direct that satisfactory arrangements are put in hand for the purchase of the interests of the dissentient shareholders.

4　The fact that the liability of members is limited.

5　The amount of the nominal capital of the company. For example, it might be stated that 'the share capital of the company is £1,000,000 divided into 2,000,000 shares of 50p each'. In some cases the different classes of shares are defined but this may be dealt with in the Articles.

The Articles lay down what may be described as the internal rules for the running of the company. The 1948 Companies Act provides a model constitution known as Table A which automatically applies if a company has no Articles of its own. For private companies incorporated on or after 1 July 1985 a new Table 'A' published in The Companies (Tables A to F) Regulations 1985 is applicable. In practice most companies have adopted Articles which, by and large, are very similar to Table A.

The Articles usually detail the various classes of share capital, defining their rights both as to participation in profits and ranking in a winding-up. They also cover such matters as the alteration of share capital, the number of directors, their qualification shares, their duties and powers including those related to borrowing, shareholders' meeting and voting rights, and other detailed procedure for the conduct of the company. The Articles can be altered by special resolution at a general meeting.

4.24　The directors

The position of company directors requires some consideration. The directors are elected by shareholders to run the business on their behalf and accordingly hold a position of trust. They must not make a secret profit out of their office, and if a director has an interest in contracts to which the company is a party this must be disclosed to his/her co-directors who, if they consider it to be a matter of sufficient importance, must make further disclosure to the members in their report. Directors are personally liable to the company in the case of negligence in the exercise of their duties but not where only errors of judgement are concerned.

Should a public company incur a serious loss of capital, the directors must convene a general meeting for this to be discussed by shareholders. The directors' duties are further stated to include having regard to the interests of the employees in general as well as to the interests of members.

Directors normally retire in rotation every third year but may be re-elected by shareholders in general meeting. However, on attaining the age of seventy a director must retire at the conclusion of the annual general meeting following his/her birthday unless his/her re-election is approved at that meeting after 'special notice' has been given.

4.25 Rights of shareholders

Shareholders appoint directors to control the company's affairs on their behalf and have themselves no right to interfere in the day-to-day running of the company. They have the right to receive the annual report and accounts, to attend, vote, and speak on any matter on the agenda at general meetings. Perhaps most important of all they have the right to share in distributed profits.

4.3 Meetings

Before any meeting can be validly held there must be a quorum of members present. The exact number required is a matter for the company's Articles. If Table A is adopted three members must be present in person.

4.31 Annual general meeting

A company must hold an annual general meeting at least once in each calendar year and within fifteen months of the previous annual general meeting. It is called by giving shareholders not less than twenty-one days' notice in writing. The business is usually confined to the following routine matters:

1 To receive and, if approved, adopt the directors' report and accounts for the year.
2 To declare a dividend.
3 To elect the directors.
4 To appoint (or re-appoint) the auditors and authorize the directors to fix their remuneration.
5 To transact any other competent business.

Other business may be transacted, but if so twenty-one days' special notice of this must be given in the notice convening the meeting. For example, a director may be removed by ordinary resolution in this way before the expiration of his/her term of office. Even in face of opposition from the board, matters can be placed on the agenda under a procedure (Companies Act 1985, section 376, formerly the Companies Act 1948, section 140) available to holders of not less than one-twentieth of the total voting rights, or alternatively by any one hundred members representing between them at least £10,000 of paid-up capital.

With regard to the payment of dividends the rate is recommended by the directors in their report and approved by the shareholders who could if they so wished vote a reduction of rate but not an increase. The normal practice is for an interim dividend to be declared by the directors between the annual general meetings leaving the final to be passed at the meeting.

4.32 Extraordinary general meeting

Frequently the Articles restrict the business that can be dealt with at an annual general meeting, although not where shareholders' rights under section 376 have been exercised, and any other business is regarded as being special and must be transacted at an extraordinary general meeting. As the result of this it is often the practice for an extraordinary general meeting to commence immediately after the conclusion of the annual general meeting. An extraordinary meeting may be called by the directors at any time by giving fourteen days' notice except when a special resolution is to be passed in which event twenty-one days' notice is required.

Normally, extraordinary general meetings are convened by the board but they can also be requisitioned by shareholders representing one-tenth of the total voting rights. The requisitionists, who are obviously dissatisfied about some important aspect of the running of the company, must clearly define the purpose of the meeting which commonly involves removal of directors. Minority holders of 10% of the voting capital can also make application to the Department of Trade for the appointment of inspectors to investigate the company's affairs.

4.33 Resolutions

There are three kinds of resolution which may be passed at company meetings – an ordinary resolution which requires a simple majority, and extraordinary and special resolutions both of which require a 75% majority. To decide which type is appropriate it may be necessary at times to consult both the Companies Act and the Articles. For instance, it does not follow that special business requires a special resolution as the share capital of a company can be increased or subdivided by an ordinary resolution. The main use of an extraordinary resolution is for the voluntary winding-up of a company on the grounds that it cannot continue its business by reason of its liabilities. Special resolutions are, among other things, required for alterations to the Memorandum or Articles, to change the name of a company, and for reductions of capital. For the latter the consent of the Court is required.

4.34 Class meetings

As well as annual general meetings and extraordinary general meetings sometimes class meetings are held, for example of preference shareholders. When this happens only holders of the specified class of shares are entitled to attend. Such meetings are held when a variation of the shareholders' rights is proposed. Should the necessary resolution be passed it is binding on all the shareholders, but persons holding 15% of the shares of the class may apply to the Court to cancel the variation.

4.35 Votes and proxies

Voting is normally conducted in the first instance by a show of hands, each shareholder present being entitled to cast one vote irrespective of the size of his/her holding. This is a satisfactory enough method of dealing expeditiously with routine or non-controversial business. However, where differences of opinion exist a poll may be demanded, in which event the relative voting power of each shareholder depends upon the size of his/her holding. The Articles usually define the voting rights but should they make no such provision a shareholder has, on a poll, one vote for each share or £10 of stock held.

One vital factor which must be provided for is that the vast majority of members may be scattered all over the country and therefore may be prevented by distance from being able to attend meetings. It is accordingly laid down by statute that any member of a company entitled to attend and vote at a meeting may appoint another person, known as a 'proxy', to vote on his/her behalf. Proxies may or may not themselves be members of the company, but unless he/she is a member a proxy cannot speak at a public company meeting except to demand a poll.

The notice calling the meeting must state that a proxy can be appointed. The Articles usually provide that the form appointing the proxy must reach the registered office before the meeting. However, any such provision is void which required the form of proxy to be received by the company more than forty-eight hours before the meeting. Should a shareholder after having appointed a proxy turn up at the meeting the authority of the proxy may be revoked at any time before voting has taken place.

Proxies can only vote on a poll, not on a show of hands. To meet this situation the Companies Act 1985 provides that except on the question of the election of a chairman and the adjournment of the meeting, both matters which must be decided on the spot, a poll may be demanded by:

(a) Any five members entitled to vote at the meeting.
(b) Any member or members holding not less than one-tenth of the voting strength, or one-tenth of the paid-up capital conferring a right to vote.

For this purpose a proxy stands in the shoes of the shareholder he represents.

The Articles may make it easier to demand a poll but not more difficult. The time to demand a poll is before, or on the declaration of, the result of the show of hands, but it cannot validly be demanded until there has been a show of hands. Most Articles also give power to the chairman to insist on a poll and it is always he who decides when and where it will be taken. This may be at once unless the Articles provide to the contrary.

4.4 Annual report and accounts

Not less than twenty-one days before the annual general meeting a company is required to send to its shareholders and also to the holders of its loan capital a copy of its balance sheet, profit and loss account, a statement of the source and application of funds, and directors' report for the year under review. Where a company has subsidiaries, group or consolidated accounts consisting of a consolidated balance sheet, a consolidated profit and loss account, and the balance sheet of the parent company must be produced. As the result of cumulative legislation the annual report and accounts has now become an impressive and informative document.

4.41 Auditor's report

Before the passing of the Companies Act 1948 it was possible to conceal much vital information, but the Act made compulsory the publishing of accounts with greater detail. It also required the company to appoint auditors, who must be members of a body of accountants established in the United Kingdom and recognized by the Department of Trade, to examine the accounts and report to the members.

This report is issued with the accounts and should be read carefully, particular attention being paid to any qualifications which might creep in thus suggesting that the auditors are not entirely satisfied with the treatment of some items in the accounts or have not been able to vouch for certain entries. In practice any divergence from orthodox phraseology usually constitutes a qualification. A typical report of satisfied auditors would read something like the following:

'We have audited the accounts of AB Public Limited Company on pages 14 to 23 in accordance with approved Auditing Standards.

In our opinion the accounts which have been prepared under the historical cost convention give under that convention a true and fair view of the state of affairs of the Company at 31 December 1985 and of the profit and source and application of funds of the Company for the period then ended and comply with the Companies Act 1985.

In our opinion the supplementary current cost accounts on pages 24 and 25 have been properly prepared, in accordance with the methods set out in the notes.

XY & Co.,
Chartered Accountants

The Companies Act 1985 lays down that if auditors are to continue in office they must now be reappointed by ordinary resolution of the shareholders at every general meeting before which the accounts are laid. If they are to be replaced at least twenty-eight days special notice of the resolution to be placed before a general meeting must be given. Should auditors resign before completion of their term of office they are obliged to state whether or not there are any circumstances connected with their resignation which they consider should be brought to the attention of shareholders or creditors and, if so, what they are. In the event of there being a 'resignation statement' the auditors can demand that an extraordinary general meeting be called in order that they may explain the circumstances.

Auditors are therefore answerable to the shareholders and when reporting are in a position to take an independent view free from directorial pressure.

4.42 Further disclosure

Although the Companies Act 1948 was a milestone in the direction of improved accounting and revelation of a company's state of affairs, it was soon evident that the amount of information which a company was compelled by law to publish fell short of the requirements of those concerned with a detailed study of such matters. After much official consideration the Companies Act 1967 (now Companies Act 1985) became law, increasing substantially the amount of company disclosure. Important items which must now be revealed include turnover, the basis of valuation of the company's assets, a list of subsidiary and associated companies (an associated company being one in which one-tenth of the nominal equity capital is held) with their principal activities and the proportion of shares held, the emoluments of the chairman or the highest paid director with details of the emolument brackets of the remaining directors without mentioning them by name, and the directors' interests in the company's share or loan capital at the beginning and end of the financial year.

4.43 Chairman's statement

Usually there is incorporated in the annual report a statement by the chairman. This amplifies and interprets where necessary the information provided by the directors' reports and the accounts. It may also survey general economic and political factors which are influencing the company's performance in its different spheres of activity.

Often perhaps the most interesting features of the report are that it comments on how the company is faring in its current accounting year and makes some forecast of future trends. Sometimes the statement is not released until the chairman's speech at the annual general meeting, in which event it is sent to shareholders as a separate document.

4.44 Interim reports

Although not a legal requirement, companies quoted on the Stock Exchange now issue interim reports providing a summary of their progress for the first six months of each accounting period, thus keeping the shareholders more up-to-date with their company's affairs.

4.5 Capital alterations

A company may sometimes decide for various reasons to make alterations to its share capital.

4.51 Reduction of capital

Misfortune may sometimes strike a company with the result that capital assets may be lost without hope of recovery. As a result of this the nominal amount of a company's capital may be ridiculously high compared with its real value. The company may therefore decide to reduce the nominal value of its share capital. To effect this a special resolution must be passed and confirmation of the Court received.

The mechanics might be that each ordinary £1.00 is written down to, say,

10p share. If the company's nominal issued ordinary capital had consisted of £1,000,000 made up of 1,000,000 £1.00 shares it would, after the reduction, consist of £100,000 made up of 1,000,000 shares of 10p each. Where creditors are not concerned the Court in granting its sanction has regard to the interests of the members of the public, who were induced to take shares in the company, and also to the fairness of the reduction as between different classes of shareholder.

Sometimes, however, a company may find that the assets which it has acquired over the years can no longer be used profitably. It may therefore decide to reduce its capital and make a repayment to shareholders of such paid-up capital. In this instance the same procedure applies but the Court will also require to be satisfied that the interests of creditors are being in no way prejudiced.

4.52 Capital reconstructions

A reconstruction takes place when a company transfers the whole of its undertaking and assets to another company under an arrangement whereby the shares of that company are distributed *pro rata* to the shareholders of the old company. Thereafter the old company winds-up. This arrangement may be carried out under the provisions of section 582 of the Companies Act 1985, formerly section 287 of the Companies Act 1948.

It is, of course, quite possible that a minority of members of the old company may not wish to become shareholders of the other company and their interests are protected under section 582. Accordingly, if any member who did not vote for the special resolution expresses his/her dissent therefrom in writing to the liquidator within seven days after the passing of the resolution, the liquidator must either abstain from carrying the resolution into effect or purchase such member's shares at a price to be determined by agreement or by arbitration. This right is of particular value in cases where partly paid shares carrying a liability for further calls are being distributed in exchange for fully paid shares.

The reason for reconstructions may be in fact a device to raise further capital by what is in effect an assessment on the holders of the fully paid-up capital of the old company. On the other hand a reconstruction may be for the purpose of merging two businesses into a larger and more effective economic unit.

4.53 Takeover bids

Few happenings in the City receive as much publicity as takeover bids which in recent years have become a very common occurrence. This is a method whereby one company obtains control of another by acquiring a majority of its voting share capital. The taken over company does not go into liquidation but remains in existence as a subsidiary of the company which made the bid.

The bidding company may be satisfied with obtaining a majority holding of the taken over company as this will enable it to determine the composition of the board of directors. However, if it wishes to be in a position to be sure of passing special or extraordinary resolutions, it requires a 75% holding. Frequently, bidding companies wish to obtain the whole of the voting capital and there are provisions under section 428 of the Companies Act 1985, formerly section 209 of the 1948 Companies Act, to prevent small minorities from frustrating this.

Where 90% by value of the holders of the class of shares subject to the offer accept it within four months of its being made the bidding company (otherwise known as the transferee company or the offeror company) may within a further two months compulsorily acquire such of the remaining 10% of the shares as it wishes on the same terms as the original offer. In calculating the 90% there must be excluded any shares owned or controlled by the bidding company at the date of the offer.

A practice has developed in certain instances whereby a bidder does not initially reveal its identity when preparing to take over a company. Instead it surreptitiously builds up a holding or holdings in the target company under the cover of nominee holdings. Alternatively, by a process known as 'warehousing' separate holdings in a company are built up apparently independent of each other but in effect by parties acting in concert with a view to their coming together as a prelude to a takeover bid.

To counter such manoeuvres it is a legal requirement that holders of shares carrying unrestricted voting rights inform the company if they have acquired shares amounting to 5% or more of the nominal value of that share capital. This extends to persons who acting in concert together acquire 5% of the shares. Such holders must thereafter inform the company within five days of any changes which result in their holdings being increased or decreased to the next unit percentage point. The Companies Act 1985 also gives companies whose shares are quoted on the Stock Exchange the right to require any member to indicate the capacity in which he/she holds the shares if this is other than that of a straightforward beneficial owner.

Example

Issued voting capital of the company for which bid is being made: £1,000,000 made up of 1,000,000 ordinary £1.00 shares.

Shares held by the bidding company at date of offer: 50,000.

Therefore if 90% of the remaining independent holders by value – i.e. 90% of 950,000 = holders of 855,000 shares – accept, the bidding company can compulsorily acquire the remaining 95,000 shares.

However, where the bidding company already holds shares to a value greater than one-tenth of all the shares affected it must before section 428 applies offer the same terms to all the other holders (see also Section 16.4), and acceptance must be by holders who not only (a) hold not less than nine-tenths in value of the outstanding shares, but also (b) are not less than three-quarters in number of those holders.

Within one month of receiving the notice of compulsory acquisition from the company a dissenting shareholder has the right to appeal to the Court against such acquisition.

On the other hand an unsatisfactory position could arise for shareholders who originally did not wish to accept the offer but as the result of its success found themselves in a minority of less than 10%. A minority under this size loses certain privileges, such as the right to requisition an extraordinary general meeting. Accordingly section 429, Companies Act 1985, formerly section 209, Companies Act 1948, also provides that on obtaining 90% of the shares the bidding company must notify this fact to the non-accepting shareholders who thereupon have the right within three months of receiving such notice to require the bidding company to accept their shares under the terms of the original offer.

4.6 Insider trading

Not unnaturally a matter which for a long time has generated much heat has been the possibility of a person with inside knowledge of a company's affairs being able to deal advantageously in its shares in the light of this knowledge which is not available to the general body of shareholders or for that matter to the public. While such activity has been officially frowned upon for many years, practical difficulties deferred the introduction of legal prohibition until the passing of the 1980 Companies Act (now 1985 Companies Act).

Insider dealing is now a criminal offence, punishable either by a fine or prison sentence of up to two years. Such an offence is deemed to occur if an individual, then or at any time during the preceding six months knowingly connected with a company, deals in its securities if by virtue of his so being connected with the company he has information which he knows is unpublished, price-sensitive information. It also occurs if he advises or procures deals in the securities of the company by disclosing information to parties other than those to whom he might reasonably be expected to do so in the proper performance of duties connected with the company. An individual acting on price-sensitive information knowing it to be obtained from a 'connected source' is likewise deemed to commit an offence.

Already in existence are the provisions of the Companies Act 1976 (now 1985 Companies Act) whereby a company is obliged without delay to inform the Stock Exchange of any changes in the director holdings of its quoted share or loan capital. These together with any other unusual price movements or transactions which may be observed are scrutinized by the appropriate officials of the Stock Exchange and may lead to the detection of offenders.

Typical questions

1 In what way is the voting power attaching to shares usually fixed?
2 In what circumstances at a company meeting may members demand a poll?

3   What restrictions, if any, may be placed by the Articles of Association of a company upon the rights of members to demand a poll at a company meeting?

(The Chartered Institute of Secretaries, *Scots Company Law*)

Suggested answers

1   The voting power attaching to shares is normally defined in the Articles of Association. If the Articles are silent a shareholder has, on a poll, one vote for each share or £10 of stock held.

2   The circumstances in which a poll will be demanded are where the result of a vote on a show of hands, in which each member has one vote, does not reflect the wishes of the majority of members holding the greater proportion by value of the voting shares. In this connection there is the important factor that proxies can only vote on a poll, not on a show of hands.

A poll may be demanded by members before or on the declaration by the chairman of the result of the vote on the show of hands. It cannot validly be demanded until there has been a show of hands.

3   The Companies Act 1985 provides that except on the questions of the election of a chairman and the adjournment of the meeting, both matters which must be decided on the spot, a poll may be demanded by:

(a)   Any five members entitled to vote at the meeting; *or*

(b)   Any member or members holding not less than one-tenth of the voting strength, or one-tenth of the paid-up capital conferring the right to vote. Restrictions can only effectively be imposed by the Articles in so far as they do not conflict with these provisions.

Additional questions

1   (a)   In what circumstances, and in what manner, may a company carry out a scheme for its reconstruction under Section 582 of the Companies Act 1985?

(b)   What are the rights of members of the company who dissent from the scheme?

(The Chartered Institute of Secretaries, *English Company Law*)

2   (a)   Summarize the circumstances in which the shares of non-accepting shareholders in an offer may be acquired under Section 428 of the Companies Act 1985.

(b)   After an offer has been made, in what circumstances is a minority shareholder in the offeree company entitled to require the offeror company to buy his/her shares?

(The Institute of Bankers, *Principles and Practice of Investment*)

3   (a)   Distinguish between an ordinary resolution, an extraordinary resolution, and a special resolution proposed at a general meeting of a company.

(b) What are the provisions of the Companies Act 1985 regarding the holding of annual general meetings?

(The Institute of Bankers, *Principles and Practice of Investment*)

4 What is the advantage of 'limited liability' as far as shareholders and companies are concerned? When might a further payment be required in respect of shares held?

5 Outline the information you would expect to find in a company's Memorandum and Articles of Association.

6 (a) In what way are shareholders safeguarded against inaccurate or misleading company accounts?

(b) What useful information might be gleaned from perusal of the chairman's statement?

7 There are restrictions on certain employees of a company dealing in the shares of the company. What are they? Are other parties also affected by these restrictions?

5 The Stock Exchange

Over the years the demand for the buying and selling of stocks and shares in the United Kingdom has reached substantial proportions. In order to satisfy this, independent stock exchanges or in other words market places were formed in various parts of the country. Eventually, however, it became apparent that share dealing facilities required to be rationalized and although problems arose in protecting the interests of members of the individual exchanges a process of regionalization and federation which commenced in 1964 led to the establishment of one united stock exchange for Great Britain and Ireland in March 1973.

At the time of writing in 1986 major changes are taking place in the way the Stock Exchange conducts its affairs, these having been triggered off by the agreement between the Government and the Stock Exchange in 1983 whereby the Office of Fair Trading called off its action in the Restrictive Practices Court on condition that the Stock Exchange would abandon its fixed commission structure and make various other important alterations in its rules and regulations. For sometime, however, a more fundamental pressure for change existed in that Stock Exchange jobbers were under capitalized in relation to the size of bargains being dealt in as the institutions, instead of private investors, have come to dominate the market. Also security dealing has become an internationalized twenty-four hours a day business and if this country is to compete with overseas markets it must provide a modern highly efficient service.

October 27 1986 has been indicated as a crucial date when many of these changes will become effective which occasion has been dubbed the 'Big Bang'. Nevertheless many aspects of this 'City revolution' have already commenced and will also continue well beyond that date.

5.1 Organization and membership

The Stock Exchange is governed by a Council comprising of elected members from all the former exchanges plus a number of lay members limited to no more than a quarter of the Council and who must be approved by the Governor of the Bank of England. The central administration is in London but there are six other administrative units, the Midlands and Western, the Northern, Belfast, the Scottish, the Irish, and the Provincial Unit which represents stockbrokers operating in smaller centres throughout England and

Wales. Each regional unit has its own chairman, committees, and officials working in conjunction with the central administration and the Council.

Although the greatest amount by far of Stock Exchange business is carried out in London there are active trading floors in Birmingham, Dublin, Glasgow and Liverpool. Stockbroking fraternities also flourish in centres such as Aberdeen, Belfast, Edinburgh, Huddersfield, Leeds, Manchester, Newcastle, Oldham, Sheffield, Bristol, Cardiff, and Nottingham while many other towns up and down the country have at least one resident firm of stockbrokers.

A high standard of integrity is required of Stock Exchange members in the conduct of their business. Dishonesty in any form will not be tolerated whether it be for the object of personal gain to the member or, for instance, for the protection of a client who is known to be dealing improperly on an 'insider' basis. A stringent set of rules has been drawn up governing members' behaviour and should any member be discovered transgressing these in any way he will find himself censured, suspended, or expelled by the Council according to the seriousness of the offence. Within the Stock Exchange there is a surveillance department responsible for identifying possible abuses or breaches of its procedures.

If a member is unable to meet his obligations he is publicly declared to be a defaulter, whereupon his membership lapses. The process by which he is removed is known as 'hammering' and this is the Stock Exchange equivalent of bankruptcy. The investor is protected by the Stock Exchange Compensation Fund against loss as the result of such default of any member.

The Stock Exchange insists that firms submit monthly statements as well as quarterly balance sheet returns to the Exchange Accountant. Among the various points to be watched is the solvency margin, i.e. excess of assets over liabilities.

A major innovation in 1986 was the removal of the restriction preventing outsiders, i.e. non-Stock Exchange members, from wholly owning Stock Exchange firms. Following on this banks and other financial conglomerates both UK and overseas purchased control of most of the large firms with the partners, although remaining members of the Stock Exchange, thereafter becoming employees. In order that the Stock Exchange can ensure that its regulatory powers can be extended to cover these outsiders as well as its approximately 4500 current members a new class of 'external membership' is to be created. Entry fees are being proposed on a sliding scale from £50,000 to £10,000 for new members depending upon the number of approved personnel involved.

5.11 Brokers and jobbers

For many years members of the Stock Exchange were split into two distinct categories – stockbrokers and stockjobbers. A member had to be one or the other. He could not be both and neither could there be a partnership between brokers and jobbers. The division was not equal as there were many times more brokers than jobbers particularly so in the regions. As from the 'Big

Bang', coincident with the ending of the minimum commission rules thereby opening the door for competitive rates, this separation of function will no longer be necessary and members of the Stock Exchange will be able to act in either capacity or both. However as features of the old system may continue for some time it is worth describing the individual functions of the broker and the jobber.

5.111 *Brokers*
The function of a stockbroker is easily understood. He acts as an agent for the buying and selling of shares on behalf of his clients, who in technical language are described as his principals. He earns his living by charging his clients a commission on the transactions which he carries out. He also gives advice to and perhaps manages the portfolios of his clients. Although some brokers have built up reputations for special knowledge in a particular type of security, for example in gilt-edged, insurance, stores, or investment trust shares, etc., they will purchase or sell all quoted investments on behalf of their clients.

A further important function of a broker is in connection with new issues when he advises on the price, submits the necessary documentation to the Quotations Department of the Stock Exchange, and may be involved in the arranging of funds for their subscription.

5.112 *Jobbers*
The reasons for the existence of jobbers are perhaps a little more difficult to grasp. First of all they have some clearly distinguishing features from brokers. They do not come into contact with the public but deal solely with brokers and other jobbers. They do not deal in all the securities quoted on the Stock Exchange but specialize in one or more categories, for example industrials, textiles, oils, land and property, breweries, etc. This specialization has, however, been reduced in recent years by the merger of firms dealing in the various types of stocks. The jobber acts as a principal himself and his profit is the difference, called his 'turn', between his buying price and his selling price.

Jobbers dealing in the various types of stocks are located at recognized positions on the floor of the Stock Exchange and here they 'make prices' at which they are prepared to buy or sell normal amounts of those particular stocks. They take stocks on their books when brokers have predominantly selling orders and sell short, i.e. sell stocks which they do not hold at the time but which they will purchase and deliver in due course, when the balance swings the other way and brokers are mainly engaged in buying.

5.113 *Jobbers' prices*
Jobbers, of course, do not wish to go on either buying a stock or, alternatively, selling it short indefinitely. They therefore adjust their prices

from time to time either to encourage or discourage buyers or sellers in order to balance their books.

A jobber, when asked, quotes two prices for a share, e.g. 87p–90p. The former is his 'bid' price at which he is willing to buy the share from the broker and the latter is his 'offer' price at which he is willing to sell the share. It is important to note that when a broker makes an enquiry about the price of a share he does not at that stage reveal whether he is a buyer or a seller.

If the jobber has more of the particular share on his books than he wishes to hold he will lower his price in order to encourage buyers and discourage sellers, but if he is short he will raise his prices in order to encourage sellers and discourage buyers. The principle may be illustrated by the following imaginary transaction.

If a broker has an order from a client to buy 500 XY shares he will go to that part of the floor where XY shares are dealt in and enquire: 'What are XY?'

The jobber may reply: '87–90'.

If the broker considers that 90p is a reasonable price to pay he will say: 'Buy 500'.

It is only at this stage that the jobber knows that the broker is a buyer and that is the bargain fixed.

The jobber has now sold 500 XY shares at 90p and for the purpose of illustration it is assumed that he does not hold any of the shares. He therefore now wishes to acquire some and in order to do so will adjust his prices. Accordingly, when the next enquiry is made of him regarding XY shares he may quote '88–91'. This increase in price is to encourage sellers, 88p being a more attractive price than 87p, and discourage buyers, 91p being more expensive than 90p.

Should the second enquirer be a broker wishing to sell XY shares he may say: 'Sell 500'.

In this event the jobber will now have bought 500 shares at 88p to cover the shares which he sold at 90p. His 'turn' would therefore be 2p per share.

If the second broker had also been a buyer the jobber would have sold a further 500 shares but at a higher price, 91p, to compensate him for the greater risk he is assuming by now being obliged to deliver 1,000 instead of only 500 shares.

Supposing that the first broker had been a seller and the jobber had bought the 500 shares, then in order to try and balance his books the jobber's next quotation might well have been '86–89'.

When the deal is completed both the broker and the jobber make an entry in their notebooks but no written contract is made between them. Transactions are carried out by word of mouth and once completed are always upheld even although there is an immediate change in market prices. The motto of the Stock Exchange is 'dictum meum pactum' – my word is my bond.

In practice, dealings are not so simple as in the above illustration. For instance the broker may make enquiries at several jobbers dealing in XY shares before effecting the transaction at the most favourable price. It is most unlikely that one transaction will be matched so neatly immediately afterwards in the opposite direction. Even though a buying broker is followed by a selling broker the number of shares being dealt in would probably differ.

A jobber may, of course, not consider it necessary to vary his prices as the result of one transaction in 500 shares, particularly if these are the shares of one of the larger companies where there is a steady flow of business in the course of a normal working day. He will only make the change when he sees his 'position' in the shares building up too much in one direction.

A jobber is not always bound to give a quotation in any of the shares in which he trades. However, once he does quote he obliges himself to deal one way or another in a reasonable amount of the shares. What is reasonable depends on the size of the company whose shares are being dealt in. Also, when very marketable shares are involved the jobber's prices will be closer together than in the case of a company in whose shares there is only an occasional transaction. The wider price is to protect the jobber who may have to hold on to the shares himself for a long time before a buyer comes along, or alternatively to enable him to raise his prices by a considerable margin in order to attract a seller of shares which he has obligated himself to deliver.

In the case of a share with a narrow market the jobber may give a single bid or offer price, meaning that he will deal in one direction only because he has none of the shares, or is not prepared to buy any. Jobbers sometimes, of course, make losses, but obviously if they are to stay in business their overall trading must be profitable.

It will be observed that the jobber exposes himself to two risks. Firstly of time before he can undo a bargain he has completed by a reciprocal transaction in the other direction, and secondly of price which may change for or against him before the second bargain can be effected.

5.12 Dual capacity

Under the proposed restructuring of the trading system all Stock Exchange member firms will be deemed to be broker-dealers and permitted to combine the functions of both stockbroking and market making (formerly known as jobbing). They are not required to perform this dual role but can if they so wish continue to act solely as stockbrokers or market makers. A stockbroker although not becoming a market maker in any stock will, subject to certain restrictions, be able to deal as a principal, thus replacing income lost following the abandonment of minimum commission rules.

Broker-dealers who wish to become market makers in specific securities can apply to do so in which connection they must meet Stock Exchange requirements, for example as regards sufficiency of capital. This obviously should not give rise to any problem where firms are now owned by the powerful banks etc. They will then be obliged to maintain two way prices in at least a prescribed minimum size of order in all securities in which they are so registered. This prescribed minimum will vary according to the size of the issue involved, and competitiveness of prices should be maintained for securities where there are a sufficient number of market makers.

While dealing will continue in traditional fashion from pitches on the Stock Exchange floors it is anticipated that this will diminish and increasingly transactions will be carried out through screen based systems and telephones. Fundamental to the new trading arrangements is the installation of a computer system known as the Stock Exchange Automated Computer System (SEAQ), on which the market makers competing two way prices in all the leading UK equities will appear. These prices will be available to members on screens either in their offices or on the Stock Exchange floor. More advanced computerized systems are planned for the future.

Actual dealing must be done only by members of the Stock Exchange or by a firm's registered representatives who before being granted this status must satisfy the Council as to their suitability. Authorized clerks under the old system will still continue to deal as before so long as some single capacity dealing remains in force on the trading floor.

5.13 Client protection

With the introduction of dual capacity concern has been expressed that a client's interests may not be looked after so single mindedly as hitherto by stockbrokers, who once they can act as principals, could at times be influenced to the client's detriment by their own position in certain stocks. To protect the investor against this the Stock Exchange proposes to introduce a number of built-in safeguards.

In the first place broker-dealers will be required to disclose on the contract note the time at which a deal was done and whether they were acting as agents or principals. Details of all transactions must be supplied to the officials of the Stock Exchange monitoring dealings and these will be publicized on the SEAQ system except in shares where there are only a few market makers and their position would be prejudiced by such disclosure.

In any event all such information will be electronically stored so that the pattern of quotations in the market at a particular time can be reconstructed to ensure that the 'best execution rule', to which all broker-dealers will be subject, has been followed. Under this a broker-dealer who is not a market maker in a security will only be able to trade in it as a principal if he can improve on the price which is currently being offered by a market maker in the number of shares.

5.14 Dealing in gilts

A new system is being introduced for dealing in gilt-edged stocks, the principal role being played by substantial financial groups who will act as market makers or as they are likely to be called 'primary dealers'. These market makers will require to be accorded some form of membership of the Stock Exchange in order to come within its trading practices and standards but they will also be subject to prudential supervision by the Bank of England as to the amount of risk they take on in relation to their capital.

The market makers will as one of their functions help the Bank of England to sell Government Stock and they will be granted special borrowing facilities with the Bank. It is also envisaged that there will be a number of both money brokers who will lend either money or stock to the market makers depending upon requirements, and inter-dealer brokers who will act as arbitrageurs between market makers thus assisting them in the proficient structuring of their positions in the stocks on their books.

An essential requirement of market makers is that they will make two way prices on demand. As it is the institutions who dominate the gilt-edged market with their large transactions it is expected that dealings will take place directly between institutions and market makers by telephone or other electronic means. More modest investors will use the services of broker-dealers who will be able to deal both as principal and agent but may choose to act only in one capacity. Many of such transactions may continue to be conducted on the floor of the Stock Exchange.

5.2 Quotations

5.21 Advantages of quotation

Mention has already been made of the function of the Stock Exchange in providing market places for stocks and shares. It will be appreciated that shareholders in companies whose shares can be bought and sold on the Stock Exchange have a much more realizable asset than a holding in an unquoted company where a sale or purchase may only be arranged after perhaps a lengthy period of private enquiry.

Also the value of quoted shares can be ascertained from day to day from the Official Lists of quotations and prices issued by the Stock Exchange. The value of shares in an unquoted company is often not easily determined, and the price for a transaction may be the subject of protracted negotiation. There is, therefore, considerable attraction for a company to have its shares quoted on the Stock Exchange as they then become more acceptable to investors and the company in turn finds it easier and cheaper to raise further capital. They are often an essential prerequisite before a company can enter the field of take-over bids.

5.211 The family company

Frequently the shares in a successful private company are nearly all held by members of one family, but such shares may be the only assets of substantial value owned by that family. This raises awkward problems when a shareholder dies, first of all from the point of view of valuing the shares and then, more important, in the raising of cash to meet the severe impact of capital transfer tax. One of the ways of providing for this eventuality is to make a considerable block of the shares available to the public at the same time obtaining a Stock Exchange quotation.

5.212 Stock Exchange requirements

A company must have reached a certain size before an application for a quotation will be entertained by the Stock Exchange. The general requirements are that its capital must have a market value of not less than £500,000, with any one security having a minimum market value of £200,000. The Stock Exchange also insists on sufficient shares being released from private ownership in order that there really will be a market in the shares, and demands certain standards of disclosure regarding the company's affairs both at the time of the initial grant of quotation and thereafter during the company's existence. The procedures by which the shares of a company may be brought to the market are discussed in Chapter 8.

As a condition of receiving a quotation a company must sign a Listing Agreement binding itself to certain standards and procedures, many of which are similar to those covered by the Companies Acts. Additional requirements include advising the Stock Exchange without delay of the dates of Board meetings at which dividends are being considered. Also, immediately after the relevant meeting is held a company must inform the Stock Exchange of all dividends, preliminary profit figures, details of any new capital issues or capital changes, and any other information necessary to enable shareholders to appraise the position of a company and to avoid the establishment of a false market in its shares. Announcements of take-over bids are required at an early stage and where it appears that such bids are impending the Stock Exchange may temporarily suspend quotation of the shares in question until a satisfactory statement is made.

5.22 The Stock Exchange Daily Official List

Whenever a security is granted a quotation on the Stock Exchange it appears on the Official List published in London for every business day. The regional lists, which were previously in existence, have now for economy reasons amalgamated with London. The stocks and shares are grouped together in their various categories starting with British Government stocks on the first page. By far the largest section is that covering Commercial and Industrial. Against each security is its official quotation for that particular day.

Although the quotations are official it does not mean that these are the actual quotations being made by market makers. In practice the market makers' prices will be within the official quotations and closer together. The Quotations Department of the Stock Exchange which publishes the Official List does, of course, base its prices on those ruling in the market, and if a broker finds he is unable to deal within the official prices he can insist that they be altered.

Since March 1981, the Official List has been available in microfiche as well as in paper form.

5.221 Ex dividend

The quotation 'x d', short for 'ex dividend', denotes a significant stage in the life of a security. When a dividend is going to be paid by a company there is a lot of work involved to ensure that the dividend warrants and tax counterfoils are all prepared in time for the day when payment is due. It would be an impossible task for large companies to complete this work if right up to the last minute changes were taking place in the register of shareholders. Accordingly, some time before the payment day the transfer books are closed and the dividend is paid to the holders on the register at the date of closure, no matter what sales and purchases are effected between that date and the date when the dividend is paid.

The Stock Exchange takes this situation into consideration and tries to arrange that anyone who purchases shares too late to be registered as a holder in time to get the next dividend purchases the shares 'x d'. As soon as dealings on the Stock Exchange switch from 'c d' (cum dividend) to 'x d' the price of the shares falls by the net amount of the dividend. The seller, therefore, who will be on the company's register at the vital date gets the dividend and receives less for his shares, while the buyer pays a lower price because he is not getting the dividend.

Gilt-edged stocks are made 'x d' on the last day on which transfers will be accepted for registration cum dividend, which is normally about five or six weeks before the payment date. For example, the interest on 3½% Conversion Loan is paid on 1 April and 1 October. For the April payment the 'x d' date will be around 24 February. In this instance a purchaser on or after 24 February will not receive his first interest payment until 1 October.*

Company securities are usually made 'x d' on the first day of a Stock Exchange Account (see Chapter 6.2) shortly before the transfer books close. It sometimes happens in practice that cum dividend sales are not registered with the company before the books close. In this event the dividend is paid to the seller as the result of which the buying broker may deduct the net amount of the dividend when paying the selling broker, or if he has settled in full with the selling broker he will lodge a subsequent claim with him for the dividend.

The 'c d' quotation is not used very frequently in practice. Securities are 'cum' all future dividends until they are specifically made 'ex' a particular dividend, i.e. the next one. When a security is on the point of going 'ex' a

---

* With certain exceptions such as short dated stocks and 3½% War Loan it is possible optionally to deal 'x d' in gilt-edged stocks for a period of twenty-one days prior to the normal 'x d' date.

dividend it may sometimes be quoted 'c d' for a brief period to make sure there is no misunderstanding.

5.222 *Business done*

Next to the 'Quotations' column in the Official List there is a heading 'Business Done'. Under this is recorded, in ascending order, the actual prices at which deals were carried out, this information being taken from input to the settlement computer system. If no business was done in a share on a particular day the prices on the last day when dealings took place are provided.

Late transactions appear on the next day's list with an appropriate sign to indicate that the bargains were effected on the previous day. Only one bargain at a particular price is published although each bargain is included in the totals for each section and the grand total for the day. The order in which the prices are recorded is not the order in which they were carried out and there is no indication as to their size or whether they represent buying or selling by the public.

The Official List also reveals the turnover in and the number of bargains carried out in equities in the previous day and the total number of bargains, while further information regarding turnover and the number of bargains struck is published monthly in the financial press shortly after the end of the month under the following eight classifications:

(a) British Government and British Government Guaranteed Short-dated Stocks
(b) Other British Government and British Government Guaranteed Stocks
(c) Irish Government Short-dated Stocks
(d) Other Irish Government Stocks
(e) United Kingdom Local Authority Stocks
(f) Overseas Government Provincial and Municipal Stocks
(g) Fixed Interest Stocks, Preference and Preferred Ordinary Shares
(h) Ordinary Shares.

Since February 1974 the Stock Exchange has also been publishing this information for each account.

5.223 *Special markings and further information*

A symbol beside a price may indicate that there is some unusual feature about the underlying deal and this can be interpreted by reference to the notes on the Official List. A special marking which may be encountered is that referring to 'bargains done at special prices'. These may arise either when a very large order is involved or where a broker is selling such a trivial quantity of shares as to make the deal at the normal price unremunerative to the market maker. Special markings may be outside the current official quotations.

By the use of symbols, numbers, and letters against individual securities the Official List also provides much useful information, for example whether the security is subject to drawings or if conversion rights have expired.

5.224 Inland Revenue valuations

When valuations require to be made for capital transfer tax, stamp duty, and capital gains tax deemed disposals it is usually the '¼ up' price taken from the official quotations which applies. In the case of capital transfer tax, however, if the death occurred between the dates under the headings in the Official List 'When last x d' and 'Pay date' (or 'Interest due') then the net amount of the relative dividend must be added to the value of the shares as calculated. Suppose that 100 shares of £1 each were held, they were 'last x d' on 25 April, the dividend of 5% was payable on 1 June, and the death occurred on 15 May when the quotation was 125p–135p. The value for capital transfer tax purposes assuming that the '¼ up' price applies would be:

100 shares at 1.27½, i.e. $1.25 + \frac{1}{4}(1.35 - 1.25)$	£127.50
Add net amount of dividend due 1 June*	5.00
	£132.50

For the alternative price which is occasionally applicable see Chapter 10.53.

Where death or the otherwise relevant date occurs on a non-business day the quotations from either the last previous or the next following Official List may be used.

Some foreign securities are quoted on the London Official List and where this is so the price to be taken for Inland Revenue valuations is determined in the same way as for United Kingdom securities. However, where there is no London quotation the price to be taken for, say, United States or Canadian securities is the sterling equivalent of the New York or Canadian price, this being the middle price if dealings are recorded or the bid price if there were no dealings. The rate of exchange applicable is given on the last page of the Official List.

5.23 Unlisted securities market

A facility has been available for many years whereby dealings can be carried out on the Stock Exchange, under its Rule 535(2) formerly 163(2), in shares

---

* An interest payment of 5% would require to have tax deducted.

Amount of interest due 1 June	£5.00
Less tax at 30%	1.50
	£3.50

of United Kingdom companies which are not officially listed. This Rule was, and now emphatically is, intended to enable stockbrokers to match occasional deals in inactive shares such as those of football clubs and small businesses. The Stock Exchange's monitoring of the affairs of these companies is minimal and its specific permission is required for each transaction.

Having to some extent encouraged dealings under this Rule in order to attact and keep business within its domain the Stock Exchange became disturbed at the increased activity in the shares of a number of companies which, as indicated above, were under no obligation to conform to the standards of disclosure for a full quotation but which might as the result of this trading appear to have acquired a status in some degree similar to listed companies. Aware that such companies might be unwilling to meet the expense and stringent requirements for a full quotation, the Stock Exchange in November 1980 introduced a medium for dealing known as the Unlisted Securities Market (USM).

The principal difference between the USM and the main market in listed companies lies in the requirements for admission. When a company entering the USM is not raising new money it does not need to publish a full prospectus (see 8.214) and even if it is, large-scale advertising in the press is not mandatory. Also a company may not have been in existence long enough to produce the trading records which the Quotations Department of the Stock Exchange might consider necessary for a full listing and in this event the USM would in the meantime be appropriate.

For a full listing 25% of a company's shares must be made available to the public but for the USM there is flexibility around a guideline figure of 10%, thus allowing the directors of the company who may so wish to retain a higher proportion for themselves and their families. A full listing is available only to companies with a market value of at least £500,000 whereas for the USM there is no minimum size.

Before being granted admission to the USM the Stock Exchange insists that companies enter into a General Undertaking which is very similar to the Listing Agreement signed by listed companies. Having obtained easier access to the market, companies will require to conform to almost identical standards to those admitted to full listing, although it may be pertinent to note that in the disclosure and acquisition of assets they are not so exacting. Provision is also made for the movement of shares from one market to the other but when 'relegation' is sought from a full listing to the USM, shareholders' consent is required.

The business done each day in the USM, which is conducted by Stock Exchange members also dealing in the main market, is recorded at the end of the Official List. The Inland Revenue have indicated that for tax purposes these bargains will be initial evidence of share values but that other factors may require to be taken into account to establish the open market value at the relevant date.

Although falling far short of rivalling the principal market in the volume of its business the USM has made substantial progress during the first five years of its existence and has been involved with over four hundred companies a number of which have moved on to a full listing. Others have met with varied fortunes some having failed to fulfil the optimistic expectations prevailing at the time of their first appearance, a feature, of course, not unknown to the main market.

While not detracting unduly from the undoubted overall success of the USM it has so far been a fairly common experience that immediately after the launch of a company there has been a substantial turnover in its shares which frequently dwindles drastically within a few weeks. This lack of interest results in poor marketability with consequent widening price spreads and volatility.

5.3 Over the counter market

The over the counter market (OTC) is a market for dealing in shares completely outside the jurisdiction of the Stock Exchange* and, notwithstanding its name, business is carried out almost wholly by telephone. Although this type of market is well established in the United States until recently there was only one firm in this country providing such a service. In the past few years the number of dealers has steadily increased some of whom are most anxious to build up a clientele among private investors.

OTC dealers tend to specialize in small but new and hopefully fast growing businesses which they themselves have brought to the market and which are often at a much more speculative stage in their development than the shares dealt in on the main Stock Exchange market or the USM. Dealers' methods of operating their respective markets vary from merely a matching service on a commission basis between buyers and sellers of a particular stock or combining this with running a book themselves and like jobbers or market makers on the Stock Exchange obtaining their remuneration from the difference between their buying and selling prices.

Inherent in either arrangement are certain snags, for example marketability in the case of the matching service where a seller may have to wait for a considerable time before a buyer is found. With the market making OTC dealer the client may be at some disadvantage if what he/she wishes to do does not suit the dealer's book, particularly as is not infrequently the case of there being only one dealer in the share involved.

As a sideline OTC dealers may transact business in Stock Exchange listed

---

* In April 1986 the Stock Exchange announced its intention to set up a third tier market in October 1986 with the objective of bringing at least some OTC shares within its ambit. The requirements for eligibility for this market will be less stringent than those for the USM and it would appear that responsibility for vetting prospectuses and supervising companies will lie with the sponsoring Stock Exchange member firms.

shares but often they will require to do this through a Stock Exchange broker. However to attract new clients many such dealers have been providing an active market in large new issues especially those arising from privatization such as British Telecom and Britoil, in which instances their services may compare favourably with those obtainable from a Stock Exchange broker.

This third tier market is very much in its infancy and lacks regulation and protection for the investor. These defects may perhaps soon be rectified following the passage of the Financial Services Bill through Parliament in 1986 (see Chapter 16) and OTC dealers could play an increasingly valuable role in producing development capital for emerging companies which would otherwise not be readily available.

5.4 Ariel

In the early 1970s the large merchant banks and their institutional clients felt dissatisfied with the high rates of commission being charged on their Stock Exchange transactions. As a result the members of the Accepting Houses Committee initiated an alternative market familiarly known as Ariel (automated real-time investments exchange limited) which became operative in February 1974 with dealing charges less than those on the Stock Exchange. However the size of the annual membership fee ensured that it was attractive only to institutions transacting a substantial volume of business.

Ariel provides dealing facilities for a much smaller number of shares than those available on the Stock Exchange, one obvious reason for this being that the institutional investors are only interested in acquiring large amounts of stock which accordingly rules out the smaller company. Originally buying and selling orders were matched by computer but this has been discarded owing to lack of the system's success and most deals are now effected discreetly by telephone.

At one time postulated as a possible rival to the Stock Exchange it does not seem likely that Ariel will have other than a minor role in the securities industry.

Typical question

What do you understand by 'dual capacity'? How could an investor be exploited by the introduction of this system and what rules have the Stock Exchange proposed to prevent this?

Suggested answer

Until the 'Big Bang' on the Stock Exchange in 1986 a stockbroker acted as an agent for his client, earned his living by charging commission, and was not permitted to deal as a principal. He carried out his clients' instructions by dealing through another type of Stock Exchange member known as a jobber who acted as a principal, did not deal direct with the public, and who was required to deal in normal amounts in those securities in which he specialized.

The jobber made a market in these shares and obtained his profit, called his 'turn', by the difference between his buying and selling prices.

As from the 'Big Bang' members of the Stock Exchange can if they wish act both as agents and principals, i.e. in a dual capacity. They are all broker-dealers and those who wish can apply to become market makers (previously known as jobbers) in specific shares.

A danger inherent in this system is that a stockbroker who is also dealing in a share might not give his client the best price available in a transaction as he might be tempted to maximize his own profit at the expense of his client.

To safeguard the client against this the Stock Exchange have made a rule that the broker-dealer will only be able to trade in the security himself, i.e. act as a principal, if he can improve upon the price which is currently being offered by a registered market maker in the number of shares. On every contract note the broker-dealer must disclose the time at which a transaction is carried out and whether he is acting as an agent or as a principal. Details of all transactions must be supplied to the officials of the Stock Exchange monitoring dealings and these will be publicized on the SEAQ system except in the case of securities where there are very few market makers and their position would be prejudiced by such disclosure. This information will be electronically stored so that the pattern of quotations in the market at a particular time can be reconstructed to ensure that compliance has been made with the 'best execution rule'.

Additional questions

1 A jobber or market maker aims to keep his 'book' even. Illustrate by means of a simple transaction the action he will take to achieve this.
2 Comment on the functions of the Stock Exchange in the financial and economic life of the community.
   Note: See also Section 8.214 and Section 17.1.
          (The Savings Banks Institute, *Personal Savings and Investment*)
3 (a) Explain the significance of the quotation 'x d'.
   (b) What particular relevance does 'x d' have with regard to capital transfer tax valuations?
4 Distinguish between the USM and the main market on the Stock Exchange. What provision is made to cater for very occasional dealing in a company's shares?
5 Briefly describe the share dealing facilities in this country which are outside the jurisdiction of the Stock Exchange.

6 Settlement

6.1 The contract

When a deal is completed by a broker and a jobber no formal document is drawn up setting down what has been agreed between them. However, between broker and the client the position is different. The broker passes details of the transaction back to his office where a contract note is prepared and sent to the client who normally receives it on the following day.

The contract note is legally binding on the broker and by accepting it the client confirms the broker's action on his behalf and assumes liability for the transaction. Should the client consider that his instructions have not been correctly carried out he should immediately get in touch with the broker.

A most important point to remember is that the ownership of shares bought and sold is effective as from the date on the contract note, the date being that of the day on which the deal was transacted. The buyer becomes entitled to all future dividends, scrip issues, rights issues, etc., pertaining to the shares as from that date unless the deal was made 'ex' any of these items. The fact that delivery of documents of title may be postponed for some time is irrelevant as far as ownership is concerned.

The essential information on contract notes is set out along the lines shown in Figures 6.1, 6.2, and 6.3. The contract note would also be headed with the name and address of the firm, and the names of the individual partners are listed. It would, of course, be signed on behalf of the firm. As it may be required either as proof of acquisition cost or sale proceeds in connection with capital gains tax it should not be mislaid (see also Section 5.3).

It will be observed that no transfer stamp duty is charged in Figures 6.1 and 6.3. This is because British Government stocks and, in fact, nearly all gilt-edged stocks are transferred free of duty. Also, where transfer stamp duty is payable it is met by the purchaser, not the seller.

The entry against 'Settlement' demands careful attention as it informs the client when he/she must pay for, or expect to receive the proceeds of the transactions. With the 9% Treasury Loan 1994 purchased in Figure 6.1 settlement is 'cash' which means that it takes place, theoretically at least, on the business day following that on which the deal was carried out. In any event, as soon as he/she receives the contract note a purchaser of a 'cash' stock should remit the sum due to his/her broker. Stocks that are dealt in for

Bought by order of John Smith Esq.

| Date 9 September 19...... | | Stock 9% Treasury Loan 1994 | | Settlement Cash | | |
Amount	Price	Consideration	Transfer stamp	Commission	Fees	VAT	Total
830	$95\frac{1}{2}$	792.65	—	4.95	—	0.74	798.34

Plus accrued interest from 17 May to 10 September 116 days   23.55

Subject to the Rules and Regulations of the Stock Exchange   821.89

Figure 6.1

Bought by order of John Smith Esq.

| Date 18 November 19...... | | Stock Bentalls Ltd Ord. 10p Units | | Settlement 2 December 19...... | | |
Amount	Price	Consideration	Transfer stamp	Commission	Fees	VAT	Total
1530	$0.56\frac{7}{8}$	870.19	9.00	13.05	—	1.96	894.20

Subject to the Rules and Regulations of the Stock Exchange

Figure 6.2

Sold by order of John Smith Esq.

| Date 18 November 19...... | | Stock British Insulated Callenders Cables Ltd Ord. 50p Shares | | Settlement 2 December | | |
Amount	Price	Consideration	Transfer stamp	Commission	Fees	VAT	Total
733	$1.23\frac{1}{8}$	902.50	—	13.54	—	2.03	886.93

Subject to the Rules and Regulations of the Stock Exchange

Figure 6.3

cash are those comprising the gilt-edged market (except those subject to stamp duty) and new issues transferable in allotment letter form.

Other stocks and shares are dealt in for the Account, and settlement takes place on the date indicated, i.e. 2 December in Figures 6.2 and 6.3.

6.2 The account system

The Stock Exchange divides its year into 'Accounts' which are usually periods of a fortnight, commencing on the Monday of one week and ending on the Friday of the next week. There are, however, some three-weekly Accounts covering Easter, the Whitsun and August Bank Holidays, and the Christmas and New Year Holidays. All dealing in non-cash stocks* which take place within one Account are settled on one day, known as the 'Account day' or the 'Settlement day', which for the normal fortnightly Account is the second Monday after the close of that Account. Dates of typical Accounts might be:

First dealings	*Last dealings*	*Account day*
10 November (Monday)	21 November (Friday)	1 December (Monday)
24 November	5 December	15 December

Therefore all dealings which took place between 10 November and 21 November inclusive would be settled on 1 December. If a client both bought and sold shares within the Account it would only be the net position arising from these transactions which would require to be settled on the Account day.

6.21 Bulls and bears

The period during which bargains do not require to be settled individually but may be set off against each other is taken advantage of by speculators, known in Stock Exchange parlance as 'bulls' and 'bears'. A bull, in the narrower use of the term, is someone who anticipates that there will be a rise in price of shares and buys them, but not with the intention of paying for them and holding them as a permanent investment. Under the Account system a bull could buy shares at the beginning of the Account and sell them at the end at a higher price and, if all goes according to plan he will receive a cheque from his broker on Account day for his net profit.

A bear, on the other hand, thinks that the price of shares is going to fall and although he does not possess the shares sells them in the hope of buying them back before the end of the Account at a lower price. Again, the only payment which requires to be made as the result of a successful 'bear operation' is the net profit paid by the broker to the speculator.

Profit making is, of course, by no means automatic and frequently bulls and bears go 'stale'. In other words they have made an error of judgment and

---

* If specially requested, settlement of gilt-edged transactions may be deferred until the Account day with an appropriate adjustment being made to the price to cover the delay in payment.

prices move in the wrong direction as the result of which they close their original transaction at a loss and must themselves make payment of the net amount of this to their brokers.

It should be observed that a bear takes a potentially greater risk than a bull. The most the latter can lose is the amount he has obligated himself to pay for his shares, whereas in theory at least there is no limit to the price a bear might have to pay for shares should they unobligingly shoot upwards. This arises from the different nature of the original obligation undertaken by a bull and a bear. The bull incurs a fixed cash debt but the bear has to deliver shares which are continually changing in value.

6.22 New time

On the last two day of an Account an exception may be made to the rule that all transactions entered into during an Account must be settled on the Account day for that Account. Referring to the Account dates on page 77 it would therefore be possible to deal for new time on Thursday 20 and Friday 21 November with settlement taking place on 15 December. To deal for new time a client must specially instruct his/her broker that he/she wishes this done. A buyer for new time may have to pay a slightly higher price than normal in return for this concession of postponed settlement.*

6.23 Contangos

A fortnight is, of course, a relatively short time for a substantial change to take place in the price of a share. At the end of the Account a bull may find that a share which he purchased has not risen in price, or at any rate perhaps not to the heights he anticipated. If he is still optimistic regarding its prospects he is sometimes able to carry the transaction over to the next and subsequent Accounts. This is done by arranging a contango.

The mechanics of the transaction are the selling of the shares for settlement on the normal Account day and an immediate repurchase of the shares for settlement on the following Account day. Both the sale and repurchase of the shares are effected at the same price, known as the 'making-up price', which is based on prices ruling at the close of business on the second last day of the Account and published on the morning of the first day of the new Account, i.e. the Preliminary day.

For the privilege the bull normally pays a rate of interest or a 'contango' which includes the broker's commission. On the Account day the broker will

---

* This facility is sometimes taken advantage of by speculators to close a deal for an account and immediately re-open it at a small difference in price for the subsequent account. On settlement day only the difference between the two transactions (including costs) within the account is settled between the stockbroker and client and the original transaction is in effect carried forward to the next account. Such dealings, described as 'cash and new', is only permitted to a limited extent.

let the bull have a cheque for the difference between his original purchase cost and the proceeds of the sale at the making-up price, if these are the greater. Should the shares have fallen in value the difference, of course, would be due by the bull to the broker.

Example

10 November 100 XY shares purchased for settlement on December at cost of	£545
At close of Account contango is arranged	
100 XY shares sold at making-up price for settlement on 2 December	£572
Due by broker to client on 2 December	£27
100 XY shares purchased at making-up price for settlement on 16 December	£572
Add interest for 14 days at, say, 10%	2.19
	£574.19

During the Account 24 November to 5 December a further rise in the share price takes place and the client sells, the net proceeds of the sale being £602. On 15 December he receives a cheque from his broker for £27.81, his total profit from the transaction being £54.81.

A bear may also be able to arrange a contango. In this event the carry-over transaction would be a closing purchase for the first Account and a re-opening sale for the next Account, again both at the making-up price.

In order to effect a contango a broker must find a market maker or another broker who is willing to carry the stock over in the opposite direction. Usually there are more bulls than bears about and this is why bulls normally pay a rate of interest in order to compensate the seller for the delay in receiving payment. However, if bulls and bears are around in equal strength no interest is given or taken, the rate being said to be even. On the infrequent occasions when bears predominate they have to pay a 'backwardation' to buyers to induce them to defer their right to have the shares delivered. A 'backwardation' is not calculated as a rate of interest but as so much, say, 2p per share.

Contango business is not practised on any great scale on the Stock Exchange nowadays and in fact many firms of stockbrokers are unwilling to accept carry-over instructions, certainly for other than substantial customers. Clients should therefore not assume that contango arrangements will be automatically available to them.

6.3 Options

The acquiring of options is a method whereby in return for a cash sum called 'option money', an investor, or perhaps the term speculator is more appropriate, obtains the right to purchase or sell shares at a fixed price in the future. Under the rules of the Stock Exchange the longest option permitted is for completion on the seventh Account day ahead, and is known as a three month option. This is the most popular period although options for shorter periods are also available.

By far the largest amount of option business is done in what are known as 'call' options. These entitle the holder to buy the shares in question, whereas the right to sell is obtained by means of a 'put' option. Obviously a speculator will only give money for a call option when he/she thinks the price of the share will rise and vice versa for a put option when he/she considers a fall to be very much on the cards.

To acquire an option the speculator must pay option money, the amount of which depends on the share being dealt in. The more volatile the share the higher the cost of the option. It may, however, normally be somewhere within the range of 5–10% of the share price, say, 17p for a share price of 200p.

6.31 Striking price

The fixed price at which the option may be exercised, known as the 'striking price', is based on the current quoted prices. With a call option the striking price is the higher quoted price plus a further small sum called the contango to recompense the option dealer, through whom the broker arranges the option, for financing the shares during the period of the option. In theory, at least, the option dealer might buy the shares and contango them at the end of each Account for so long as they are the subject of the option. With a put option the striking price is usually the current lower quoted price. There is no contango money, although it is possible that occasionally the striking price will be slightly under the lower price as a precaution by the option dealer against having to pay a backwardation on the shares.

6.32 Declaration day

At the end of the period the holder either abandons his/her option or claims his/her rights under it. The time for doing this is the 'Declaration day' which is the second last day in the Account before the final Account day on which completion of the option may take place. This may be illustrated as follows:

Typical option dealing dates

First dealings	Last dealings	Last declaration	For settlement
17 Nov. (Mon.)	28 Nov. (Fri.)	19 Feb. (Thurs.)	2 Mar. (Mon.)
1 Dec.	12 Dec.	5 Mar.	16 Mar.

Any options taken out between 1 December (an Account day) and 12 December can be exercised on 5 March for settlement on 16 March (an Account day). Declaration days on the normal fortnightly Account are always Thursdays. Options may also be exercised during their currency on declaration days for previous Accounts. For example, it could be possible for an option taken out between 1 December and 12 December to be exercised on 19 February.

5.33 Dealing against options

Option money is mostly given by speculators whose intention is to deal at a profit against the option before it expires. Should his judgement prove wrong and prices move adversely a speculator will abandon his option, his loss being the option money together with the commission charged him by the broker.

Suppose a speculator wishes to take out a call option on 400 shares where the jobber's current quotation is 195p–200p, the option cost is 12p, and the contango is 5p. He will give 12p per share for the call of 400 shares at a striking price of 205. His outlays will be:

400 shares at 12p	...	...	...	...	...	...	£48.00
Brokerage* 1½% on (2.05 × 400)		...	...	...	...		12.30
VAT	...	...	...	...	...	...	1.84
							£62.14

The brokerage is calculated as if the shares were being purchased in the normal way at the striking price.

If the price of the shares has risen to, say, 225p–230p by the time of the Account for which the option must be settled, the speculator will sell the shares and exercise the option. His profit will be as follows:

400 shares sold at 2.25	...	...	...	...	...		£900.00
400 shares purchased at 2.05	...	...	...	£820.00		
Cost of obtaining option		...	...	...	62.14		
						882.14	
Profit	...	...	...	...	...	...	£17.86

It will be observed that no further brokerage is charged when the option is exercised, or in the dealing against it.

Sometimes although no profit can be made from an option it should be exercised in order to reduce the speculator's loss. For instance, suppose the shares had only risen to 215p–220p.

Total cost when option exercised		...	...	...	...		£882.14
400 shares sold at 2.15	...	...	...	...	...	...	860.00
Loss	...	...	...	...	...	...	...	£22.14

If the option had not been exercised the loss would have been £62.14, the total cost of the option which incidentally is the maximum loss the speculator

---

As from 'Big Bang' brokerage variable.

could suffer. When exercising the option would result in a larger loss than this it would, tax considerations apart, not be exercised but abandoned.

The position has, however, now been complicated by the tax on capital gains. When an option is abandoned the cost is not an allowable loss to set off against other gains. It may, overall, be profitable to exercise the option even though a larger but allowable loss is thereby sustained. An allowable loss of, say, £80.00 may be more useful (see Sections 10.11 and 10.12) than a non-allowable one of £62.14 where the former results in a saving of capital gains tax on £80 at 30%, i.e. £24.

A point to note is that although options can be exercised only on a declaration day, they can be dealt against at any time during that Account, as settlement for both transactions is on the same Account day.

Indexation for capital gains tax purchases will apply to expenditure on call options if the option is exercised in which event the option price and acquisition cost will be separately indexed when the respective items of expenditure are incurred.

6.34 Double options

As well as call and put options it is also possible to obtain a double option which is a combination of both. The holder has the right either to buy or sell the shares subject to the option at the striking price which in this case will probably be around the middle of the current quoted prices. The option money is exactly twice that of the single option.

A double option in a share may be attractive when an event is about to take place within the following three months, which will make a strong impact one way or another on the share. For example, the announcement of the result of an important drilling by a mining company.

6.35 Limiting the risk

Options are expensive and in order to be profitable require a fairly sharp short-term price movement. The costs to be covered are the jobber's turn, the option money, the broker's commission, and in the case of a call option the contango in the striking price. They do, however, substantially reduce the speculator's risk of loss. Suppose that instead of giving for a call option in the above example the speculator had purchased the shares. His/her total outlay and possible loss, at least in theory, would have been:

400 shares at 2.00	...	...	...	...	...	...	...	£800.00
Brokerage	...	...	...	...	...	...	...	12.00
VAT	...	...	...	...	...	...	...	1.80
Transfer stamp	...	...	...	...	...	...	...	8.00
								£821.80

as opposed to £62.14.

Another aspect of options is that they may be regarded as a form of insurance. This is particularly apparent where an investor holds a share which has risen strongly in price. He may consider that basically the prospects for the share remain good, but some event which is about to occur may cause him apprehension. He may therefore protect his profit by giving option money for the put of his shares. The occasion for this could be a general election, either at home or in overseas territories where the company carries on business, resulting in the coming to power of a new government which may introduce legislation inimical to the company's interests.

6.4 Traded options

Since April 1978 a further dimension has been available in United Kingdom option dealing by the introduction of traded options in the Stock Exchange in London. Greater flexibility is available to the holder of traded options than with the options previously described in that he/she has the additional alternative of being able to sell the traded option in the market during its currency.

The number of traded options, originally available in only a handful of large United Kingdom companies, is cautiously being increased and in early 1986 they were obtainable in the shares of thirty-five companies, two British Government stocks, the FT-SE Index (see Section 14.23) as well as two currency options (the dollar/sterling rate and the dollar/deutschmark rate).

No double options are available but calls and puts can both be purchased at the same exercise price. This is a strategy known as a 'straddle' and may be employed where a substantial movement is likely in a share price but the direction is uncertain.

Unlike conventional options, traded options abandoned or disposed of after 5 April 1980 are treated as chargeable disposals for capital gains tax purposes (see Section 10.11) with the result that loss relief is now available.

6.41 Series available

Although the same fundamental principles largely apply to traded options the rules vary considerably. For instance they have a maximum life of nine months with expiry dates being arranged in a three-monthly cycle so that there are always three expiry dates available.* For each expiry date there are at least two exercise prices for the option and as there are three expiry dates there are always in existence a minimum of six series of options in the shares of a particular company. This may be more readily understandable by

---

* Except the FT-SE Index option which has a maximum life of four months with four expiry dates at monthly intervals.

referring to the published closing offer prices for the options in British Petroleum on 29 May 1981.

	Exercise Price	July Option price	October Option price	January Option price	Price of Ordinary shares
Call	360	40	54	70	384
Call	390	22	37	54	
Call	420	11	20	38	
Put	360	9	20	24	
Put	390	20	32	36	
Put	420	42	48	50	

While the cost of an option varies with supply and demand, it is influenced by the exercise price, the length of time until the option expires, and the market price of the shares. Other factors are the volatility of the shares, current interest rates, and dividends likely to be paid on the shares.

In the above example for obvious reasons the cost of the July call option exercisable at 360p at 40p was more than the cost of the options exercisable at 390p and 420p. All three of these options were cheaper than their October and January counterparts by which time there was deemed to be more scope for a greater rise in the share price. The options exercisable at 360p are called 'in the money' options as the share price is above the exercise price. The July option price of 40p is regarded as being made up of two elements, intrinsic value 24p (384p–360p) and 16p time value. Likewise the October and January 360s have intrinsic values of 24p but time values of 30p and 46p respectively.

On the other hand the share price at 384p is less than the call options exercisable at 390p and 420p, which options are said to be 'out of the money'. These options had no intrinsic value, only time value which in essence is the measure of hope existing for a rise in the price of the share during the remainder of their lives.

Put options, although the opposite of call options, mirror their characteristics. The cost of the July put option exercisable at 360p at 9p was less than the options exercisable at 390p and 420p. All three of these options were cheaper than their October and January counterparts by dint of the longer time available to the latter for a fall in the share price.

The put options exercisable at 360p are out of the money and have no intrinsic value as the share price at 384p is above the exercise price. They have only time value. The 390p options all had intrinsic values of 6p (390p–384p) and time values of 14p, 26p, and 30p respectively. The 420p options had intrinsic values of 36p and time values of 6p, 12p, and 14p.

At the end of July the July series of options expired and were replaced by an April series. New series of options are also introduced if the price of the underlying security varies to the extent of its closing on two consecutive days above or below the current maximum or minimum exercise price.

6.42 Gearing

Percentage-wise the price movements of a traded option are far more extreme than those of the underlying share. The holder of an option is thus exposed to a higher risk but on the other hand could reap greater rewards in relation to the amount of his/her investment. These possibilities can be illustrated by reference to the price of British Petroleum on 19 June 1981, 326p, and the call and put prices for the July 360p series of 4p and 36p respectively. While the share price had fallen since 29 May by 15% the price of the call option had dropped by 90%. However the put option had risen to 36p, an increase of 300%.

As with conventional options (see Section 6.35) the motives for the acquisition of traded options may be of an 'insurance' rather than of a speculative nature in order that an investor may protect him/herself from the serious effects of making a major error of judgment, either in a purchase or in the failure to sell at the right time.

6.43 Dealing

As well as the uniformity to which traded options must conform with regard to exercise prices and expiry dates, they also can only be dealt in units called contracts. A contract normally represents 1000 shares in a company although this will be reduced to 100 if the share price is exceptionally 'heavy'. The gilt contracts are for £50,000 nominal worth of stock while the underlying position for a dollar/sterling contract is £12,500. As with other traded securities market makers have a spread between their bid and offer prices.

FT-SE Index options are rather unusual. They do not give the holder of the option the right to buy or sell all the shares comprising the Index. Rather they give investors the opportunity of protecting themselves against or gambling on movements on the stock market generally, based on striking prices of the Index spaced at intervals of 25, rather than in individual securities. Each contract is worth a notional £10 and the price quoted for an option relates to a 1p unit.

Suppose in January when the FT-SE Index is 1396 an investor pays 50p for an April call option at 1400 and by March the Index is standing 1495 and the price of a 1400 April call option is then 106. He/she may decide to sell the option and the arithmetic, ignoring expenses, would be as follows:

Proceeds of sale 106 × 1000	...	...	...	...	...		£1,060
Cost of purchase 50 × 1000	...	...	...	...	...		500
Profit	...	...	...	...	...	...	£560

A unique feature of the FT-SE Index option is that there is never any question of delivery of stock. Settlement is always implemented in cash.

6.44 Safeguards for the investor

While a conventional option is basically a contract between two parties aware of each other's identity (or their agents are so aware), the holder of a traded option does not know the identity of the party from whom he will be acquiring the shares until he actually exercises the option. He can feel assured, however, that with his call option the underlying shares will be forthcoming as the writer, i.e. the creator, of a traded option must deposit with the London Options Clearing House (LOCH) either the shares to which the option relates or a sum of money, known as margin, equivalent to 25% of their value adjusted for whether the option is in or out of the money.* The writer of a put option must deposit the cash margin. Besides this investors can regard themselves as being safeguarded ultimately by the financial guarantees of the Stock Exchange.

All deals must be channelled through LOCH which acts as a registrar for the contracts. No certificates are issued in respect of traded options and all deals are for settlement the following day.

The writer of the call option who has undertaken in return for his receiving a premium to sell a specific number of shares at a fixed price may already be the holder of the underlying shares. Alternatively he may be an uncovered or 'naked' writer which means that he is at a much greater risk because, if the share price should rise and the option be exercised, he will have to buy the shares in the market.

Typical questions

1 The 25p shares of XYZ Metal Company Limited are presently priced at 125p–132p. An investor wishes to take out a three months 'put' option on 200 shares. Explain concisely what this means and state what conditions would probably have to prevail before the investor would exercise the option. Assume the option is fixed at 10p per share.
2 State the merits of options.
3 Explain the significance of Declaration day.
   (The Institute of Bankers in Scotland, *Theory and Practice of Investment*)

Suggested answers

1 An investor who gave 10p per share option money for a three months 'put' option in 200 XYZ Metal Company Limited 25p shares would be entitled to sell the shares at 125, the striking price, during the following three months, after which the option would lapse. The striking price for put options is usually the current bid price when the options are taken out, although occasionally it is a little below this.

   Most options are taken out with a view to dealing against them at a

---

* For FT-SE options the margin is 12½% of the Index value with similar adjustments.

profit. In this particular instance the position would probably be that the investor does not hold any XYZ Metal Company shares, but as he thinks the price is going to fall substantially within the next three months he has acquired a put option and hopes to buy the shares well below the option striking price before the option lapses. The arithmetic might be as follows:

Cost of acquiring option

200 shares at 10p	...	...	...	...	...	£20.00
Brokerage (minimum)		...	...	...	...	7.00
VAT	...	...	...	...	...	1.05
						£28.05

Suppose that within three months the price of the shares falls to 100p–107p, 200 shares are purchased, and the option is exercised in the same Account.

Proceeds of sale

200 shares sold at 1.25	...	...	...	...	...	£250.00
Cost of obtaining option		...	...	...	...	28.05
Cost of purchase						£221.95
200 shares at 1.07	...	...	...	...	...	214.00
Profit	...	...	...	...	...	£7.95

The investor would also exercise his option even though the price had not fallen sufficiently to make a profit if by doing so he would make a smaller loss than if he allowed the option to lapse, thus forfeiting the whole cost of the option, £28.05. For example, if the share price was 112–120p the cost of purchasing the shares would be:

200 at 1.20	...	...	...	...	...	...	£240.00

The loss would be £240.00–£221.95 = £18.05, i.e. less than if the option had been allowed to lapse.

2 The merit of options is that they allow speculation to take place with a small capital outlay. The maximum loss that can be suffered is the cost of acquiring the option. If in the above example the investor had sold the shares, meaning to buy them back in time to deliver, there is no limit to what he might have had to pay for them if his judgement had erred and the price had risen sharply. If the share price had doubled he would have lost nearly £300 instead of only his option money.

A put option is also a useful way of ensuring the profit on a share already held should there be a possibility of an event taking place in the next three months which might bring about a sharp drop in the price.

3   Options can only be exercised on a declaration day which is the second
    last day of an Account, usually a Thursday. The normal declaration day
    for an option is the last one before it lapses, but it may also be exercised
    on any declaration day during its currency. Although options can only be
    exercised on declaration days, dealing against them can take place at any
    time during the same Account.

Additional questions

1   Why is a contract note an important document? Detail the information it
    provides.
2   When does the buyer of a British Government stock require to pay for
    his/her purchase? For what other securities would this also apply?
3   Explain what is meant by the Account system. Illustrate your answer.
4   When may one deal for 'new time' and what advantages does it confer?
    (The Institute of Bankers in Scotland, *Theory and Practice of Investment*)
5   How may a 'bull' without paying for shares that he has purchased be able
    to let his profit run for more than one Account? Explain the mechanics of
    the arrangement.
6   (a)   What is the maximum period allowed for options on the Stock
          Exchange?
    (b)   How is the striking price for a 'call' option fixed?
    (c)   What sort of situation might give rise to a demand for double
          options?
7   What are the distinguishing features of traded options? How does the
    price of a traded option react to changes in the price of the underlying
    share?

7 Transfer of title

7.1 Registered securities

Practically all the securities issued by United Kingdom public authorities and companies are registered securities. This means that the issuing body maintains a register on which the names and addresses of holders and the amount of stock or shares held is recorded. The shareholder receives a certificate in his/her name stating that he/she is the owner of so many shares. When a change of ownership takes place certain procedures must be adhered to in order that the new owner may be registered in place of the old one.

7.11 Talisman

In April 1979 a new computerized system for transferring the title to the stock and shares of Stock Exchange listed United Kingdom companies became operational. It has been named 'Talisman' in recognition of the functions it performs: transfer accounting, lodgement for jobbers*, stock management for jobbers. Initially the system embraced only a limited number of stocks but by the middle of 1981 it covered practically all listed United Kingdom securities. It also embraced stocks dealt in on the Unlisted Security market, Irish registered stocks, South African stocks both for London delivery and South African delivery – the Stock Exchange maintaining an Agency in Johannesburg for the latter – and a few Australian stocks for London delivery, i.e. where there is a United Kingdom register. It has been further extended to cover settlement in London in US dollars and Irish punts.

7.111 Sepon
Fundamental to the system is a Stock Exchange nominee company called 'Sepon' into which name are transferred all shares sold by investors and out of which name are transferred all shares purchased by investors. The name 'Sepon' is pre-printed on the transfer form (see Figure 7.1) to be signed by the seller, and company registrars have on record Sepon as being the holder of a continually changing pool of shares. Jobbers have trading accounts with Sepon in respect of the stocks in which they deal.

---

* Market makers after 'Big Bang'.

TALISMAN SOLD TRANSFER

This transfer is pursuant to a Stock Exchange transaction, and is exempt from Transfer Stamp Duty.

Above this line for Registrar's use only.

Bargain Reference No:

Certificate lodged with Registrar

Name of Undertaking

United Biscuits (Holdings) Limited

Description of Security

Ordinary Shares of 25p

(for completion by the Registrars/ Stock Exchange)

Amount of Stock or number of Stock units or shares or other security in words

Three thousand

Figures

3,000

In the name(s) of

Andrew Seller
40 North Road
Edingow
Midlothian

Name(s) of registered holder(s) should be given in full: the address should be given where there is only one holder

If the transfer is not made by the registered holder(s) insert also the name(s) and capacity (e.g. Executor(s) of the

Account Designation (if any)

I/We hereby transfer the above security out of the name(s) aforesaid into the name of SEPON LIMITED and request the necessary entries to be made in the register.

Bodies corporate should affix their common seal and each signatory should state his/her representative capacity (e.g. 'Company Secretary' 'Director') against his/her signature.

1 'Andrew Seller'

2

3

4

Balance Certificate Required for (amount or number in figures)

Stamp and Firm Code of Selling Broker

A.W. & Co.

RD NP OR 102

Date   17 October 1979

SEPON LIMITED is lodging this Transfer at the direction and on behalf of the Member Firm whose stamp appears herein ('the Original Lodging Agent') and does not in any manner or to any extent warrant or represent the validity or genuineness of the transfer instructions contained herein or the genuineness of the Transferor's signature. The Original Lodging Agent by delivering this Transfer to SEPON LIMITED authorises SEPON LIMITED to lodge this Transfer for registration and agrees to be deemed for all purposes to be the person(s) actually lodging this Transfer for registration.

Stock Exchange Operating Account Number (if applicable)

TAL 112/1

PLEASE SIGN HERE

Figure 7.1

Shortly after giving his instructions to sell, a shareholder receives a Talisman Sold Transfer form covering the details of his sale and this he returns signed to his broker together with the relative share certificate(s) if this has not already been sent. The broker forwards the certificate and the transfer form to the Stock Exchange Centre where they are checked for good delivery, i.e. that everything is in order, and then passed on to the company registrar for registration into the Sepon account. On Settlement day the Centre allocates pool shares (those registered in the name of Sepon) to the jobber's trading account and the selling broker receives payment not directly from the jobber but from the Centre on the jobber's behalf.

The system is dependent on the early delivery of stock and the selling broker only receives payment on Settlement day for stock deposited at the Centre by noon on the Friday prior to Settlement day. Thereafter all other settlements take place on the day following that on which the sold stock is deposited at the Centre.

The standard stock transfer form cannot be used for Talisman sales even though it is completed in favour of Sepon as transferee, and company registrars will reject any sold Talisman transfer which is not received directly from the Centre or on which any alteration has been made to 'Sepon Limited'.

Where a seller has sold only part of his holding and has forwarded a certificate for more shares than he has sold the amount for which a balance certificate is required is entered on the Talisman transfer. The balance certificate for the shares retained is issued by the company registrar direct to the Centre (except in the case of an operating account holder) which passes it to the selling broker for onward transmission to his client.

When shares are purchased the broker advises the Centre of the buyer's registration details and it is essential that these are submitted by the last day before Settlement day. Shares to meet each purchase are apportioned from the jobber's trading account in the amounts, or to use Stock Exchange language 'the shapes', required to meet the purchases made from him. Buying brokers on behalf of their clients make payment to the Centre and transfers authorizing the removal of shares from Sepon into the name of purchasers are prepared by the Centre and sent to the company registrar in order that he can issue a share certificate in each purchaser's name.

Under Talisman the Centre has full details of every transaction, these being transmitted from terminals in brokers' offices, and thus is able to allocate dividends, scrip issues, rights issues, etc. to the investor entitled thereto when these occur around the time when a bargain is effected and the danger of some confusion might possibly otherwise arise. Brokers, however, remain responsible for the actual claiming from and remitting to their clients. As hitherto stamp duty is payable by the purchaser but with Talisman this will be collected centrally on behalf of the Inland Revenue under a composition agreement instead of each transfer form being individually stamped.

7.112 Stock notes

A stock note (see Figure 7.2) is an Advice issued by the Talisman Centre giving details of a purchase and registration particulars. It contains an undertaking that a Talisman Bought Transfer will be produced by the Centre and that it will be lodged for registration in accordance with the details submitted by the stockbroker to the Centre. In certain circumstances, such as purchases to be registered in name of a bank's nominee company, payment will be made only against delivery of a stock note.

7.113 Operating account numbers

The facility of an operating account number within the Talisman system is available to institutional investors. The advantages of these include:

1 When the selling broker delivers stock to the Stock Exchange it will be held by the Stock Exchange in the operating account to the order of the account holder until delivered by allocation to the jobber's trading account on Settlement day. The Stock Exchange is accountable to the account holder for the stock sold while it is awaiting delivery.

2 An operating account holder can request the selling broker to instruct the Stock Exchange to issue a Stock Receipt as evidence that the stock has been received at the Stock Exchange. The receipt is then forwarded by the broker to the account holder.

3 An operating account holder can request the selling broker to arrange for payment on Settlement day in the form of a cheque drawn by the Stock Exchange in favour of the account holder. This facility is known as a Centre Cheque and, to qualify, the individual bargain must have a minimum value of £25,000 or £5,000 for continuation business where the initial bargain value was not less than £25,000.

4 An operating account holder can use the Stock Exchange's Certification Office* to certify Talisman sold transfers (i.e. verify that a certificate(s) covering the shares sold is being forwarded by the Stock Exchange to the company registrar) where the share certificate is for an amount greater than is being sold or where a single certificate is held but sales have been carried out through more than one broker. Balance certificates will be sent direct to the account holder by the company registrar.

5 The operating account holder can provide stand-by registration details which will be applied to any purchase for which registration details have not been provided by Settlement day.

6 In the event of a suspension of Talisman the Stock Exchange will

---

* Should the account holder, while awaiting a balance certificate, effect a further sale, certification can then only be done by the company registrar and not by the Stock Exchange. This also applies if shares purchased in a previous account are sold before the stock certificate is received.

THE STOCK EXCHANGE
LONDON EC2N 1HP
Telephone: 01-588 2355

Date of Issue: 19 JUN 79

Serial No: **M 02599**

Name of Undertaking								
BEECHAM GROUP								

Description of Security						Security Code No.		
ORD 25P						0-088-006		

AMOUNT OF STOCK OR NUMBER OF STOCK UNITS/SHARES OR OTHER SECURITY IN WORDS

Hundred Millions	Ten Millions	Millions	Hundred Thousands	Ten Thousands	Thousands	Hundreds	Tens	Units
*****	*****	*****	*****	*****	*****	THREE	FIVE	ZERO

Firm Name & Code	Transaction Ref.	Deal Date	Settlement Date	Quantity
RD NP OR 102	9LE8164	23MAY79	12JUN79	350

Client	A/c. No.	Stamp Rate	Stamping Consideration	Stamp Duty
2VRRO19YA06		2%*	£2,345.00	£47.00

AMOUNT PAYABLE *(This may be completed by member firm at its option)* £

Transferee Details	Designation
K.B.SECURITIES LIMITED, P.O.BOX 50, 81,ST.ANDREW SQUARE, EASTBURGH.	

Other Details

This is to certify that the stock specified above has been apportioned pursuant to the transaction referred to above and that The Stock Exchange will lodge a TALISMAN Bought Transfer comprising that stock for registration into the name of the transferee specified above. Until such transfer is lodged the transferee shall have a beneficial interest to the extent of the stock specified above in all the stock of the same description registered or accepted by The Stock Exchange for registration into the name of SEPON Limited. The Stock Exchange shall not be responsible for any certificate relating to the stock.

If in the case of any bought bargain the stock is for any reason not registered in the name of the transferee pursuant to that bought bargain, The Stock Exchange will repay to the broker named above, as agent for the transferee, the amount specified above (being the amount paid as consideration for the stock plus any stamp duty thereon). The Stock Exchange shall not be concerned with the manner in which the broker applies any such payment.

In the case of apportionments pursuant to bought bargains, this Stock Note shall be of no effect for any purpose unless and until the broker named above has been paid the gross purchase consideration payable for the stock.

The Stock Exchange reserves the right in exceptional circumstances to reverse any apportionment in the event of bad delivery to SEPON Limited.

This Stock Note is issued subject to, and the expressions used herein are to be construed in accordance with, the Rules and Regulations of The Stock Exchange and, where appropriate, the Standard Conditions of Service for the time being in force between The Stock Exchange and the client named above.

For and on behalf of The Stock Exchange

Authorised Signature

This Stock Note is not a document of title and cannot be transferred or negotiated whether absolutely or by way of security

* See Appendix B.

Figure 7.2

compensate an account holder on the net sold position of the account in accordance with agreed conditions.

7.12 *Transfer of gilt-edged stocks*

Until the commencement of Talisman all United Kingdom registered securities were, following the passing of the Stock Transfer Act 1963, transferred by means of a standard stock transfer form, this being supplemented by the use of brokers' transfer forms where stock sold by a single stockholder was in due course deliverable to two or more purchasers. Apart from non-market transactions the stock transfer form will, once Talisman has embraced all company securities, be used only for gilt-edged transfers.

When an investor sells a gilt holding he will receive from his broker a stock transfer form (see Figure 7.3) completed at this stage only with his name and address and the nominal amount and description of the stock being sold. The seller signs the transfer and returns it to his broker along with the stock certificate if this has not already been forwarded.

Frequently the stock will be taken into the name of the jobber (or his nominees) and accordingly on delivery of the stock transfer form with the relative scrip the jobber will complete the lower part of the form with the relevant registration particulars. This forms a pool holding out of which sales by the jobber are delivered.

Alternatively the selling broker may deliver to the buying broker or brokers and where he has to deliver to more than one broker a complication arises in that he has only one stock transfer form signed by the seller and perhaps only one stock certificate. In this event the broker cancels the bottom part of the stock transfer form and completes part one of two (or more) brokers' transfer forms (see Figure 7.5), entering the amounts appropriate to each delivery. He then takes the stock transfer form, the two (or more) brokers' transfer forms and the certificate to the Certification Office of the Stock Exchange to have the brokers' transfer forms certified.

The brokers' transfer forms once certified are good delivery and they are presented to the respective buying brokers for payment. The certificate and stock transfer form with the advice form on the reverse completed (see Figure 7.4) are forwarded by the Stock Exchange to the Bank of England to await the presentation of the brokers' transfer forms after the registration particulars of the purchasers have been completed by the buying brokers.

Thus when an investor buys a gilt-edged stock his broker will receive either a stock transfer form with the relative stock certificate, or a certified stock (where part of holding is sold and only one buyer is involved) or brokers' transfer form according to the circumstances of the transaction. In all cases the action he takes is the same, i.e. he completes the bottom section of the form with his/her client's registration details and sends it to the Bank of England for registration accompanied with the relative stock certificate where the stock transfer form has not been certified. Shortly thereafter a new certificate for the stock purchased will be sent to the broker for onward transmission to his/her client or delivery elsewhere for safe keeping on his/her client's behalf.

7.13 Overseas registered stocks

The securities of some overseas countries are still subject to the procedure in force before the Stock Transfer Act 1963 was passed. This means that the buyer as well as the seller must sign the transfer form and both their signatures require to be witnessed. Where a holding is sold to more than one purchaser separate transfer forms must be signed both by seller and buyer for each individual purchase. For overseas registered stocks quoted in the United Kingdom, reference should be made to the Stock Exchange Daily Official List and the Stock Exchange Official Year Book to verify transfer requirements.

7.2 Bearer securities

With bearer securities the issuing body does not keep a register of shareholders; neither does the shareholder's name appear on the certificate, or the bearer bond as it is commonly called. Actual possession of bearer securities denotes ownership and all that is necessary in a sale to transfer title is for the seller to deliver the stock to the buyer. Stamp duty is payable only on the first occasion that the bonds are negotiated.

One complication arising from there being no record of shareholders is that interest or dividend payments cannot be paid by the issuing body without claims being made by holders entitled to receive them. This difficulty is overcome by each bearer bond having a sheet of numbered coupons attached to it. When a dividend is about to be paid an advertisement appears in the financial press informing holders that in order to receive payment they should lodge coupon number such and such with a named paying agent on or after a certain date. When a sheet of coupons has been completely used up in this way provision must be made for replacing it. This is usually done by having attached to the sheet a slip known as a 'talon' which is lodged in exchange for a new coupon sheet.

A serious disadvantage of bearer securities is that loss of title, i.e. certificate and coupons, means complete forfeiture of both capital and income rights. Holders receive no notice of meetings, circulars, or reports which the company issue, and there is also the inherent danger of forgery of documents. Dividends must also be claimed instead of coming in automatically as with registered stock. For safety, bearer securities are usually held by the beneficial owner's bank which also attends to the claiming of dividends in his behalf.

For bearer bonds to be good delivery they must be in good condition and not badly torn or the wording materially obliterated. Where doubt exists

STOCK TRANSFER FORM

WADDIE & CO. LTD
EDINBURGH & LONDON

(Above this line for Registrars only)

Certificate lodged with the Registrar

Consideration Money £ 8,000

(For completion by the Registrar Stock Exchange)

Full name of Undertaking.	9% Treasury Loan 1994

Full description of Security.	

Number or amount of Shares, Stock or other security and, in figures column only, number and denomination of units, if any.	Words	Figures
	Ten thousand	£10,000
		(units of)

Name(s) of registered holder(s) should be given in full; the address should be given where there is only one holder.

If the transfer is not made by the registered holder(s) insert also the name(s) and capacity (e.g., Executor(s)) of the person(s) making the transfer

In the name(s) of

Andrew Seller
40 North Road
Edingow
Midlothian

person(s) named below or to the several persons named in *Parts 2 of Brokers Transfer Forms relating to the above security:*

not stock exchange transactions, of Agent(s), if any, acting for the Transferor(s).

Delete words in italics except for stock exchange transactions

Signature(s) of transferor(s)

1. ....'Andrew Seller'.........

A.W. & Co.

2. ....

3. ....

4. ....

Date..13.June.1979.......

Bodies corporate should execute under their common seal.

Full name(s) and full postal addresses(es) (including County or, if applicable, Postal District number) of the person(s) to whom the security is transferred.

Please state title, if any, or whether Mr., Mrs., or Miss.

Please complete in type-writing or in Block Capitals.

Mr. James Buyer
72 Ivy Avenue
Plymhampton
Devon

I/We request that such entries be made on the register as are necessary to give effect to this transfer.

Stamp of Buying Broker(s) (if any)

Stamp or name and address of person lodging this form
(if other than the Buying Broker(s))

J.M.C. & Co.

Figure 7.3

The security represented by the Stock Transfer form has been sold as follows:

...........................Shares/Stock	6,000 ....Shares/Stock	
...........................Shares/Stock	4,000 ....Shares/Stock	
...........................Shares/Stock	....................Shares/Stock	
...........................Shares/Stock	....................Shares/Stock	
...........................Shares/Stock	....................Shares/Stock	
...........................Shares/Stock	....................Shares/Stock	
...........................Shares/Stock	....................Shares/Stock	
...........................Shares/Stock	....................Shares/Stock	
...........................Shares/Stock	....................Shares/Stock	
...........................Shares/Stock	....................Shares/Stock	

10,000

Balance (if any) due to Selling Broker(s)

Amount of Certificate(s)

10,000

Brokers Transfer Forms for above amounts certified

Stamp of certifying Stock Exchange   *Stamp of Selling Broker(s)*

A.W. & Co

Figure 7.4

reference must be made to the Council of the Stock Exchange for their ruling. All coupons subsequent to the last one lodged for payment must be attached and the bonds must, when appropriate, be properly stamped.

Bearer securities are not very numerous as far as British companies are concerned. However, there are still some in existence, Rio Tinto-Zinc Corporation and Shell Transport and Trading Company for example, both having equity issues in bearer as well as in registered form. Quite a few British Government stocks, for instance $3\frac{1}{2}$% War Loan, have a small part of the amount on issue in bearer form. They are more popular abroad and the majority of foreign government loans in London are bearer securities.

7.3 American and Canadian certificates

Shares in United States and Canadian companies are, so far as United Kingdom investors are concerned, a mixture between registered and bearer form. There is a register of shareholders to whom dividends are paid and reports, etc., sent. The front of the share certificate shows the name of the shareholder and is more or less similar in layout to a British share certificate. However, on the reverse of the certificate (Figure 7.6) there is a form of transfer. When a change of ownership takes place, if this form is completed in full and forwarded to the company's transfer agent in America or Canada, a fresh certificate will be issued in the name of the new owner.

Alternatively, if the registered holder has signed the form (before a witness who also signs) but the remainder of the form is left blank it becomes a bearer document and passes from seller to buyer in the same way as bearer bonds. Because of this they are sometimes described as 'hand to hand' certificates. The dividends are of course paid to the registered holder and subsequent owners must claim them from him/her.

7.31 Marking names

It will be appreciated that difficulties can arise in collecting dividends when the registered owner is a private individual who could well move about the country. It has, therefore, become the normal practice for American and Canadian securities owned by residents in the United Kingdom to be registered in 'recognized marking names'. These are the names of stockbrokers, jobbers, banks, and other financial institutions whose business includes dealing in such shares. To qualify as a recognized marking name, which is a status granted by the Stock Exchange, an undertaking must be given to pay dividends to the owners of the shares at the rate of exchange fixed by the Stock Exchange.

When a sale takes place all that usually happens is that the certificate, which having been signed by the marking name is in bearer form, passes from one bank* to another where it is held on behalf of the beneficial owner. The bank, which must keep an eye on payment dates, claims all dividends from the marking name.

There is nothing to prevent an investor who has purchased shares in a marking name from him/herself becoming registered as the owner. He will of course require to meet the costs involved in sending the securities abroad for registration. Another snag is that when it comes to selling shares in 'other names' a lower price is received than when they are in marking names. It is not a course of action to be recommended.

---

* With the removal of Exchange Control regulations in 1979 it is no longer necessary for the certificates to be held by the bodies such as banks formerly designated as authorized depositaries but for safety and convenience most investors will wish to avail themselves of this facility.

BROKERS TRANSFER FORM

(Above this line for Registrars only)

Certificate lodged with the Registrar

Consideration Money £ 4,800 ....

(For completion by the Registrar/Stock Exchange)

Part 1

Full name of Undertaking.	9% Treasury Stock 1994
Full description of Security.	
Number or amount of Shares, Stock or other security and, in figures column only, number and denomination of units, if any.	Words Six thousand Figures £6,000 (units of)
Name(s) of registered holder(s) should be given in full; the address should be given where there is only one holder. If the transfer is not made by the registered holder(s) insert also the name(s) and capacity (e.g. Executor(s)) of the person(s) making the transfer.	In the name(s) of Andrew Seller 40 North Road Edingow Midlothian

I/we confirm that the Stock Transfer Form relating to the security set out above has been lodged with the Registrar, and that the said security has been sold by me/us by a stock exchange transaction within the meaning of the Stock Transfer Act 1963.

A.W. & Co.

13 June 1979

Date and Stamp of Selling Broker(s)

Part 2

Full name(s) and full postal address(es) (including County or, if applicable, Postal District number) of the person(s) to whom the security is transferred.

Please state title, if any, or whether Mr., Mrs. or Miss.

Please complete in type-writing or in Block Capitals.

Mr. James Part-Buyer
50 Green Terrace
Ashburgh
Northumberland

I/We confirm that the security set out in Part 1 above has been purchased by a stock exchange transaction within the meaning of the Stock Transfer Act 1963, and I/we request that such entries be made in the register as are necessary to give effect to this transfer.

Stamp of Buying Broker(s)

T.R. & Co.

Stamp of Lodging Agent (if other than the Buying Broker(s))

Figure 7.5

For Value received...hereby sell, assign and transfer unto

....

....

....

.... **Shares**

of the Capital Stock represented by the within Certificate, and do hereby irrevocably
constitute and appoint...Attorney
to transfer the said stock on the books of the within named Corporation with full
power of substitution in the premises.

Dated...

....

In presence of

....

Figure 7.6

7.32 No par value

A point which may be observed when dealing with American and Canadian
shares is that while the shares of some companies may have a nominal value,
for example $5 shares, others may be described as shares of no nominal or
par value. This is in contrast to this country where by law all shares must
have a nominal value. Where shares have no par value dividends must be
declared as so much cash per share and not in percentage terms.

7.4 Australian securities

Owing to extreme delays being incurred in receiving certificates for
Australian shares purchased in London a Bearer Deposit Receipt Scheme for
Australian securities was introduced in March 1970.

The Bearer Deposit Receipts are fully bearer documents and are issued in
London against Australian securities which are registered in names of
nominees of certain Australian banks (the depositary banks) and are lodged
with the depositary banks in Australia.

Only the stocks of a limited number of Australian companies are at present
in the scheme but it is anticipated that further companies will be added from
time to time.

7.5 American deposit receipts

American deposit receipts (ADRs) provide a means whereby American investors can own UK securities without being involved in the administrative procedure of having their holdings registered in their own names in the UK. They arise from Americans purchasing shares in the normal way in this country except that the shares are registered and held in name of an American bank. On each occasion that this happens the bank issues an ADR for the relevant number of shares and this is a negotiable bearer instrument, priced in dollars, which thereafter can be traded in the United States. The holders from time to time are entitled to the dividends which must be claimed from the registered bank.

In recent years there has been a considerable increase in the number of ADRs in existence although there is an active market only in the shares of a few major UK companies. There is nothing to prevent a UK resident from buying ADRs.

Typical questions

1 What is meant by a 'good marking name'? In what type of security is it most usual to find this method of registration and why has the practice gained ground? How are dividends received by the beneficial owner?
2 The price of 'Shell' Transport and Trading Ordinary shares is quoted as:

410 (registered) and
$411\frac{1}{4}$ (bearer)

Why should there be this difference in price? State how you would obtain a good title in each case.

(The Institute of Bankers in Scotland, *Theory and Practice of Investment*)

Suggested answers

1 A 'good marking name' (alternatively known as a recognized marking name) is the name of a firm of stockbrokers or market makers, or a bank, or other financial institution which has been granted this status by the Stock Exchange.

It is usual for American and Canadian securities owned by residents in the United Kingdom to be registered in a good marking name. When the registered holder of such shares has endorsed the form of transfer in blank on the back of the certificate it becomes a bearer document and ownership passes by delivery. This is a satisfactory arrangement when the registered owner is a good marking name but gives rise to difficulties if the registered owner is a private individual since dividends, etc., are paid to the registered holder and must be claimed therefrom by the beneficial owner. As the result of this American and Canadian securities registered in marking names command a higher price on the Stock Exchange than identical securities in other names. The difference approximates to the cost involved should a purchaser of shares in other names decide to send the certificate to the transfer agent overseas to have the shares registered either in his/her own name or in a recognized marking name.

Once the shares are in a marking name there is little point in a purchaser going to the trouble and expense of having them registered in his own name when the outcome will be that he will thereby have reduced the value of the holding.

Dividends claimed by the beneficial owner from a marking name must be paid at a rate of exchange fixed by the Stock Exchange. In practice it is usually the beneficial owner's bank which claims the dividends on his behalf from the marking name.

2 The reason for the difference in price is that the purchaser of Shell registered has to meet *ad valorem* stamp duty of £1% (see Appendix B) on the consideration which he pays for the shares. No such impost falls on the purchaser of Shell bearer as the result of which the price is slightly higher.

For a buyer to obtain a good title to the registered shares it is necessary for there to be delivered to him (or his agent) a stamped transfer form signed by the seller either certified or together with the relative share certificate. The buyer's registration particulars are then entered on the transfer form and the document(s) lodged with the company's registrar. The buyer is entered on the company's register as owner of the shares and in due course he receives a share certificate in his own name.

In the case of the bearer shares a good title is obtained on delivery of the share certificates with relative coupons attached, all in good condition. As bearer securities in this country are usually held by a bank for safety, delivery is effected between the seller's bank and the buyer's bank.

Additional questions

1 What is the difference between a standard stock transfer form and a Talisman Sold Transfer form and for what type of transaction are they respectively brought into use?

2 Detail the procedure following the execution by a seller of a Talisman Sold Transfer form which will result in the seller being paid and the purchaser receiving his/her share certificate.

3 What are the advantages of an operating account number and to whom is this facility available?

4 Specify the circumstances which give rise to the certification of transfers.

5 What differences in procedure may be involved in the transfer of overseas registered stocks?

6 Why are coupons attached to bearer securities and what happens when they are used up? State the disadvantages of bearer securities.

8 New issues

8.1 To shareholders

A rather dismal note was struck in Chapter 4 when dealing with capital reduction arising from the loss of assets. Fortunately, a happier state of affairs often exists with a company steadily ploughing back a proportion of its profits in order to expand the business. As a result, in the course of time both its assets and reserves build up while its nominal issued capital may remain unchanged. This situation could give rise to a balance sheet moulded in the following pattern.

Capital issued					
100,000 Ordinary Shares			*Fixed assets*	...	...£190,000
of £1 each ...	...£100,000				
Reserves			*Current assets*	...	160,000
Revenue ...	... 250,000				
	£350,000				£350,000

8.11 Bonus issues

The company may decide to capitalize a portion of the reserves by increasing the issued capital, thus recording in the balance sheet what has actually taken place, i.e. that profits have been used to acquire assets which are now part of the capital of the business. Suppose that £100,000 is the amount to be treated in this way. Each shareholder will receive one new share for each share already held in what is described as a bonus, capitalization, or scrip issue. When this has been done it will be reflected as follows in the balance sheet.

Capital issued					
200,000 Ordinary Shares			*Fixed assets*	...	...£190,000
of £1 each ...	...£200,000				
Reserves			*Current assets*	...	160,000
Revenue ...	... 150,000				
	£350,000				£350,000

It will be observed that although each shareholder has twice the number of shares previously held there is no change in the total assets of the company. The shareholder has paid nothing for his new shares and his proportionate ownership of the company has not altered. If each of the £1 shares before the bonus issue had been worth £3 they should now be worth £1.50, and the total value of his holding would be the same. Similarly, if he had been receiving a $17\frac{1}{2}$% dividend on his pre-bonus shares he would expect to receive a dividend in the region of $8\frac{3}{4}$% on the increased holding. Basically all that has taken place has been a book-keeping adjustment.

There are one or two points worthy of note. First of all a bonus issue allows a lower rate of dividend to be declared on the nominal capital while paying the shareholder the same amount of cash. Obviously $17\frac{1}{2}$% of £100 is exactly the same as $8\frac{3}{4}$% of £200. However, to the uninformed on investment matters the $17\frac{1}{2}$% may appear to be an outrageously high rate of dividend and the $8\frac{3}{4}$% comparatively reasonable. The fact that all shareholders acquiring holdings in the recent past have almost certainly paid well over par is overlooked. For instance a buyer at £3 would only be receiving a yield of 5.8% ($17.5 \times \frac{1}{3}$) on the money invested, which is a far cry from the 17.5% yield applicable to anyone who had obtained his shares at par. In any event should such a shareholder exist he would, in all probability, have acquired his shares many years ago when a much lower rate was being paid, and the increases which have ensued must be seen in the light of the steady fall in the purchasing power of money. However, be that as it may, in the interests of industrial harmony there is something to be said for occasional bonus issues and consequent reduction in the rate of dividend.

A bonus issue is, of course, not completely devoid of real significance to the shareholder. It can usually be taken as a sign that the company's affairs are progressing favourably, and it may also be the occasion for a small increase in dividend, as where fractional percentages are involved the consequent rate of dividend may be rounded up to the nearest whole number. In the example quoted above the rate after the issue might well have been 9%.

Another aspect of a bonus issue which may benefit shareholders is that, for no strictly logical reason, investors tend to be biased against heavy (highly priced) shares and a bonus issue, particularly a substantial one, brings a company's shares into a more popular range. For example, suppose a share is worth £5 and a four for one bonus issue is made. Logically each share should then be worth £1 but in practice it may be found that they are worth, say, £1.05 and the shareholders' capital has increased a little in value.

8.12 Rights issues

A common situation to arise is for a company to find itself in need of additional funds to further some project which the directors have in mind, or perhaps to repay temporary borrowing with which the project has already been financed. It may be decided that the best method of doing this is by a rights issue of ordinary shares. This means that shareholders will be provisionally allotted new shares again in strict proportion to their holdings. The difference between this and a bonus issue is that if the shareholders wish to accept the new shares allotted to them they will have to pay a certain amount per share to the company.

For instance, a company with an issued capital of 1,000,000 ordinary shares of £1 each may require to raise £250,000, the ordinary shares at this time being worth £2.50. The cash could, therefore, be raised by issuing 250,000 new £1 shares at par, i.e. a one for four rights issue, or by issuing 125,000 new ordinary £1 shares at £2, a one for eight rights issue.

It is, of course, essential that the price of the new shares is below that of the old shares otherwise no one would subscribe for them as they could be purchased more cheaply in the market. Because of this lower price it is necessary that such an issue is made to the company's shareholders* and not to the general public who would then be acquiring shares at below the market price and the existing shareholders' stake in the company would be worth less as the result of this gift to outsiders.

All the shareholders are unlikely both to wish to subscribe for the shares and to have sufficient cash available to enable them to do so. Such shareholders not accepting their shares can sell their 'rights' to subscribe for them and it is the purchaser who in this event pays the amount required by the company. As soon as the terms of a rights issue are announced it is possible to estimate what the value of the rights per old share and the value of the new shares (nil paid) will be when dealings in the new shares eventually commence. Suppose the above-mentioned company decides to make the one for four issue at par.

Cost of four old shares (before the issue) at £2.50 each			...		£10.00
Cost of subscribing for one new share at £1.00	...	...	...		1.00
Five shares therefore cost	...	...	...	...	...	£11.00
Each of these shares is worth	...	...	...	...	...	£2.20

The value of each old share shows an estimated drop of 30p and this is known as the value of the rights per old share. As £1.00 must be subscribed for each new share the price of a new share (nil paid) will be estimated to be £1.20 (£2.20–£1.00). This £1.20 is also referred to as the premium on the new shares, i.e. the amount by which they are above their issue price.

These calculations are, of course, only theoretical as the actual prices are affected by normal market forces of supply and demand when actual

---

* As well as being a stock exchange requirement for listed companies, this is now necessary in terms of the 1980 Companies Act unless the shareholders determine otherwise.

transactions take place. Also, the prices of the old and new shares will not be exactly the same as for a limited period after issue the new shares can be purchased free of stamp duty.*

Dealings normally begin in the new shares on the day after the allotment letters are posted by the company to its shareholders. It may in fact be an advantageous time for the purchase of a holding in the company, as no matter how attractive the issue there will almost certainly be some shareholders who do not have sufficient cash to subscribe for the shares provisionally allotted to them. This will increase the number of sellers in the market and, until they have unloaded, the price may be temporarily depressed.

Payment for the new shares to the company does not usually require to be made for a few weeks after they have been issued. Most frequently the payment must be made in one lump sum, but there are other occasions when all the cash may not be needed by the company immediately and the payment may be made in two or more separate instalments. For example, the new shares may be provisionally allotted at £1.00, payable as to 50p on or before 26 March and 50p on or before 26 June. During this time the shares may be sold and purchased first of all in nil paid form, subsequently in partly paid form.

It is important for the original allottee either to pay the call or calls on the shares not later than the appointed dates, or alternatively to sell them to someone else who thereupon assumes this responsibility. If this is not done the relative provisional allotment will be deemed to have been declined and will be cancelled with the possible loss to the holder of all value pertaining thereto. However, there is an increasing tendency nowadays for companies to sell in the market new shares which have not been taken up and any excess over the subscription price after deduction of expenses is distributed *pro rata* among the shareholders to whom such shares were provisionally allotted.

Rights issues may often be described as being made on 'generous' or 'bonus' terms when the amount to be subscribed for the new shares is well below the price of the old ones. This can be misleading as it implies that the shareholders are being given something by the company which is not the case at all. For instance, in the example given, before the rights issue a shareholder with 100 shares owned 100/1,000,000 of the assets of the company valued by the market at £2,500,000. Should the shareholder take up his new shares he will own 125/1,250,000 of the assets of the company, which is exactly the same proportion. That his total holding is now (normal market forces apart) theoretically worth £25 more is due to the fact that the company's assets have been increased by the receipt of £250,000 cash of which his contribution has been £25. It should be noted that if the shareholder does not subscribe for the full allotment his proportionate ownership of the company is inevitably reduced.

When deciding whether or not to take up shares provisionally allotted, what

---

* Under the 1986 Finance Bill proposals this will no longer be the case after 27 October 1986.

matters is not the relationship of the issue price to the price of the old shares but how profitably the company will utilize the new capital raised. If earnings on capital employed are likely to be maintained or increased then the new shares offer the prospect of increased participation in the company's prosperity. If not, the shareholder should look around and consider if the proceeds of the sale of the new shares (nil paid) could not be more usefully invested elsewhere.

The announcement of a rights issue is usually accompanied by a forecast of the rate of dividend likely to be paid on the enlarged capital. Naturally if the rights issue is a substantial one well below the market price a drop in the rate will be inevitable. If it is a small issue the dividend rate may be maintained, particularly if the issue price of the new is not far below the market price.

8.13 Excess shares and fractions

Along with the provision allotment letter in a rights issue the shareholder may also receive a form for application of excess shares. This form has no marketable value but may be used by the shareholder to apply for further new shares over and above his/her *pro rata* entitlement. The excess shares may arise when other shareholders ignore their allotments and also where fractions are involved.

Both bonus and rights issues by their terms sometimes produce fractions of shares. For example, in a one for three bonus issue a holder of 100 shares would be entitled to $33\frac{1}{3}$ new shares. Fractions are, however, not issued and in bonus issues the invariable practice is for the company to arrange for the sale of all shares remaining in its hands as the result of these fractions and to distribute the proceeds proportionately among the shareholders concerned. In rights issues fractions are often ignored. In this case the individual shareholder suffers a small disadvantage when his holding is not divisible into a whole number and his allotment is slightly less than his strict entitlement.

8.2 To the general public

New issues are made to the public either because a quoted company requires to raise further capital or because an unquoted company, usually a private company, wishes to change its status and receive a stock exchange quotation. There are various methods employed.

8.21 Public invitation to subscribe

8.211 Issue by prospectus

This is where a company offers share or loan capital direct to the public at a fixed price. It is commonly used by a quoted company for new loan capital issues, but share capital issues by this method are now rare. Practically all government and other public authority issues are made by prospectus.

Before making the issue the company will consult with an issuing house as to the terms and conditions by which the required capital is most likely to be raised in the light of the current market conditions.

8.212 *Offer for sale*

Most of the larger issues of ordinary shares become quoted on the Stock Exchange and available to the public for the first time through an offer for sale. This is where an issuing house itself offers shares to the public at a fixed price of so much per share.

The issuing house in all probability will have just acquired the shares from the company or from one or two major shareholders at a slightly lower price than that at which it is now offering them. Alternatively it may offer them to the public at the same price, its remuneration being obtained by way of a fee from the company. It is quite possible that the shares, in fact, may have been recently created as the result of which the company has had funds made available to it by the issuing house. On other occasions all that may be taking place is a change in ownership of the shares for the purposes of a quotation.

8.213 *Issue by tender*

This is a method normally associated with water companies seeking new capital, but from time to time it is also used by other bodies.* Its distinguishing feature is that the shares are offered at a minimum fixed price but applicants may apply for shares at any higher price per share, such price being usually restricted to a multiple of 5p.

With water companies, which have a maximum rate of dividend and are akin to fixed interest stocks, allotments are made from the highest price downwards until the issue is fully allocated. In practice there is seldom a wide divergence between the highest and lowest prices as the restriction of the dividend to a fixed maximum tends to promote uniformity in applicants' assessments of the worth of the stocks.

In the case of other companies the shares are usually allotted all at the same price, this being the highest price at which the number of shares tendered for, together with those tendered for at a higher price, is equal to or exceeds the number of shares offered. If this basis of allocation does not result in a spread of the shares among a sufficiently large number of holders to create reasonable prospects of their being a market in the shares the Stock Exchange will insist on the larger allotments being scaled down, with the result that the 'striking' price will be reduced and applicants at this lower price will also receive shares.

Example

In an offer for sale by tender 375,000 ordinary 25p shares were offered at a minimum price of 130p per share. The issue proved a popular one, being oversubscribed twenty-six times, and the striking price was 175p. The basis of allotment was as follows:

---

* In 1979 the Government issued several new stocks by tender and since then it has come into more general use.

Shares applied for	Allotted
100	25
200	50
500	75
1000–25,000	10% of application
30,000 and upwards	$8\frac{1}{2}$% of application (approximate)

this issue applications were only allowed for the following numbers of
shares: 100, 200, 500, 1000, 2000, 5000, and multiples of 5000.

disadvantage of the issue by tender method is that the small investor may
have difficulty in deciding the price at which he/she should apply for the
shares. The investor will, of course, be able to seek guidance from his/her
stockbroker and the financial press.

.214 General procedure and disclosure*

he rules and regulations regarding the issue of shares in the above-
mentioned three ways are largely similar and, accordingly, they may be dealt
with together. In all issues at a comparatively early stage in the proceedings
the company or issuing house will approach the Stock Exchange through its
stockbroker with a view to ensuring that, in due course, the Stock Exchange
will grant permission for the shares to be dealt in. Permission is not actually
granted until after the issue has been made, but if the usual processes of
consultation have been adhered to it is unlikely to be withheld. However,
should permission be refused all subscription money will have to be returned
to applicants.

Money is being handed over by the public in exchange for shares. To
protect the public from unwittingly subscribing for what are dubious
ventures, perhaps right from the start, the Companies Acts and the Stock
Exchange both insist that certain information regarding the company must be
disclosed. This does not guarantee that the company will prosper in the future
but it does give the public the opportunity of coming to a reasonable
conclusion regarding the company's prospects. The public are further
protected by the fact that no reputable issuing house will risk lending its name
to the issue of shares on a company whose affairs are other than satisfactory.
In fact, the quality of an issue may to some extent be gauged by the auspices
under which it is making its appearance.

Copies of the document offering the shares must be published in at least
two leading newspapers, one of which must be a national. A form of
application is incorporated in the advertisement with full instructions on how
to apply, the minimum amount that may be subscribed for, and the sum
payable on application and allotment. In order to give time for the proper

---

See also Section 5.23.

examination of the information and for comment in the financial press, application lists cannot be opened until at least the third business day after the advertisement. They usually stay open at most for one day, but frequently when offers are oversubscribed close within a few minutes. Once an intending subscriber has submitted his/her application he/she cannot withdraw it until after the close of the third business day after the opening of the lists. Copies of the offer document together with an application form may also be obtained from the issuing house, the stockbrokers, and the branches of the bankers to the issue.

The offer document itself contains a mass of information, such as full details of the company's capital now being issued together with relevant particulars of other classes of capital, if any; the history and business of the company and its future prospects with any profits forecast given being accompanied by a report from the auditors or reporting accountants and the issuing house on the assumptions on which the forecast is made; the auditor's report on the company's profits together with their report on the balance sheet in summarized form for a minimum of the last five years, or such lesser period as may be agreed with the Stock Exchange; the holdings of directors and their families; the costs of the issue and to whom payable; details of any options and to whom they have been granted; and a summary of any material contracts other than in the normal course of business entered into during the previous two years.

The ordinary investor by him/herself may have difficulty in assimilating all the information provided, but he/she will receive considerable assistance in interpretation from the financial press. Should any false or misleading statements be made, a subscriber influenced by such statements has legal rights against the perpetrators who may find themselves fined, or imprisoned, or both.

It should be noted that while loan capital may be issued at par, at a discount or at a premium, share capital is invariably issued at par or at a premium. In theory it is possible to issue share capital at a discount but various conditions must be complied with and the sanction of the Court obtained.

8.215 Allotment

In order to ensure as far as possible the success of issues the terms to the public, particularly in offers for sale, tend to be on the generous side as the result of which they are often oversubscribed and the market price when dealings begin is above the issue price, i.e. at a premium. For instance, a share issued at 110p might be quoted at around 135p.

This oversubscription means, of course, that all applications cannot be met in full and some scheme of allotment which is duly announced must be resorted to. There is usually a bias in favour of small investors, but with heavy oversubscriptions, even allowing for drastic scaling down of the large applications, frequently a ballot is required and only a minority of lucky applicants actually receive an allotment.

All the allotment letters or letters of acceptance must be issued simultaneously in order that as far as is practical all allottees are in the same position when dealings begin on the following business day. Unsuccessful applicants receive letters of regret usually a day or two later together with the refund of their subscription money.

8.216 *Underwriting*

When a company or any other body is involved in an issue it wishes to make sure that it will receive the money which it requires. Although the terms of the issue may have been arranged to guarantee its almost certain success, market sentiment may be changed very suddenly by political or economic factors in the short period between the price being fixed and the offer being made. It is, therefore, the normal practice for issues to be underwritten, which in other words is the taking out of a form of insurance for their success.

A rate of underwriting commission, perhaps in the region of 2% of the total sum to be raised, is paid to the house handling the issue. This makes the issuing house responsible in the last resort to take up any shares not subscribed for by the public. The issuing house, however, does not carry all this risk itself but will farm out part or perhaps the whole of the underwriting at a reduced commission of, say, $1\frac{1}{2}$% to sub-underwriters who may be other issuing houses, insurance companies, banks, investment trusts, etc. These sub-underwriters become primarily responsible for the subscription *pro rata* of shares not taken up by the public. Should any of the sub-underwriters fail to meet their obligations these then devolve on the principal underwriter, which is the reason for the retention of the $\frac{1}{2}$% 'overriding' commission by the issuing house.

8.217 *The stag*

This is the term used to denote a subscriber for a new issue who applies for shares, not with the intention of retaining them as a permanent investment but with a view to selling them at a profit either during initial dealings or very shortly thereafter. Obviously stags only apply for issues in which they think dealings will commence at a premium over the issue price.

Stags are sometimes rather a nuisance in that they cause heavy oversubscription and thus much extra work for whoever is handling the issue. They may also prevent genuine investors from receiving an allotment. However, they do at times perform a useful function in helping a large issue to be marketed when it is too big to be absorbed by permanent investors in a single day. In this event it is unlikely that the stags will be able to sell the shares at a premium in early dealings, and they must take an immediate loss or retain their shares in the hope that in the near future the price will pick up and they will be able to sell at a profit.

As the stag expects the issue to be oversubscribed and anticipates receiving no more than a scaled down allotment he often exposes himself to the risk of heavy loss by applying for more shares than he can afford to hold. If he has misjudged the situation and the issue is a flop he will receive his full allotment which he may have to sell at once at a substantial loss.

In offers for sale by tender the scope for successful stagging is, of course, considerably reduced.

8.22 Not quite so public

8.221 A placing

This occurs where a stockbroker, either alone or in conjunction with an issuing house, arranges for shares to be placed at the issue price with a number of clients among whom the institutions such as investment trusts and insurance companies are often predominant. Where a quotation is sought the Stock Exchange can insist that at least 25% of any placing of ordinary shares and 20% of any placing of fixed interest stock is made available to clients of brokers other than the placing broker thus ensuring a 'market', at least in initial dealings.

The advantage of this method is that it is much cheaper than an offer for sale. It is, however, difficult for ordinary members of the public to obtain shares at the placing price, and as this is usually lower than the opening price in the market such appreciation is a windfall for a favoured few. The Stock Exchange, therefore, does not allow placings of equity capital except in the case of relatively small issues where the cost of an offer for sale would be disproportionately high. This restriction does not apply to fixed interest issues as these arouse less widespread demand and the main participants are pension funds and insurance companies. Where placings are permitted the Stock Exchange insists on a statement of information being published in the press, but as the public are not being invited to subscribe there is no application form attached.

Placings may arise because new shares have been created by the companies concerned in order to raise fresh funds. On the other hand the shares may only be changing hands as the result of large shareholders reducing their holdings, the main objective being a Stock Exchange quotation.

8.222 An introduction

Sometimes there is a relatively large number of individual shareholders in an unquoted company and there is a reasonable spread of shares among them. The directors may decide that it is now desirable to have a Stock Exchange quotation and this may be accomplished by means of an introduction.

As always the approach to the Stock Exchange is made through the company's stockbroker. Once the Stock Exchange is satisfied with the company's affairs it grants permission for dealings to take place in the shares. As a prerequisite of this it will insist that a sufficient number of shares may be made available, probably from one or two of the larger shareholders, to the market makers in order that they may create a reasonably free market in the shares. Again there is the usual Stock Exchange requirement of a statement of the company's affairs being published in the press.

With an introduction there is no question of additional funds being raised by the company, at least not at that particular stage.

8.3 The allotment letter

Fundamentally the same principles apply for dealings with allotment letters arising from the various types of issue. The provisional allotment letter in a rights issue probably gives rise to most problems, and merits some detailed consideration of the situations encountered.

8.31 Rights issues

On receiving his/her provisional allotment letter the shareholder should study the general information and instructions contained therein. The hard core of this is provided in box form on the front page and is along the lines typified in Figure 8.1.

Ordinary Shares registered in your name on 14 February 19........	Number of new Shares provisionally Allotted	Amount Payable at £1·25 per Share
1,000	200	£250

At	Name and address of bank
Latest time for Acceptance and Payment 3 p.m. on 20 March 19...........	

At	Name and address of company's registrar.
Latest times for:	
Splitting:	
Nil paid	3 p.m. on 18 March 19..........
Fully paid	3 p.m. on 28 April 19..........
Registration of Renunciation	3 p.m. on 30 April 19..........
Certificates Ready	on 28 May 19..........

Figure 8.1

8.311 Acceptance of full allotment

If the shareholder is going to take up the 200 shares he must pay the £250 to the bank handling the issue not later than the latest time stated, 3 p.m. on 20 March. The allotment letter will be returned to him receipted, and thereafter all he need do is present the fully paid letter on or after 28 May to the company's registrar (or otherwise as instructed), whereupon he will receive his share certificate in exchange. In fact it is not even necessary to do this, as around 27 June the allotment letter will cease to be valid for any purpose and certificates will automatically be sent to all registered holders who have not presented their allotment letters.

8.312 Renunciation of full allotment

It may be, however, that the shareholder does not wish to accept the new shares. Accordingly he should sign the Form of Renunciation (Figure 8.2) which is printed on the allotment letter and send the allotment letter to his stockbroker with instructions to sell the shares nil paid on his behalf. Shortly afterwards the shareholder will receive a remittance for the proceeds from his stockbroker.

The person who has purchased the shares must pay the amount due on acceptance not later than on the appointed time. The purchaser must also complete the Registration Application Form (Figure 8.3), also printed on the allotment letter, and lodge the allotment letter as instructed in order that the renunciation may be recorded not later than 3 p.m. on 30 April. The

---

Form X   **Form of Renunciation**
To the Directors of
                        NAME OF COMPANY

I/We hereby renounce my/our right to the Shares comprised in this Allotment Letter in favour of the person(s) named in the Registration Application Form Y relating to or including such Shares.

Dated this..day of................................19..........

Signature(s)
of allottee(s)

(In the case of joint allottees ALL must sign)
(A Corporation must affix its Seal)

Figure 8.2

Form Y   **Registration Application Form**

THIS FORM SHOULD NOT BE COMPLETED BY OR ON BEHALF OF ORIGINAL ALLOTTEES

To the Directors of

NAME OF COMPANY

FULL NAME(S). (Please state title, if any, or whether Mr., Mrs. or Miss.) AND FULL POSTAL ADDRESS(ES) (including County, or, if applicable, Postal District number) OF THE PERSON(S) IN WHOSE NAME(S) THE STOCK IS TO BE REGISTERED.	**Please complete in typewriting or in Block Capitals**

I/We request registration in the above name(s) of the Shares specified in this Allotment Letter (‡*and in the several Allotment Letters attached hereto and amounting to* ☐ *Shares in all, as shown in the Consolidation Listing Form*).

> **Stamp or name and address of person lodging this Form.**

‡ Delete words in italics if not required. Where several Allotment Letters are consolidated the total amount of Shares included in the consolidation must be inserted.

Figure 8.3

purchaser's stockbroker or bank will probably attend to these matters on his/her behalf.

It should perhaps be mentioned that dealings do not necessarily require to take place through the medium of the Stock Exchange. Quite often a rights or a scrip issue may be an opportune occasion for the holder to gift shares to members of his/her family or to place them in a trust.

It is important that the renunciation is registered as otherwise the certificate for the new shares will be sent to the original allottee and not to the purchaser, even though he/she has paid for them. The purchaser will be able to compel the original allottee to make the shares over to him/her, but a normal stock transfer form will require to be completed.

While the shares are being dealt in in allotment letter form, i.e. up until renunciation has been registered or the last time for it has elapsed, the shares pass free of stamp duty. It is proposed in the 1986 Finance Bill that after 27 October 1986 *ad valorem* stamp duty must be paid when shares are traded in allotment letter form. This applies whether the shares are being dealt in nil paid or fully paid. Once the Form of Renunciation has been signed it is possible, if the initial purchasers do not wish to retain them, for the shares to be the subject of a succession of sales and the allotment letter is in effect a bearer document until the renunciation has been registered. It is, of course, also possible for the original allottee to accept the shares and then sell them fully paid while still in allotment letter form. In this event the payment he/she had made on the shares would be reflected in the price received from the purchaser who would not now have to pay the amount due on acceptance. Otherwise the same procedure applies as with the sale nil paid.

8.313 Part acceptance, part renunciation

There is a further alternative open to the shareholder receiving the provisional allotment letter. He may wish to take up some of the shares but not all, probably because he has not sufficient cash available. In this case the shareholder again signs the Form of Renunciation and sends the allotment letter to his stockbroker with instructions of what he wishes done. In deciding how may shares to take up he will probably take into the reckoning what he will receive from those he is selling nil paid. The shareholder may in practice leave the exact details of the transaction to his broker, who is in any event closer to the market.

When the number of shares being sold and accepted is determined the broker sends the renounced allotment letter to whoever is attending to the splitting, i.e. the company's registrar (or otherwise as instructed) and asks for two split allotment letters for, say, 125 shares to be accepted by his client and 75 shares being sold. On receiving these the broker sends the split allotment letter for the 125 shares to his client together with the proceeds of the 75 shares.

The original allottee now proceeds along the same lines as if he had accepted the full allotment except that he pays the sum due on 125 shares, i.e. £156.25, not the sum due on 200 shares. The stockbroker may, of course, attend to everything on his client's behalf. The split allotment letter for 75 shares is delivered to the purchaser against payment.

Split allotment letters have the words 'Original duly renounced' stamped across the Form of Renunciation and no further renunciation is required in respect of shares not being accepted.

8.32 Bonus issues

A bonus issue may be made by means of a fully paid allotment letter which can be dealt with by the original allottee in the same manner as the provisional allotment letter in the rights issue, with the important difference that no cash requires to be paid in acceptance of the shares. The allottee may retain the shares, sell, or gift them, wholly or in part, according to his/her wishes.

It has, however, become increasingly common for bonus issues to be issued by way of a renounceable certificate instead of a fully paid allotment letter. The normal allotment letter forms of renunciation and registration application are printed on the back of the certificate, and for a few weeks the shares can be dealt in just as if they were issued by fully paid allotment letter. If the original allottee wishes to retain the new shares he need take no further action as in due course he will be registered as the owner of the shares, and the certificate which will have ceased to be renounceable will be his document of title.

The advantage of this method is that it saves a considerable amount of work, since instead of issuing definitive certificates to replace all allotment letters they only require to be prepared and issued to replace certificates that have been renounced.

8.33 Prospectus offers, offers for sale

In prospectus offers successful applicants receive allotment letters, and in offers for sale letters of acceptance. If the issues have called for full payment on application the letters will be fully paid, and if the allottees wish to retain their holdings they are in the same position as the original allottee who holds a fully paid allotment letter in a rights issue. Should they wish to dispose of all or part of their shares the Form of Renunciation must be signed and the same procedures adhered to as with a fully paid rights issue. Where letters are only partly paid the original allottee or subsequent purchaser must ensure that the further call or calls are met on time.

Typical question

There are three principal ways of obtaining a Stock Exchange quotation for a class of securities not previously quoted.

What are they and what are the differences between them?

(The Institute of Bankers, *Investment*)

Suggested answers

The three principal ways are:
1   *An offer for sale*   This is where an issuing house acquires the shares from principal shareholders in a company and then offers them at a fixed price to the public. Copies of the document offering the shares must be advertised in at least two leading newspapers, one of which must be a

'national'. A form of application, with the appropriate instructions, is incorporated in the advertisement. Copies of the offer document together with an application form may also be obtained from the issuing house, the stockbrokers, and the branches of the bankers to the issue.

2   *A placing*   This occurs where a stockbroker, either alone or in collaboration with an issuing house, arranges for shares to be placed at a fixed price with a number of its clients. The shares will again have been made available from the holdings of principal shareholders.

Although the issue must be advertised in the press there is, of course, no application form as the public is not being invited to subscribe. In order that there will be a 'market' when dealings start the Stock Exchange can insist that at least 25% of any placing of ordinary shares and 20% of any placing of fixed interest stock is made available to clients of brokers other than the placing broker. Any member of the public wishing to obtain shares in a placing must ask his stockbroker to try and get them for him. His chances, however, of obtaining them at the placing price are not very bright.

The expenses of a placing issue are much lower than in an offer for sale and this is the main reason why they are permitted where relatively small issues of equity capital are concerned. With larger issues the Stock Exchange insists on an offer for sale, although this does not apply in the case of fixed interest securities where the demand is less widespread and may be confined largely to insurance companies and pension funds.

3   *An introduction*   In an introduction very few shares may change hands at all if the Stock Exchange is satisfied that there already is a reasonable spread of the shares among the present holders. Before allowing dealings to commence, however, the Stock Exchange may insist that a small number of the shares are made available to the market makers in order that they may create a reasonably free market in the shares.

Any member of the public wishing to acquire shares will do so by giving normal 'buy' instructions to his stockbroker. He will have been made aware of the existence of the shares by advertisement in the press.

Additional questions

1   (a)   Analyse the factors requiring consideration in order to determine the terms upon which a rights issues should be made. Explain the courses of action which are open to an existing shareholder when a rights issue is made.

(b)   The £1 ordinary shares of X Limited are currently quoted at 340p. A rights issue of three for ten is to be made at 250p. Calculate the equilibrium price 'ex rights' and the value of the rights. Ignore stamp duty.

(The Chartered Institute of Secretaries, *Secretarial and Administrative Practice-II*)

2 A large public company raises cash from the public by means of an issue at 97½ of an 8% Debenture Stock. 10 per cent is due on application, 20% on allotment and the remainder in three months' time. Your customer applies for £1,000 stock and receives an allotment of £200 which he immediately renounces in favour of his wife. Explain in detail how this transaction would be carried out from the completion of the application form in your customer's name to the issue of the certificate in his wife's name.

(The Institute of Bankers in Scotland, *Theory and Practice of Investment*)

3 You have been accused of becoming richer as the result of a company in which you hold shares making a bonus issue. Is there any truth in this accusation? Draft a suitable reply.

4 Describe the significance to shareholders of 'excess' shares and 'fractions'.

5 Outline the position as regards the issuing of capital at a discount or at a premium.

6 What are the distinctive features of an issue by tender?

7 (a) Why is underwriting necessary? Explain, briefly, how it is effected.
   (b) Do you consider that stags perform any useful function or are they just a nuisance? Elaborate.

8 What should the investor look for in trying to assess the merits of a new issue from the prospectus?

(The Savings Bank Institute, *Personal Savings and Investment*)

9 Taxation – some relevant aspects

A major force in financial affairs nowadays in undoubtedly that of taxation. The investor or businessman or woman who fails to appreciate the relevant fundamentals of this vast, increasingly complicated, and ever-changing subject will be the poorer for his/her omission. It is, of course, impossible to deal comprehensively with the subject in a book of this nature. However, some aspects pertinent to investment are touched on in the following pages.

9.1 Personal taxation

In 1973/74 a new system of taxation was introduced in the United Kingdom under the name of 'Unified Tax' whereby the former income tax and surtax liabilities which were calculated under different sets of rules were merged into one tax. However, according to his/her circumstances an individual is still granted certain allowances before he/she is required to pay tax. These vary from year to year as do also the rates of tax and may be ascertained by consulting the pamphlets issued by the Inland Revenue.

9.11 Rates and allowances

For 1985/86 every single person in this country was granted a personal allowance of £2205 which meant that the first £2205 of income was exempt from tax. Further exempt amounts could be added to this if, for example, the individual was married, was elderly, supported a dependent relative, etc.

The income of a husband and wife 'living together' is treated as one for the purpose of calculating the total tax payable except in circumstances applicable to better-off working couples where it is beneficial for a specific election to be made for a wife's earned income to be assessed on her alone as if she were a single person. In this event the husband receives only the single personal allowance, not the married personal allowance, and the wife's investment income still falls to be treated as that of her husband.

A child's investment income has been a matter of political sensitivity, the Labour Party view sometimes being that it should be lumped with the parents' income irrespective of the source whereas the Conservatives hitherto have considered that it should be assessed on the child as an individual except in the event of it being derived from a source provided by either parent.

After the various allowances are set against an individual's income he/she pays tax on the balance. For 1985/86 the first £16,200 of such income was taxed at 30% (basic rate), the next £3,000 band at 40% and so on by stages until £40,200 was reached over which figure the impost was levied at 60%.

9.12 Influence on policy

It will readily be appreciated that the rich investor who is paying income tax at the top rate of 60% is not greatly concerned in investing for income purposes when every pound of interest or dividend paid to him only benefits him to the extent of 40p. His obvious alternative is to look for an investment which does not produce a high income but which over the years will increase in capital value. As will be seen in Chapter 10 when he realizes his investment the maximum rate of capital gains for which he will be liable is 30p in the pound, a much lighter impost.

Long before an investor is paying the top rate of tax he will be weighing up the relative advantages to himself of investing for high income or capital appreciation.* The sheer size of his contributions to the Inland Revenue will have impressed upon him the necessity for this. However, at the other end of the scale the non-taxpayer does not always understand that by not considering his own particular circumstances as regards tax he is not investing to best advantage.

For example, the investor may have invested savings with a building society attracted by a rate of interest of, say, 8.75% free of income tax. If he is not liable to any tax at all the 'free of tax' benefit is valueless to him. For every £100 invested he will receive each year £8.75. Without using any particular ingenuity the same investor could have received a return of around 12.5% on the money by investing it in an investment account with the National Savings Bank. As the investor pays no tax he receives and keeps each year £12.50 for each £100 invested. By venturing further afield to, say, gilt-edged and debenture stocks, the investor may well be able to obtain a still higher return on his money.

The relative attractions of building societies on the one hand and the National Savings Bank and similar high yielding investments on the other may not be so clear cut for the basic rate taxpayer. From his £12.50 received from the National Savings Bank he/she would have to pay £3.75 tax (basic rate at 30%) leaving him with £8.75 in his pocket. Frequently, however, as interest and tax rates vary he may find that his net of tax amount is less than he would receive from the building society.

A point to remember with building society interest (and interest from banks apart from the National Savings Bank) is that the exemption does not

---

* The substantial tax reductions introduced by the Conservative Government have, in the meantime at least, decreased although by no means eliminated the attractions of capital appreciation for investors with large incomes.

extend to the excess of higher rates of tax over basic rate. Where higher rate taxpayers are in receipt of building society or bank interest they are liable for tax in the grossed up amount. That is, on the equivalent amount of gross income which after deducting tax at the basic rate would have produced the amount of interest received. For example, if a higher rate taxpayer liable at 60% on the top slice of his investment income had received £8.75 building society interest he would effectively pay higher rate tax on £8.75 × 100/100 − 30 = £12.50 at 30%.

Various other examples of investments suitable for tax and non-taxpayers are given elsewhere in this book. Meantime it is impressed on the investor the necessity for keeping tax considerations well to the fore in his mind. As a general rule it is worth emphasizing that tax exemptions or concessions attaching to investments are of greatest value to the top rate taxpayer and their relative importance descends with the rate of tax paid until the non-taxpayer is reached when they have no value at all.

9.2 Corporation tax

Note: The calculations in this chapter are based on corporation tax rate of 50% and basic/ACT rate of 30%.

Since April 1973 companies in this country have been taxed under the imputation system thus ending the complete separation of the taxing of a company and its shareholders which had existed since 1965 under the previous system.

A company pays corporation tax on all its profits whether retained or distributed by way of dividend. The rate of corporation tax for the preceding financial year is normally announced in the annual Budget proposals, a financial year being that ending on 31 March. Assessments to corporation tax are for a company's accounting year which, unless it also ends on 31 March, will span two financial years. Therefore, if the rate of corporation tax changes a company may pay two different rates of corporation tax on the profits of one accounting year.

For example, for the financial year ending 31 March 1983 (officially known as the financial year 1982) corporation tax was at the rate of 52% and for the year ending 31 March 1984 it changed to 50%. If a company's accounting year ends on 31 December then for the year to 31 December 1983 three-twelfths of its profits would be taxed at 52% and 9/12ths at 50%.

When a company pays a dividend to its shareholders it does not under the imputation system require to deduct any further tax. It does, however, make an advance payment of corporation tax (known as 'ACT') to the Inland Revenue equal to three-sevenths of the dividend being distributed. This payment, which corresponds to a personal basic tax rate of 30%, is regarded as being made on behalf of shareholders and each shareholder is assessed for income tax purposes on the total dividend plus the tax paid by the company.* However, because the company has paid tax on the dividend there will be a tax credit of the same amount attributable to each shareholder.

Example

Dividend paid to shareholder	Tax credit (Tax at 30% of total income)	Total income for tax purposes
£7	£3	£10

The basic rate taxpayer will not be liable for any further tax in respect of the dividend. The higher rate taxpayer will have to pay further tax at his/her appropriate rate on £10. The non-taxpayer will be able to reclaim £3.

The company having paid ACT in respect of the dividend can normally offset this against its total liability for corporation tax on its income for the accounting year (or period) during which the distribution is made regardless of the year to which the dividend purports to relate. The resultant net liability is known as the mainstream corporation tax.

Example

In May 1979 company pays out £70,000 to its shareholders being dividend for year to 31 December 1978 (for simplicity it is assumed that company pays one annual dividend not an interim and final dividend which is frequently the case). Its taxable income for the year to 31 December 1979 is £200,000.

1   On paying dividend it will require to account for three-sevenths of the amount paid to the Inland Revenue, i.e. ACT of £30,000.
2   Corporation tax assessment for 1979:

£200,000 at 50%	£100,000
Deduct ACT paid during 1979	30,000
Mainstream corporation tax for 1979	£70,000

There is, however, a limit imposed on the extent to which ACT can be used to offset a company's corporation tax liability to cover the situation where a company makes distributions which are disproportionately large relative to the taxable profits of the accounting year. This could arise, for example, when distributions are being made out of previous years profits or because its commercial profits have been reduced for tax purposes by capital allowances. It would be quite possible in such circumstances for a company's mainstream corporation tax to be eliminated altogether and for dividends to be paid out of profits which have suffered corporation tax only at the rate of three-sevenths necessary to frank the tax credit as compared with the 50% rate for companies generally. It is not the intention to favour distributions to such an

---

* ACT varies with basic rate tax. If the latter was 33% the ACT payment would be $^{33}/_{67}$ of the dividend distributed.

extent and accordingly the amount of advance corporation tax which can be set off in any accounting period is restricted to an amount which, with the distribution to which it relates, absorbs the whole of the company's taxable income for the period. The effect of this is that with corporation tax at 50% the set off of ACT may never reduce the mainstream liability to below 20%.

Example
A company has taxable income of £200,000 on which its total corporation tax liability would be £100,000. It pays dividends during the same accounting year of £420,000.

1 On paying dividends company will account for £180,000 ACT to Inland Revenue.

2 ACT available to offset corporation tax liability
Maximum distribution out of £200,000 after allowing for ACT £140,000

ACT thereon (three-sevenths)	£60,000

3 Corporation tax assessment

£200,000 at 50%	...£100,000
Deduct available ACT	60,000
Mainstream corporation tax	£40,000

4 Unrelieved ACT £120,000

Unrelieved or surplus ACT can be carried back for two years or carried forward indefinitely to future years and set off against the corporation tax liability for these years.

9.21 Overseas income

ACT can only be used as an advance payment of United Kingdom corporation tax. It cannot be used to offset foreign taxes. This puts a company with a large proportion of its earnings overseas on which a high rate of foreign tax has been paid at a considerable disadvantage relative to a company with United Kingdom earnings. In the extreme case of a company earning all its profits overseas and paying overseas corporation tax at the rate of 50% or more no United Kingdom corporation tax would as the result of double taxation relief be paid if no distributions were made. However, the ACT which would require to be deducted on the payment of a dividend would be set against the mainstream corporation tax liability in priority to the application of double taxation relief, thus resulting in unrelieved foreign tax (see example 2(a) below).

Where a company has 'mixed' income it would be at no disadvantage where it is able to pay its dividend from United Kingdom income and use its overseas income as retentions. There is in fact a considerable attraction for overseas trading companies to obtain a source of United Kingdom income by means of a merger or takeover.

The following examples illustrate the position.

1 No distribution made

Profits all earned overseas		£100
Overseas corporation tax at, say, 50%		50
		£50
UK corporation tax at 50%	£50	
Less double taxation relief	50	
(Overseas tax attracting full relief)	—	
Profits retained		£50

2 Distribution of £21 made

(a)

Profits all earned overseas		£100
Overseas corporation tax at, say, 50% ... (50)		50
		£50
UK corporation tax at 50%	£50	
Less ACT	9	
	£41	
Less double taxation relief	41	
Dividend paid	£21	
ACT	9 (9)	30
Profits retained		£20
(Total tax paid) ... ... (59)		

(b)

Profits all earned in UK		£100
UK corporation tax at 50%	£50	
Less ACT	9(41)	41
	—	£59
Dividend paid	£21	
ACT	9 (9)	30
Profits retained		£29
(Total tax paid) ... ... (50)		

(c)

Profits earned overseas		£50
Profits earned in UK		50
		£100

Overseas corporation tax at, say, 50%...	(25)	25

UK corporation tax on UK income at 50%	£25	£75
Less ACT	9(16)	16

UK corporation tax on overseas income	£25
Less double taxation relief	25

	£59
Dividend paid	£21
ACT	9 (9)	30

Profits retained		£29

(Total tax paid)	(50)

When a dividend as in 2(a) gives rise to the payment of ACT the resultant unrelieved tax is not available for carry forward.

Frequently foreign profits are taxed at rates of at least 50% which means that with United Kingdom corporation tax at 50% double taxation agreements exclude the payment of mainstream United Kingdom tax. However, where a lower rate of foreign tax is payable there is a United Kingdom corporation tax charge on the overseas income against which ACT can be offset. In fact, so long as the foreign rate does not exceed 28.57% the whole of the net profit could be distributed without there being any unrelieved foreign tax.

Example

Profits all earned overseas	£100
Overseas corporation tax at 28.57%	28.57

	£71.43
UK corporation tax at 50% £50	
ACT 21.43	

	£28.57
Less double taxation relief 28.57	

	£71.43
Dividend £50	
ACT 21.43	71.43

9.22 Preference shares

Until 6 April 1973 it was the custom to declare dividends at a gross rate or as a gross amount. Under imputation tax dividends are declared net and when the relevant legislation was introduced in the 1972 Finance Act special provision was made for the adaptation of dividends of preference shares to the new system. This provided for a once and for all netting-down of the rate of preference dividends to seven-tenths of their former rate.

Thus on 100 10% Preference Shares of £1 each the dividend will be paid at the rate of 7% with tax credit of three-sevenths of this net amount being available to the shareholder. With basic rate tax and ACT at 30% he/she is therefore receiving the equivalent of 10% gross under the old system. However, should the tax rates change the preference shareholder may in the future be receiving, together with the related tax credit, either more or less than the previous gross amount.

9.23 Impact on company financing

An important feature of taxation so far as company financing is concerned is that interest on loan capital is allowed as a deduction from profits before corporation tax is charged, whereas dividends on share capital must be met out of profits as reduced by corporation tax. There is therefore an incentive to a company (not so pronounced as in the system existing between 1965 and 1973) to raise funds by means of a loan stock issue. This can be illustrated by comparing the cost to a company of servicing a £500,000 10% Loan Stock as opposed to a £500,000 7% Preference Stock (equivalent to a 10% Preference Stock under the old system).

(a)	£500,000 10% Loan stock		
	Pre-interest profits, say, … … … … …		£140,000
	Less Loan stock interest … … … … …		50,000
			£90,000
	Corporation tax at 50% … … … … …		45,000
	Profits after payment of Loan stock interest … …		£45,000
(b)	£500,000 7% Preference stock		
	Pre-tax profits, say, … … … … … …		£140,000
	Corporation tax at 50% … … …	£70,000	
	Less ACT … … … … …	15,000	
			55,000
			£85,000
	Dividend paid … … … …	£35,000	
	ACT … … … … … …	15,000	
			50,000
	Profits after payment of Preference dividend … …		£35,000

In both cases the payments received by stockholders would be effectually the same. A holder of £1,000 Loan Stock would, for instance, receive £70, basic rate tax at 30% having been deducted by the company as agent for the Inland Revenue in the collection of tax. A £1,000 Preference Stock holder would receive £70 but would be credited with a £30 payment of basic rate tax.

For similar reasons it is more advantageous for companies to raise finance by means of a loan stock issue rather than by an equity rights issue. The calculation is not so simple here as the amount to be paid away in meeting an ordinary dividend is not fixed. Initially subscribers for ordinary shares would normally be prepared to accept a lower return on their money in anticipation of increased future dividends and consequent enhanced capital values for their shares.

9.24 Already taxed

Many British companies have shareholdings in other companies in respect of which they receive dividends. As these dividends are paid out of profits which have already borne corporation tax the recipient company does not have to pay further corporation tax on this source of income. Corporation tax does, however, have to be paid by a company on income it receives from gilt-edged stocks or loan capital in other companies.

When a company receives such a dividend it will be entitled to the tax credit of three-sevenths. The net amount may be redistributed to its own shareholders without payment of ACT and the related tax credit remains attached for the benefit of its shareholders. This income received by a company is called 'franked investment income' and as defined consists of the net 'qualifying distribution' (fiscal parlance for the dividend) received together with the related tax credit.

9.3 Double taxation relief

Where a resident of the United Kingdom receives income from abroad there is the possibility that it may be taxed twice as the consequence of the operation of the two countries' tax systems. It is not the intention of the Inland Revenue that this double taxation should occur, at least not so far as the same types of taxation are concerned, and accordingly provisions have been made to prevent it from happening either under Double Taxation Agreements with overseas countries or, where this has not been possible, by granting unilateral relief.

9.31 Tax available for relief

Many of the agreements negotiated before the 1965 Finance Act enabled a shareholder to obtain relief in respect of taxes paid by an overseas company on its profits as well as for the tax actually deducted by the company when paying the dividend. However relief for tax paid by an overseas company on its profits – officially described as the 'underlying' tax – has been withdrawn and is only allowed on the direct tax deducted from the dividend, usually described as a 'withholding' tax.

9.32 Credit allowed

Relief for tax on overseas dividends is given by 'credit' or 'set off' against the United Kingdom tax on such income. There are two limits to this credit:

(a) It cannot exceed the overseas tax on the overseas income; and
(b) it must not exceed the United Kingdom tax on the overseas income at the taxpayer's marginal rate.

As most investors' marginal rate of tax, i.e. the rate of tax which they pay on the top slice of their income will normally be greater than the rate of withholding tax it is usually the first limit which will affect the credit.

Example
In 1985/86 a married man with a salary of £7,970 and United Kingdom investment income of £500 gross receives an ordinary dividend of £170 (£200 less withholding tax of £30) from an overseas company. (The overseas company has paid tax on its profits at $42\frac{1}{2}\%$ but as no relief is allowed for this underlying tax it is ignored.)

It is obvious here, as will frequently be the case, that the taxpayer will be liable for the basic rate of tax on his overseas income and the tax credit will be £30, the withholding tax being at the rate of 15%. The actual computation of liability and credit is as follows:

								Income
Salary	...	...	...	...	...	...	...	£7,970
United Kingdom investment income			...	...	...	...	500
Overseas dividend		...	...	...	...	...	...	200
								8,670
Married allowance		...	...	...	...	...	...	3,455
								5,215
Tax payable (£5,215 at 30%)		...	...	...	...	...	£1,564
Less credit for overseas tax		...	...	...	...	...	30
Net United Kingdom tax		...	...	...	...	...	...	£1,534

Example
In 1985/86 a married man has a salary of £3,365 and receives an ordinary dividend of £85 (£100 less withholding tax of £15) from an overseas company.

	Excluding overseas income	Including overseas income
Salary	£3,365	£3,365
Overseas dividend	—	100
	£3,365	£3,465
Married allowance	£3,455	£3,455
		£10
Tax payable at 30%		£3
Tax credit		£3
Net United Kingdom tax		Nil

In this case the taxpayer is not liable to tax on his United Kingdom income and his credit is restricted to the United Kingdom tax on the overseas income at his marginal rate, i.e. £10 at 30% = £3. If the taxpayer's income had all been from sources in the United Kingdom his total tax bill would have been £3. As it is he has paid £15 tax on his overseas income and is unable to receive any credit for the balance of £12.

Where there are two or more sources of income, for example dividends from countries with different rates of withholding tax, it is necessary to ensure for each source separately that the overseas tax is less than the United Kingdom tax. Frequently this will be obvious where the taxpayer has substantial income taxed at the basic rate and a relatively small amount of overseas income subject to withholding taxes in the range 10–20%.

However, in some cases it may be necessary to make calculations. This is done by comparing (a) the tax on the total income including all overseas income with (b) the tax on the total income less income from one overseas source. Thereafter a further calculation is made comparing (b), the tax on the total income less the overseas source already dealt with, with (c) the tax on the total income less the first and second sources of overseas income. The order in which the sources of income are taken may be chosen by the taxpayer to his/her best advantage.

9.33 Provisional relief

When dividends are paid by overseas companies to United Kingdom residents the payment is usually made through a paying agent in the United Kingdom or is collected by a United Kingdom bank. The general rule is that the paying agent or bank must deduct United Kingdom tax at the basic rate from the dividend, but in practice the Inland Revenue grants authority for tax to be deducted at a lesser rate, thus provisionally giving credit relief. The details on the tax counterfoil may read as follows:

Gross dividend declared	...	...	...	...	...	...	£100.00
Overseas withholding tax		...	...	...	...	...	15.00
Net dividend after deductions of overseas tax			...	...	...	85.00
Less UK tax at 15% on gross dividend of £100.00				...	...	15.00
Net payment	...	...	...	...	...	...	£70.00

The deduction of United Kingdom tax at the rate of 15% is arrived at by subtracting the withholding tax rate of 15% from the basic rate of 30%.*

9.34 Companies and double taxation relief

British companies may also receive credit for tax paid on overseas income. There are two circumstances when this may arise. Firstly when a United Kingdom company operates in an overseas country and thereby becomes liable to the taxes of that country in respect of its profits arising there, and secondly when a United Kingdom company receives dividends in respect of holdings in overseas companies.

In the case of a United Kingdom company carrying on activities overseas the credit is limited to the lesser of the United Kingdom or overseas taxes on the overseas profits.

Example

A company for the year ending 31 March has overseas trading profits of £80,000 on which overseas tax of £25,000 was paid, and £200,000 United Kingdom profits.

UK corporation tax on overseas profits £80,000 at 50%			...	£40,000
All overseas tax allowed as credit	...	...	...	25,000
Balance of corporation tax liability on overseas income			...	£15,000

If the overseas tax had been greater than the United Kingdom tax the balance would have been unrelieved.

Where a United Kingdom company receives dividends from an overseas company it may, in certain circumstances, obtain relief from the underlying as well as the direct tax. The withdrawal of the credit for underlying tax was

---

* Under the Double Taxation Agreements with some countries it may be possible on the completion and approval of the appropriate forms to have the foreign withholding tax reduced or eliminated at source.

only intended to apply to the portfolio investor and where the United Kingdom company controls a specified amount of the voting power in the overseas company it will still obtain relief for the underlying tax. The amount is at present 10% although this minimum may be breached where the company's shareholding has been diluted below 10% for reasons outside its control.

Example

A company for the year ending 31 March has United Kingdom profits of £150,000 and receives a dividend of £36,000 net after a withholding tax of 10% had been deducted from the company in which it had the specified voting power. The overseas company had paid tax at 25% on the relevant profits.

The pre-tax profits required to cover the net dividend of £36,000 must be calculated.

Dividend before withholding tax £36,000 × 100/90	...	...	£40,000
Relevant pre-tax profits £40,000 × 100/75	...	...	53,333
UK corporation tax on overseas profits £53,333 at 50%		...	£26,667
All overseas tax allowed as credit	...	...	...	17,333
Balance of corporation tax liability on overseas income		...	£9,334

Here again if the tax on the overseas income had exceeded the United Kingdom tax chargeable on it the balance would have been unrelieved as credit.

If the United Kingdom company had not held the specified voting power the relief would have been as follows:

UK corporation tax on overseas dividend £40,000 at 50%		...	£20,000
Overseas withholding tax allowed as credit	...	...	4,000
Balance of corporation tax liability on overseas income		...	£16,000

Typical questions

A United Kingdom company has an issued share capital of £8 million, £4 million of this being in 4.2% (formerly 6%) Cumulative Preference Shares of £1 each. Profits before tax shown in the latest published accounts were £2 million and the ordinary dividend was 7p per £1 share.

The directors are seeking the approval of preference shareholders to the substitution of a 7½% Unsecured Loan Stock 1990–5 for the outstanding preference share capital on the basis of £1 of loan stock for every preference share.

1 If you are a private investor in the preference shares give your reasons why you would accept or refuse this offer.
2 Illustrate by appropriating profits in two columns (before and after these proposals have taken effect) the effect on profits retained in the company.
(The Institute of Bankers, *Principles and Practice of Investment*)

Suggested answer

1 The unsecured loan stock would be accepted for the following reasons:
  (a) It would increase gross income received by £1.50 on every £100 nominal amount invested, such nominal amount remaining the same.
  (b) It provides definite dates for the redemption of the unsecured loan stock. Although these are a long way into the future they will give increasing support to the market value of the stock as the years roll by. The preference shares have no such support.
  (c) From the security angle the rights of the loan stockholders are stronger than those of the preference shareholder. In a liquidation the loan stockholders would rank along with the general body of creditors, whereas the preference shareholders are members of the company and would not receive anything until all the creditors were satisfied. Also the interest on the loan stock is a debt due by the company in contrast to the preference dividend which must be declared by the directors. There is no obligation on them to do so, even although profits are available, unless of course they wish to pay an ordinary dividend.

2

		Before	*After*
Profits before tax		£2,000,000	£2,000,000
Interest of £4 million 7½% Unsecured Loan Stock 1990/5		—	300,000
		2,000,000	1,700,000
Corporation tax at 50% ... £1,000,000			
Less ACT 192,000		808,000	
		£1,192,000	
Corporation tax at 50% ... £850,000			
Less ACT 120,000			730,000
			£970,000
Dividend on £4 million 4.2% Cumulative Preference* £1 Shares ... £168,000			
ACT 72,000		£240,000	—

	£952,000	£970,000
Dividend on £4 million Ordinary* Share		
Capital at 7p per £1 share ... £280,000		
ACT 120,000	400,000	400,000
Retained	£552,000	£570,000

Additional questions

1 (a) To what taxes on income are residents in the United Kingdom liable?
   (b) What broadly should be the investment policy of the high taxpayer?
   (c) Are there any points regarding tax which the non-taxpaying investor should keep in mind? For instance, are National Savings Certificates particularly suitable for his/her requirements?
2 Outline the basis on which British companies are now charged to tax.
3 (a) Explain what is meant by 'franked investment income'.
   (b) To what category of investor are preference shares an attractive type of fixed interest holding? Why?
4 (a) What is the principle behind double taxation relief?
   (b) From what type of overseas tax has relief been withdrawn?
   (c) The credit for double taxation relief is subject to two limits. What are they?
5 A gross dividend of £50 is paid by an overseas company from which it deducts a withholding tax of 10%. Give the details which would appear on the tax voucher received by the shareholder from the paying agent in this country.
6 Outline the double taxation relief available to United Kingdom companies. In what circumstances may they obtain relief in respect of the underlying tax.
7 What do you understand by 'surplus or unrelieved ACT'?
8 Why should a British company deriving its income largely from overseas wish to obtain a source of United Kingdom income?

---

* Assumed that the company had only two classes of issued share capital.

10 Tax on capital gains

10.1 General structure

There is now only one type of tax on capital gains realized by residents of the United Kingdom. The tax formerly known as short-term capital gains tax was abolished by the 1971 Finance Act.

Tax is payable on gains arising from many forms of property but this chapter is concerned mainly with the rules as they affect quoted Stock Exchange securities.

10.11 Taxable amount

In each fiscal year the amount liable to tax is the net gain, i.e. the total of all chargeable gains made during the year less all allowable losses. If losses exceed the gains the balance can be carried forward indefinitely to future fiscal years and used to set off against future gains. However, when tax is paid on a gain made in a fiscal year no refund can normally be claimed should a net loss arise in a future year.

When working out the gain or loss the expenses of acquisition, i.e. brokerage and stamp duty, etc., are added to the cost and the expenses of disposal are deducted from the proceeds. In other words it is the amounts actually paid to and received from the stockbroker that are used.

Where allowable losses are available for carry forward they must be deducted from taxable amounts when these arise in a subsequent year but only to the extent that such amounts are not reduced below the annual exemption (see Section 10.12).

Example

As at 5 April 1985 investor has unused allowable losses of £1,500.
In the year to 5 April 1986 he/she

has chargeable gains of ...	£10,000
and allowable losses of ...	2,000
Net gains	£8,000
Deduct carry forward losses ...	1,500
Taxable amount	£6,500

The investor's allowable losses are now all used up and he/she pays tax on £600, i.e. £6,500 less the £5,900 exemption.

Example
As at 5 April 1985 investor has unused allowable losses of £1,500.
In the year to 5 April 1986 he/she

has chargeable gains of	...	£10,000
and allowable losses of	...	3,000
Net gains	...	£7,000
Deduct carry forward losses	...	1,100
Taxable amount	... ...	£5,900

The investor still has allowable losses of £400 to carry forward to future years and for 1985/86 he/she pays no tax as the taxable amount of £5,900 covered by the £5,900 exemption.

If the investor's net gains had been £5,900 or less the whole of the allowable losses would have leap-frogged 1985/86 to subsequent years.

10.12 Rate of tax and the annual exemption

Since the introduction of capital gains tax in 1965 the charge has been at the flat rate of 30% although there was originally some alleviation of this for lower rate taxpayers. In 1980 a new system came into being whereby an individual was allowed an amount of gains each year which would be exempt from capital gains tax. For 1985/86 this amount was £5,900 and the present intention is that the exempt amount should be revised annually with reference to the Retail Prices Index.

Example
For 1985/86 investor has taxable amount of
£13,400
Exempt £5,900
Tax payable at 30% on £7,500   £2,250

Where a married woman is living with her husband the annual exemption in any tax year is divided between them in the ratio of their respective net gains calculated after setting off any losses brought forward.

The full annual exemption also applies to trusts which are mainly for the benefit of the mentally disabled or for those receiving attendance allowance. In the case of other trusts which were created before 7 June 1978, the exemption limit is half the full amount e.g. £2,950 for 1985/86. For trusts created on or after 7 June 1978 this exemption may be restricted where several trusts have been formed by the same settlor. The rule here is that the annual exemption must be divided by the total number of such trusts (excluding any trusts which are exempt from capital gains tax) but subject to a minimum of each trust which for 1985/86 was £590.

Example

Two trusts were created since 6 June 1978 by Mr Smith and over the same period six trusts were created by Mr Brown.
For 1985/86
Each of Mr Smith's trusts are entitled to £1,475 exemption.
Each of Mr Brown's trusts are entitled to £590 (minimum) exemption.

10.13 Exemptions

Non-residents, charities, and pension funds which are exempt from income tax are also free from capital gains tax.

Certain forms of National Savings such as Premium Bonds, National Savings Certificates, and terminal bonuses payable under SAYE are exempt as are British Government stocks and stocks of the public corporations guaranteed by the Treasury where realization takes place after 1 July 1986. Also exempt are corporate bonds (e.g. debenture and loan stocks) issued by companies and other entities such as foreign governments acquired after 13 March 1984 so long as they or other securities issued by the same borrower are quoted on the Stock Exchange or USM. Prior to 1 July 1986 the exemption applied to British Government stocks and qualifying corporate bonds only after they had been held for one year.

10.131 Investment and unit trusts

If they comply with certain conditions (see Section 13.17), investment and unit trusts are completely exempt from capital gains tax on their disposals made since 31 March 1980. Investors realizing shares or units are now liable to capital gains tax in the normal way, the former concessions having been removed as from 6 April 1980.

10.14 Husband and wife

In the basic situation of a husband and wife 'living together' the calculation of each spouse's gains and losses are worked out separately. At the end of the year they are lumped together and if the net result is a gain an assessment is issued in the name of the husband. On the other hand, if there is a net loss this may be carried forward and set against the future gains of either.

However, this basic arrangement may be departed from as the result of either of two distinct elections being made.

In the first place either spouse may elect to be assessed separately for capital gains tax purposes. Where this election has been made in order to determine the liability of each spouse the annual exemption is allocated between them in proportion to their taxable amounts. Notwithstanding this election the gains of one spouse may be reduced by the other's unrelieved losses.

A completely separate election, however, may be made by either spouse that his/her losses should not be made available to the other. This would be advantageous where the other spouse's gains are exempt anyway, being covered by the annual exemption.

There is no liability on investments transferred from one spouse to the other. If, for instance, a husband gives shares to his wife she would be treated as having acquired them on the same date and for the same cost at which they were acquired by the husband, her acquisition cost being enhanced by the indexation allowance available to him.*

10.2 Indexation

In order that capital gains tax should be charged only on real future gains and not inflationary gains, indexation with reference to the Retail Prices Index was introduced by the 1982 Finance Act, the specific rules being thereafter considerably amended particularly by the 1985 Finance Act. The basic principle is that when a sale is made the acquisition cost is adjusted in the same ratio as the RPI has varied between the months of acquisition and sale or optionally where holdings were acquired prior to April 1982 the variation between March 1982 and the month of sale.

The principle is theoretically straightforward and remains so in practice where an investor acquires a holding of shares in a single purchase after 31 March 1982 and subsequently disposes of it completely in one sale. The formula for working out the factor by which the acquisition value is to be increased is $\dfrac{RD - RI}{RI}$ where RD is the RPI for the month of disposal and RI is the RPI for the month of acquisition (or for March 1982).

Example

1000 shares purchased in July 1983 for £1,500...		...		RPI		336.5
1000 shares sold in May 1985 for £2,600		...	...	RPI		375.6
Proceeds of shares sold		...	...			£2,600
Cost of shares			£1,500			
Add indexation relief						

$$£1,500 \times \frac{375.6 - 336.5}{336.5} \quad ... \quad ... \quad ... \qquad 174 \qquad 1,674$$

Taxable gain						£926

---

* It should be noted, however, that unless the marriage takes place on 6 April, husband and wife are each regarded for tax purposes as being single for the year of marriage.

Indexation may now also be applied either to create a loss where otherwise there would have been a gain or to increase the value of a loss.

Example

Shares purchased for £2,000 in April 1982 and sold for £2,080 in February 1986. Assume RPI increased by 14% over period.

Cost of shares	£2,000
Add indexation relief of 14%	280
	£2,280
Sale proceeds	2,080
Allowable loss	£200

Following indexation a gain of £80 has been eliminated and an allowable loss of £200 created.

Example

Shares purchased for £2,000 in April 1982 and sold for £1,800 in February 1986. Assume RPI increase of 14% over period.

Cost of shares	£2,000
Add indexation relief of 14%	280
	£2,280
Sale proceeds	1,800
Allowable loss	£480

Following indexation a loss of £200 has been increased to an allowable loss of £480.

10.21 Pre-April 1982 holdings election

There are a variety of situations in respect of which complication can arise the most significant of these being derived from the fact that shareholdings were obviously in existence before indexation commenced in April 1982. An important rule with regard to these pre April 1982 holdings is that an investor may elect to have the indexation allowance based on the market value (see Section 10.53) of such holdings as at 31 March 1982 rather than the acquisition cost before that date. The election must be made within two years of the tax year of disposal and where the 31 March 1982 value is the higher a larger indexation allowance can be obtained by so electing.

Example

500 shares purchased in 1975 for £1,000 and worth £5,000 on 31 March 1982. 500 shares sold in January 1986 for £6,200. Assume an increase of RPI between March 1982 and January 1986 of 14%.

Proceeds of shares sold	...	...	...	...	...	...	£6,200
Cost of shares	...	...	...	...	£1,000	
Election made							
Add indexation relief 14% of £5,000			...		700	1.700
Taxable gain	...	...	...	...	...		£4,500

If no election had been made the indexation relief would have been 14% of £1,000 = £140 leaving a taxable gain of £5,060.

10.22 Identification

Where a holding of the same class of shares has been built up by several purchases over a period of time and then some of the shares are sold there are specific rules for identifying which of the shares have been sold. Such shares sold must be regarded as coming from shares (if any) acquired in the following categories in the order in which they are listed.

1 Shares bought on the same day.
2 Shares bought in the nine days before the sale on a first in first out (FIFO) basis.
3 Shares bought after 5 April 1982 (31 March 1982 in the case of companies) treated as a pool.
4 Shares acquired between 6 April 1965 and 5 April 1982 treated as a pool.
5 Shares purchased before 6 April 1965 on a last in first out (LIFO) basis. These shares may form part of the 5 April 1982 pool if an election was made under the 1968 Finance Act (see Section 10.32). The time for making this election was extended by the Finance Act 1985 to two years after the end of the tax year in which the first disposal occurs after 5 April 1985.

Example

2 April 1962	1500 XY shares purchased
7 October 1964	600 XY shares purchased
3 May 1970	500 XY shares purchased
6 October 1983	1000 XY shares purchased
5 July 1985	750 XY shares purchased
7 July 1985	1000 XY shares purchased

The following sales took place:
(a) 1000 shares on 10 July 1985. These are deemed to be the 750 shares purchased on 5 July 1985 and 250 of the shares purchased on 7 July 1985.
(b) 800 shares on 17 September 1985. The remaining shares purchased on 7 July 1985 are now in a pool with the 1000 shares purchased on 6

October 1983 and 800 of these shares are sold leaving 950 shares in this pool.

(c) 2500 on 20 November 1985.
   (i) No election made as regards the pre-6 April 1965 purchases. The shares sold are the 950 shares in the post 5 April 1982 pool, the 500 shares in the 5 April 1982 pool, the 600 shares purchased on 7 October 1964 and 450 of the shares purchased on 2 April 1962.
   (ii) An election made that the pre-6 April 1965 purchases should be included in the 5 April 1982 pool.

The shares sold are the 950 shares in the post 5 April 1982 pool and 1550 of the 2600 shares in the 5 April 1982 pool.

The significance of pooling is that when shares are in a pool they are treated as a single asset and when some of the shares comprising the pool are disposed of the disposal is treated as a disposal of part of this asset and the acquisition cost of those shares for capital gains purposes is not their actual cost but a proportionate part of the cost of all the shares in the pool.

Example

2 July 1983	500 XY shares purchased for £1,000
5 October 1984	1000 XY shares purchased for £1,800
6 May 1985	300 XY shares sold

(It is assumed that the purchase costs include the May 1985 indexation update)
As both purchases come within the post 5 April 1982 pool the acquisition cost of the shares sold will be £2,800 × 300/1500 = £560.

In future most activity will be in the post 5 April 1982 pool and the legislation requires that this indexed pool be revalued in line with the index as at 6 April 1985 and thereafter on each occasion that shares are added to or sold from the pool.

Example

15 December 1983	1000 XY shares purchased for £1,500
16 August 1986	1000 XY shares purchased for £1,700
4 December 1986	1000 XY shares purchased for £1,900
28 January 1987	1000 XY shares sold for £2,300

Assume RPIs

December 1983	343
April 1985	374
August 1986	382
December 1986	391
January 1987	395

	Holding	Unindexed cost	Indexed pool
Shares acquired before 6 April 1985	1,000	£1,500	£1,500
Indexation update			
$£1,500 \times \dfrac{374 - 343}{343}$			136
			£1,636
16 August 1986 purchase ...	1,000	£1,700	1,700
Indexation update			
$£1,636 \times \dfrac{382 - 374}{374}$			35
			£3,371
4 December 1986 purchase ...	1,000	£1,900	1,900
Indexation update			
$£3,371 \times \dfrac{391 - 382}{382}$			79
			£5,350
28 January 1987 sale			
Indexation update			
$£5,350 \times \dfrac{395 - 391}{391}$			55
			£5,405
		(1,000)	1,802
			£3,603

Sale proceeds	£2,300	
Indexed acquisition value of shares sold...	1,802	
Taxable gain	£498	

10.23 Rights and scrip issues

A similar adjustment must be made to the indexed pool whenever an event which effects the base value of the shares occurs e.g. a rights issue or a scrip issue.

Example

16 August 1986	1000 XY shares purchased for £1,700
28 January 1987	1 for 2 rights issue subscribed for at 110p per share
29 March 1987	500 XY shares purchased for £1,200

Assume RPIs
August 1986   382
January 1987   395
March 1987   398

		Holding	Unindexed cost	Indexed pool
16 August 1986 purchase	...	1,000	£1,700	£1,700
28 January 1987 rights issue	...	500	£550	550
Indexation update				
$£1,700 \times \dfrac{395 - 382}{382}$	...	...		58
				$\overline{£2,308}$
29 March 1987 purchase	...	500	£1,200	1,200
Indexation update				
$£2,308 \times \dfrac{398 - 395}{395}$	...	...		18
				$\overline{£3,526}$

As will be seen the indexation of the cost of shares arising under the rights issue starts from the time of payment although otherwise these new shares (as is also the case with scrip issues) are regarded as having been acquired at the time the original shares were bought.

Example
16March 1978   500 XY shares purchased for £800
15 May 1985   1000 XY shares purchased for £2,000
10 October 1985   1 for 2 rights subscribed for at £1.00

In this event 250 shares and 500 shares are added to the 5 April 1982 pool and the post 5 April 1982 pool respectively. An indexation update is applied to both pools and the cost of the shares taken up added thereto. In the case of a bonus or scrip issue the same procedure applies but there is, of course, no cost element to be added to the pools.

Where rights issues are sold nil paid they are treated as a capital distribution in the hands of the shareholder. This means that the net proceeds of the sale are compared with the proportion of the acquisition value that the net proceeds bear to the net proceeds plus the value of the retained shares.

Example
16 March 1978   500 XY shares purchased for £800 (Value 31 March 1982 £1,200 election made)
15 May 1985   1000 XY shares purchased for £2,000
10 October 1986   1 for 2 rights issue

750 new shares sold nil paid for £525
Value of 1500 shares retained £3,150

Assume RPIs
March 1982   313
May 1985   376
October 1986   387

1 5 April 1982 Pool	*Holding*	*Unindexed cost*	*Indexed pool*
31 March 1982	500	£1,200	£1,200
10 October 1986 rights issue			
Indexation update			
$£1,200 \times \dfrac{387 - 313}{313}$			284
			£1,484
Sale 250 new shares nil paid (proceeds £175)			212
			£1,272

2 Post 5 April 1982 Pool			
15 May 1985	1,000	£2,000	£2,000
10 October 1986 rights issue			
Indexation update			
$£2,000 \times \dfrac{387 - 376}{376}$			59
			£2,059
Sale 500 new shares nil paid (proceeds £350)			294
			£1,765

Proceeds of sale £525
Indexed cost of shares sold

5 April 1982 Pool $£1,484 \times \dfrac{175}{1,050 + 175}$ £212

Post 5 April 1982 Pool $£2,059 \times \dfrac{350}{2,100 + 350}$ 294   506

Taxable gain £19

In practice, where the proceeds are less than 5% of the value of the holding retained, the Inland Revenue are prepared to write down the cost of the holding by the amount of the proceeds and thus defer the payment of tax. For instance, if in the above example the proceeds of the rights had been £150, i.e. less than 5% of £3,150 the value of the retained holding, then the only immediate action necessary would be to index update the two pools and write them down by £50 and £100 respectively. This procedure also applies where as the result of a scrip or rights issue a shareholder receives the proceeds of a fractional share from the company.

Where rights issues are sold partly paid the position is a little more involved. For the purposes of the computation the outstanding liability on the shares is added to both the cost and the proceeds of sale.

10.24 Calls on shares

Where a call is made on shares or securities any consideration paid within twelve months of the acquisition is treated as having been paid at the time when the shares were allotted. Calls made after twelve months from the date of acquisition are deemed to be separate items of expenditure incurred when they were actually paid.

10.25 Employee share schemes

A separate post 5 April 1982 pool must be maintained in respect of shares held by a person as an employee of a company on terms which restrict his/her right to dispose of them. The separate pool is maintained so long as those terms are in force. Accordingly the rules of pooling and identification apply to the employee as if he held the shares in a different capacity from that in which he holds any other shares of the same class.

10.3 Pre-budget day 1965 holdings*

10.31 No election

Budget day 6 April 1965 is an important date as it is since then that realizations first became liable for the long-term tax. As it is not intended that gains which have accrued before long-term tax had been introduced should be liable for the tax, even though they were realized afterwards, certain rules have been laid down to cover stocks held at this date.

The taxable gain is deemed to be the lesser of either the gain since acquisition or the gain since 6 April 1965. On the other hand an allowable loss is deemed to be the smaller of either the loss since acquisition or the loss since 6 April 1965.

Example
(a) 100 shares purchased 16 June 1962 for £0.60 per share
      Price of shares 6 April 1965 £0.77½

---

* Although the importance of this section diminishes with the passage of time there are still a considerable number of pre 6 April 1965 holdings in existence for which it has practical relevance.

100 shares sold 10 October 1977 for £1.00 per share
The assessable gain per share is £0.22½

(b) 100 shares purchased 16 June 1962 for £1.25 per share
Price of shares 6 April 1965 £1.37½
100 shares sold 10 October 1977 for £1.00 per share
The allowable loss per share is £0.25.

In practice, of course, adjustment would be required for the expenses of purchase and sale.

10.311 Neutral zone

A further complication arises when a share is sold at a price in between the acquisition price and the 6 April 1965 price. In this event the share is said to be within its neutral zone and there is no assessable gain or allowable loss. For example, any transactions between £0.77½ and £1.00 in Figure 10.1 are neutral. This equally applies if the purchase price and 6 April price are reversed.

Purchase price   £0.77½ ——————————————————————
(prior to 6 April 1965)

                      no gain
                      no loss

6 April 1965 price   £1.00 ——————————————————————

Figure 10.1   *Typical Neutral Zone*

10.312 6 April 1965 price

The acquisition and disposal values of shares are based on the prices at which actual bargains took place, but for 6 April 1965 prices it has been necessary to lay down a formula for their calculation. For London quoted stocks reference is made to the Stock Exchange Official Daily List on that day and the price is taken to be the higher of:

(a) The middle closing quotation; *or*
(b) The middle market price of normal recorded bargains.

Example
Closing quotation 112½–117½
Bargains marked 112½, 113¾, 115, 116¼
The middle closing quotation is 115
The lowest bargain marked is 112½ and the highest 116¼
Halfway between is 114⅜

As the middle closing quotation is the higher, this is taken as the 6 April 1965 price, i.e. 115.

It should be noted that the London prices are not applicable where the shares are those in which one of the regional areas affords a more active market. There are available reference books showing the prices of most United Kingdom securites as determined by this formula. Appendixes are issued from time to time with the appropriate adjustments for scrip, rights issues, etc.

10.32 *Election*

Many people purchased shares or acquired them by inheritance or through gifts before capital gains tax was ever considered to be a possibility in this country. It will therefore, be readily appreciated that many investors have not kept careful records of their acquisition values. As the result of this a realization may incur much tiresome and time-consuming research through old papers, perhaps to no avail. Even if records have been kept, where there have been several transactions in the same shares together with scrip and rights issues this will add up to a considerable amount of complicated calculation.

To cover these contingencies the 1968 Finance Act provides an investor with the opportunity to make two separate elections – one for fixed interest stocks and the other for equities – to the effect that all his/her pre-6 April 1965 holdings will be treated as if they were acquired at their values at that date. The election may be made for both the defined categories or for either of them separately. Once made it is irrevocable and covers all the holdings in the category for which it is made.

The election only applies to any disposals from a pre-6 April 1965 purchase made after 19 March 1968. It must be made within two years of the close of the fiscal year in which the first relevant disposal takes place. For instance, if the first sale of a pre-6 April 1965 holding took place on 27 June 1968 the investor, if he/she wishes to elect, must do so not later than on 5 April 1971.*

It should be noted that for this purpose a participating preference share comes within the equity classification, whereas a convertible stock is regarded as fixed interest until conversion takes place when it moves into the equity category.

From the point of view of effort involved the option to elect provides an easy way out, but careful consideration may be required if the investor wishes to minimize his/her tax bill. The various permutations involved may be summarized as follows:

6 April 1965 price between acquisition and sale prices

(a)	(b)
Sale price £1.00	Acquisition price £1.00
6 April 1965 price £0.80	6 April 1965 price £0.80
Acquisition price £0.50	Sale price £0.50

---

* Period extended by 1985 Finance Act (see Section 10.22).

In both cases it is immaterial whether or not election has taken place. In (a) there is a gain of £0.20 per share and in (b) a loss of £0.30 per share.

Acquisition price between 6 April 1965 and sale prices

(a)	(b)
Sale price £1.00	6 April 1965 price £1.00
Acquisition price £0.80	Acquisition price £0.80
6 April 1965 price £0.50	Sale price £0.50

In (a) if election has taken place the taxable gain will be £0.50 whereas the actual gain is £0.20. In (b) if election has taken place the allowable loss will be £0.50 although the actual loss is £0.30.

Sale price between 6 April 1965 and acquisition prices

(a)	(b)
6 April 1965 price £1.00	Acquisition price £1.00
Sale price £0.80	Sale price £0.80
Acquisition price £0.50	6 April 1965 price £0.50

In (a) if election has taken place there will be an allowable loss of £0.20 whereas there is an actual gain of £0.30. In (b) if election has taken place there will be a taxable gain of £0.30 although there is an actual loss of £0.20.

It will be seen that election can produce some inequitable results. If all the shares in an investor's portfolio behaved in the same way the decision whether or not to elect would be simple. Unfortunately this will seldom be the case, certainly as far as equities are concerned, and the position of each pro-6 April 1965 holding should be considered before a decision is made.

10.4 Takeovers and mergers

In takeovers or amalgamations the capital gains tax position depends upon the terms. If the original shares held are merely replaced by new shares the rule is simple – the new shares stand in the shoes of the one they replace, i.e. they inherit their acquisition value and date.* However, if the offer is in cash such proceeds are liable to capital gains tax. Where the offer is partly cash and partly in shares there will be a disposal for gains tax purposes as far as the cash element of the offer is concerned.

Example
1977—2000 shares in Company A purchased for   ...   ... £1,800†

---

* For any person owning more than 5% of, or any class of, the shares or debentures this provision for, in effect, deferment of tax is conditional on approval from the Board of Inland Revenue. Approval will not be given where it is considered that one of the main reasons for the bid is avoidance of liability to tax.
† Assume indexation update to 1986 included in this figure.

1986—Company B offers one share and £0.50 cash for every two shares in Company A.

Offer is accepted and shareholder receives 1000 Company B shares and £500 cash.

It is now necessary to allocate the acquisition cost of £1,800 between the 1000 Company B shares and the £500 cash.

The value of the 1000 Company B shares based on the closing quotations on the day the offer was accepted was £1,900.

Acquisition cost of 1000 Company B shares
£1,800 × 1900/(500 + 1,900) £1,425
Acquisition cost of cash
£1,800 × 500/(500 + 1,900) £375
Assessable gain £125

10.5 Other taxable occasions

Capital gains tax is most commonly associated with actual sales of stock exchange securities and other chargeable assets. There are, however, certain other occasions when there is what is known as 'deemed' disposal which gives rise to a capital gains tax assessment. These may be summarized as follows.

10.51 Gifts

Gifts may be covered by the annual exemption so long as the gains arising when aggregated with gains from realizations do not exceed the limit. Since 21 March 1972 all gifts to charities have been exempt from capital gains tax.

Otherwise, unless an election is made by both parties (see below), a gift is regarded as a sale by the donor and a purchase by the donee. The value at which this deemed disposal for capital gains tax takes place is worked out according to a special formula (see Section 10.53). The donor is liable to meet the tax on any gain and entitled to use any loss which may arise. However, where the gift is to a connected person, for example a son, a sister, or the trustees of a settlement of which the donor is the settlor, any loss on the deemed disposal is only available to set off against gains accruing to the donor on other disposals to the same connected person.

A significant change in the capital gains tax position for gifts was introduced by the 1980 Finance Act by extending the principle of rollover relief to any gift made by one person to another provided both donor and donee jointly so elect. The effect of this is that the donor is not regarded as having made a deemed disposal but the donee acquires the asset(s) concerned at the donor's acquisition value. Should a partial payment be made for the assets transferred and the amount of such payment exceeds the cost for capital gains tax purposes the relief granted covers only the gift element.

Example

An asset costing £10,000 (indexation update included) with a market value of

£40,000 at the time of the transaction is transferred from father to daughter for £16,000

(a) *Without election*

Deemed proceeds	...	...	...	...	...	£40,000
Less cost of asset	...	...	...	...	...	10,000

Father's gain	...	...	...	...	...	£30,000

Daughter's acquisition value	...	...	...	...	£40,000

(b) *Election made*

Father's gain as above	...	...	...	...	...	£30,000
Less father's actual gain being excess of proceeds over cost,						
i.e. £16,000–£10,000	...	...	...	...	...	6,000

Held-over gain	...	...	...	...	...	£24,000

Daughter's acquisition value						
Market value	...	...	...	...	...	£40,000
Less held-over gain	...	...	...	...	...	24,000
						£16,000

The option to have indexation based on 31 March 1982 values does not extend to those who dispose of assets which they acquired after that date subject to a rollover relief claim.

Where a gift gives rise to the payment of capital transfer tax, the amount of this tax will be allowed as a deduction in computing the chargeable gain accruing to the donee on his/her subsequent disposal of the asset involved to the extent that this does not give rise to a loss.

The rules relating to gifts also apply when assets are settled in a United Kingdom resident trust, rollover relief having been made available by the 1981 Finance Act. The claim for such relief requires to be made by the settlor.

10.52 Trusts

When a beneficiary of a trust becomes absolutely entitled to assets as against the trustees there is in certain circumstances a deemed disposal for capital gains tax purposes. The occasions when such a liability may arise are, for example, the attainment of a certain age by a beneficiary, the exercise of a discretion by the trustees, or a variation of the trust.

The death of a lifetenant occurring after 31 March 1971 does not result in such a liability arising. The position now is that when a lifetenant dies the trust investments are revalued at the deemed disposal prices and any increase in value escapes capital gains tax. The aquisition values of the party or parties entitled to the investments are based on the deemed disposal prices except when they revert to the settlor who is treated as having acquired them at the original cost to the trustees.

If, when a trust comes to an end, the trustees have unrelieved losses on their hands they may pass these on to the beneficiaries who may utilize them to offset personal gains incurred in the current or future fiscal years.

Rollover relief for property leaving a trust is available for deemed disposals arising after 5 April 1982 on a joint claim by transferor and transferee.

10.53 Deemed disposal prices

In determining the values to be taken for quoted securities at death and on other occasions of a deemed disposal the formula is similar to that for obtaining the 6 April 1965 values. It is, however, not identical and the price to be taken is the lower of:

(a) The lower of the closing quotations plus one quarter of the difference between it and the higher closing quotation; *or*

(b) The middle market price of normal recorded bargains.

London quotations and prices are again taken unless there is a more active market in one of the regional areas.

Example
Closing quotation 125p–135p
Bargains marked $126\frac{1}{4}$, 130, $131\frac{1}{4}$, $133\frac{3}{4}$
The '$\frac{1}{4}$' up closing quotation is $127\frac{1}{2}$
The lowest bargain marked is $126\frac{1}{4}$ and the highest is $133\frac{3}{4}$
Half way between is 130
As the '$\frac{1}{4}$' up price is the lower this is the deemed disposal price, i.e. $1.27\frac{1}{2}$.

Where the Stock Exchange is closed on the day in question the prices are determined by reference to either the latest previous date or the earliest subsequent date.

10.6 Death

As from 31 March 1971 the death of a person has not given rise to a deemed disposal for capital gains tax purposes in respect of the assets of which the deceased was competent to dispose. The deceased's personal representatives are treated as having acquired his investments at their deemed disposal prices as at the date of his death and where such investments are transferred to legatees they also acquire them at the value as so calculated. There is thus an exemption from tax for any gain between the cost to the deceased on acquisition and the value at the date of his death.

Allowable losses sustained by an individual in the year of assessment in which he dies may be carried back and set off against net gains for any of the three preceding years of assessment, taking later years before earlier years. This is an exception to the rule that losses cannot be used to offset gains made in earlier years.

Where personal representatives realize investments they are liable to capital gains tax in the normal way. The annual exemption is available to them in the year of death and for each of the next two years. However, should they complete the administration of the estate with unrelieved losses they are unable to pass these on to the legatees.

10.7 Influence on decisions

The thought of having to meet capital gains tax on investments which have appreciated in value may tend to be a deterring factor in deciding upon the sale of holdings which have reached a level when they would otherwise appear to be too highly priced.

Admittedly, to effect a sale would result in the loss of the use of capital which must be handed over to the Inland Revenue in tax. While this is undoubtedly an addition to the various factors on which any decision must be based, it must not be given too much weight – certainly not to the extent that other normal investment considerations are disregarded. The future prospects of the company concerned together with those of alternative investments should remain what basically determines when a change should be made.

A point which should be borne in mind is that gains, once assessed, cannot be the source of a refund in the event of future losses. Therefore towards the end of a fiscal year in which profits have been realized to the extent of their being taxable the remaining holdings in the portfolio should be scrutinized to see if they are showing an allowable loss which, if taken, would reduce the forthcoming assessment. Even if there are no taxable gains the fact that losses can be carried forward may influence the sale of a share which has performed disappointingly and where there is no evidence to suggest an imminent recovery in price.

Before the end of each fiscal year investors should consider whether it would be advantageous to realize any of their holdings in order to benefit from the annual exemption even if this means doing a 'bed and breakfast', i.e. selling a stock one day and buying it back on the next. The expenses of such a transaction, although relatively light, must be weighed against the potential benefit of having established a higher acquisition value for the holding(s) involved. 'Bed and breakfasting' could also be applied to the situation envisaged in the previous paragraph where it is desired to retain a holding presently showing a loss. Here the lower acquisition value thereby established on which indexation will be based would be disadvantageous in the event of a future sale.

Finally the absence of tax charge on death coupled with the revaluation of the investment to be taken over by the legatees may justifiably to some extent inhibit investment switches where persons of advanced years are involved.

Typical question

You have a customer who inherited 1000 Ordinary Shares General Bank plc in 1963 with a Probate value of £2,130. She sells the shares in March 1986 for £7,470 and she asks you what capital gains tax she will have to pay. Calculate this using the following data.

Price of shares 6 April 1965   256p   Assume RPIs
Price of shares 31 March 1982   498p   March 1982   313
1985/86 net gains to date £4,560   March 1986   380

State what the revised position would be if you subsequently discovered that as at 6 April 1985 your customer had carry forward losses of £3,250.

Suggested answer

As the price 256p on 6 April 1985 is greater than the acquisition price (Probate value £2,130 for 1000 shares) it is the gain based on the former price which is chargeable to tax. Similarly as the 31 March market value exceeds the 6 April 1965 value your customer will elect that indexation is based on the 31 March 1982 value.

Sale proceeds	...	...	...	...	...	...	£7,470
Acquisition value of shares		...	...	...	£2,560		
March 1986 indexation update							
$£4,980 \times \dfrac{380 - 313}{313}$	...	...	...	...	1066	3,626	
						———	
						£3,844	
Add previous 1985/86 net gains	...	...	...	...	...	4,560	
Taxable amount	...	...	...	...	...	...	£8,404
Less exemption	...	...	...	...	...	...	5,900
							£2,504

Tax payable on £2,504 at 30% = £776.

If the customer had carry forward losses of £3,250 at 6 April 1985 these could be used to reduce the taxable amount to £5,900 and no tax would be payable for 1985/86. Your customer would have carry forward losses of £746 (£3,250–£2,504) available for future years.

Additional questions

1   Who is assessable to tax on capital gains? Are there any exemptions from liability? Detail the forms of investment which are exempt from tax on capital gains.

2 Explain how taxable gains are assessed. What is the position when a husband and wife both realize chargeable assets?

3 What is the significance of Budget Day, 6 April 1965? Explain the election options which have become available to investors in respect of disposals made after 19 March 1968.

4 Transactions were carried out in the shares of AB plc as undernoted.

2 July 1978	500 shares purchased for	£750
4 October 1981	900 shares purchased for	£1,500
7 October 1984	500 shares purchased for	£1,000
11 March 1986	600 shares sold for	£1,800

   (a) Identify which shares were sold on 11 March 1986.
   (b) Given the following additional information work out the gain arising from the sale.
   Price of shares 31 March 1982   170p
   Assume RPIs
   March 1982   313
   October 1984   355
   March 1986   380.

5 Using the following data calculate the gain arising from the sale of the new shares nil paid of DC plc.

17 April 1979	400 shares purchased for £700 (Value 31 March 1982 £1,000)
16 August 1985	1200 shares purchased for £2,300
15 January 1986	1 for 2 rights issue 800 new shares nil paid sold for £520
	Value of 1600 shares retained £3,200

   Assume RPIs
   March 1982   313
   August 1985   377
   January 1986   379.

5 Apart from the actual sale of investments when do taxable occasions arise? If the Stock Exchange is closed on the day in question how are the appropriate values obtained? How can the payment of tax be avoided on certain of these occasions?

6 Discuss the investment implications of the capital gains tax both from the administrative and the policy making point of view.

11 Yield

Stocks and shares are purchased with different objectives in mind. The old age pensioner with a few hundred pounds at his disposal will invest it to produce the highest income which he can obtain for him, while the young tycoon in the top tax bracket will want his investments to produce maximum capital appreciation and current income will be of lesser concern to him. In between there is a whole army of investors with varying emphasis to be placed on their income and capital requirements. All would, of course, welcome both a high current income together with prospects of rapid capital appreciation. Unfortunately this is not easily obtained unless the investor is either very shrewd or lucky, probably both, and it is up to the individual or his adviser to decide upon the sensible policy according to personal circumstances.

Except in the case of some of the sophisticated non-income paying types of investment which are from time to time introduced as a counter to penal taxation, one of the first points to consider about any prospective investment is what calculable return it gives on the capital utilized in its acquisition. This is known as the yield and in financial media it is usually expressed gross, i.e. ignoring tax. The individual must make the necessary adjustments according to the rate which he/she pays.

11.1 Flat yield

This is the yield based on the price of the stock and the rate of interest or dividend paid thereon. No account is taken of any guaranteed capital appreciation which will take place if a dated stock is held to redemption. It is alternatively known as the current, interest, or running yield. When the stock is priced below its par value the yield will be above the interest or dividend rate, and when priced above par the yield will be less. The actual calculation of flat yield is a straightforward matter and the following formula normally applies:

Yield % = Interest (or dividend) rate × par/price

Examples
A 6% fixed interest stock standing at 80
Yield = 6 × 100/80 = 7.5%

A 10% fixed interest stock standing at 125
Yield = 10 × 100/125 = 8%
A 4.9% (formerly 7%) £1 preference share standing at 80p
Yield = 7 × 100/80 = 8.75%
A 25p ordinary share with dividend rate of 26%* standing at 150p
Yield = 26 × 25/150 = 4.3%

Normally dividends on ordinary shares are not expressed in percentage terms but are declared as so much per share. In this event the formula is:

$$\text{Yield \%} = \frac{\text{Dividend (in pence or pounds)}}{\text{Price (in pence or pounds)}} \times 100$$

Example
A share at 350p, dividend 12p*
Yield = 12/350 × 100 = 3.4%

This method would, of course, require to be adopted with a share of no par value.

11.11 *Cleaning the price*†

Before a yield can be calculated accurately the price should be 'cleaned', i.e. an adjustment should be made for the accrued interest or dividend contained in the price. This is necessary because, except on the day when interest is paid right up to date, the price of the stock is based on two factors, the main one being the capital value of the stock and the other the accrued interest attaching thereto.

Take the case of a 9% debenture stock which has run four months since the last interest payment was made. It will have £3 gross interest in the price and this should be deducted from the price of the non-taxpayer. Other investors should take tax at their appropriate rate off the interest before deducting it from the price. A further adjustment should be made to the price to cover the purchase costs. These are, of course, a more important factor with company stocks than with gilt-edged.

With fixed interest stocks the procedure is straightforward, but with ordinary shares dividend dates and the amounts paid vary so that in practice adjustment to the price only takes place during the period between the declaration of the dividend and the quotation of the share 'ex div'.

---

* It has now become customary for companies to declare their dividends with reference to the net amount payable. To calculate the yield on a comparable basis it is necessary to gross this up at basic rate. Accordingly, in these examples the declared dividends would be 18.2% which grossed at 30% = 26% and 8.4p which grossed at 30% = 12p.
† Since February 1986 this has become a less universal requirement (see Section 2.3).

11.12 Estimate with ordinary

With ordinary shares dividends vary so that in the absence of comment from the board regarding future payments the calculation of yield will only be a matter of estimation. However, with most major companies any fluctuation in dividend between one year and the next is nowadays usually marginal and the latest known rate forms the basis for a reasonably accurate calculation of yield. This does not, of course, apply should there be any marked deterioration in a company's affairs in which event last year's dividend rate may be solely of historical value.

11.2 Redemption yields

Many fixed interest stocks have a date or dates when they will be redeemed, usually at par. With such stocks, as well as working out the flat yield it is possible to calculate the redemption yield which also takes into the reckoning the gain or loss on the capital value of the stock to redemption.

Example

A 5% stock redeemable at par in 1990 is standing at 85 in 1980.
The flat yield is $5 \times 100/85$ 5.88%
Also to be taken into account are the 15 points which the stock will appreciate to redemption. These can, for an approximate calculation, be divided by the period to redemption, i.e. 10 years, and the resultant figure added to the flat yield 1.50%

Gross redemption yield 7.38%

The word 'gross' is added because in this calculation no adjustment has been made for tax.

   Should a stock be standing above par the loss to redemption results in the gross redemption yield being less than the flat yield.

Example

An 8% stock redeemable at par in 1995 is standing at 105 in 1980.
Flat yield $8 \times 100/105$ 7.62%
Deduct annual capital loss 5/15   ...   .   0.33%

Gross redemption yield 7.29%

This is only an approximate method of working out redemption yields as, for instance, in the first example £1.50 is not going to be received by the holder of £100 stock each year for ten years. What happens is that at the end of ten years the holder will receive £15 of capital appreciation. This is less valuable to him/her than receiving £1.50 each year, which amount could be invested and itself earn interest.

Accurate redemption yields on a compound basis can be worked out but only after a rather complicated arithmetical exercise. In practice they are obtained from bond yield tables, or more commonly from the daily lists which are produced by specialist brokers and market makers. The actual gross redemption yields in the two examples are 7.18% and 7.44% respectively.

11.21 Adjusting for tax

Gross redemption yields are pertinent to non-taxpaying investors such as pension funds and charities but to most investors they are only of limited value. A further step must be taken to allow for tax, thus bringing out the actual net return to the investor. Not surprisingly such yields are known as net redemption yields.

Working on the approximate figures, suppose that in the first example the stock was a debenture or loan stock and that the holder was a basic rate taxpayer.

	%
Flat yield	5.88
Deduct income tax at 30%	1.76
	4.12
Capital element in yield*	1.50
Net redemption yield	5.62

The calculation for a payer of tax at, say, 65% would be as follows:

	%
Flat yield	5.88
Deduct income tax at 65%	3.82
	2.06
Capital element in yield*	1.50
Net redemption yield	3.56

---

* Assumed that debenture is a qualifying corporate bond (see Section 10.13). If not a deduction should be made for capital gains tax.

Obtaining the net redemption yield lets each investor know the merits of a stock to him/herself personally and he/she avoids making the wrong purchase in the light of superficially attractive flat and gross redemption yields. This can be illustrated by comparing the actual yields on two British Government stocks in February 1986.

	Price	Flat yield	Gross redemption yield	Net redemption yield (*tax at 55%*)
Gas 3% 1990/95	69⅝	4.31	7.66	5.29
12¾% Treasury 1995	109¼	11.67	11.16	4.74

For the non-taxpayer the 12¾% Treasury 1995 is quite clearly the more attractive as his/her return is measured by the gross redemption yield. However, for the 55% rate taxpayer the better buy would be the 3% Gas 1990/95 and this becomes more so for the even higher rate taxpayer. The reason is that there is capital appreciation in the 3% Gas 1990/95 which is more valuable to the high taxpayer than an equivalent amount of income. When wishing to purchase a fixed interest investment the high taxpayer should therefore look for a stock with a low rather than high coupon rate.

11.22 Comparing with ordinary

In assessing fixed interest stocks recourse is sometimes made to one further type of yield known as a grossed-up redemption yield or a gross equivalent yield. This is the net redemption yield grossed up at the appropriate rate of tax. What in effect gross equivalent yields do is to treat the net capital part of the yield as though it were taxed income and then see what the equivalent would be before tax.

Reverting to the 5% stock redeemable in 1990, approximate net redemption yields of 5.62% and 3.56% have been calculated for the basic rate payer and the 65% taxpayer respectively. The gross equivalent yields would be:

Basic rate payer $5.62 \times 100/(100 - 30) = 8.03\%$
65% payer $\quad 3.56 \times 100/(100 - 65) = 10.17\%$

The purpose of grossed up yields is to make possible a comparison with other investments such as ordinary shares, where the capital profit and loss cannot be estimated in advance and it is usual to quote gross yields. A grossed-up redemption yield gives the taxpayer the gross yield he/she would have to obtain on any investment where the return is all taxable as income in order to be left with the same net amount in his/her hands. The calculation again emphasizes how valuable capital growth is to the high taxpayer as compared with income.

11.23 Index-linked stocks

When appraising the merits of index-linked stocks the difficulty arises of not knowing the rates of inflation which will prevail during their lives. The potential investor must be prepared to take some view of what this will be and then, applying this rate, compare the yield which he/she will then obtain from the index-linked stock with an appropriate alternative gilt-edged stock. A practical approach is to obtain from a stockbroker or other professional adviser a list setting out the net redemption yields on conventional stocks of similar maturities at various rates of tax against the inflation rates necessary for the index-linked stocks to equal these. For example, in November 1985 2% Index-Linked Treasury Stock 1996 (price 113) and 9% Treasury Stock 1992/96 (price 92) could be compared as follows:

	9% Treasury Stock 1992/96	*Break-even inflation rate*
Tax rate	*Net redemption yield %*	*for index-linked stock %*
Nil	10.53	6.52
30%	7.57	4.11
50%	5.62	2.53

For the nil taxpayer at that time inflation over the period to redemption would have to exceed 6.52% for the index-linked stock to be the better purchase while for the 30% and 50% taxpayers inflation would require to exceed 4.11% and 2.53% respectively. The reason why the index-linked stock is more attractive the higher the rate of tax lies in the fact of its low coupon and the impact of the index-linking on its capital value at redemption. Also the return from the 9% Treasury Stock 1992/96 arises mainly from income which reduces in value as the tax rate progresses.

Of further assistance to investors are the real returns quoted in the financial press available on index-linked stocks as their prices change. The reason why these vary slightly at different rates of inflation is due to the fact that for the last eight months of their lives the stocks are unprotected by index-linking.

While index-linked stocks are most commonly regarded as alternatives to fixed interest stocks comparison should on occasion be made with the returns expected from other types of investment with claims of inflation proofing such as ordinary shares and real property.

11.3 Switching

A close watch on yields, particularly in the gilt-edged market, is kept by such of the institutions as employ part of their funds in fixed interest investment. From time to time as the result of heavy buying or selling orders the yields on two similar stocks, for example, Exchequer 12¼% 1992 and Treasury 12½% 1993, may temporarily get out of line. The wide-awake investment manager notices this and he sells the stock which has become relatively dearer and buys the cheaper one. When the yield relationship between the two stocks has reverted to normal he may deal in the opposite direction, the original stock being reinstated in his portfolio but with a capital profit having been made as the result of the transactions. Alternatively the manager may be content to stay with the new stock in order to benefit from the better yield obtained.

Switching is facilitated in the gilt-edged market owing to the exemption from transfer stamp duty and the relatively low rates of commission chargeable. Dealing in large amounts, as is possible with British Government stocks, sizeable profits can be made from small market anomalies.

A second type of switch may be profitable to an institutional investor, for example a bank, which is assessed to tax on its investment profits on a trading basis. Two stocks, say, a 9% issue and a 12% issue, may offer the same gross redemption yield, but if the 12% issue rises above par there will be a loss to redemption. This loss is of value to such an institution as it may be deducted from profits before they are assessed to tax.

Changes in tax legislation may also produce the situation where switches may advantageously be made from one type of fixed interest security to another. For example, the freedom from capital gains tax on British Government stocks could provide the incentive for an investor to take an allowable capital gains tax loss available from a non-exempt debenture or loan stock which had fallen below his acquisition cost by selling this stock and investing the proceeds in a British Government stock where the appreciation is exempt from tax. In evaluating the desirability of such a move the relative yields of the respective stocks would have to be carefully considered as well as the tax advantages.

A further occasion for switching, although not in the same strictly technical sense, is when an investor takes a view of the future trend in interest rates. If the investor thinks they are going to rise he will shorten the average life of his portfolio. Alternatively he will lengthen it should he anticipate a fall.

Typical questions

1 State concisely how flat yield differs from redemption yield.
2 Where a stock has two redemption dates, under what circumstances will the redemption yield be calculated on
   (a) the earlier date, and
   (b) the later date?
   Your reason should be given.
3 Explain why it is common practice to issue stocks with alternative dates for redemption.
   (The Institute of Bankers in Scotland, *Theory and Practice of Investment*)

Suggested answer

1 A flat yield relates the interest being paid on a stock to the price of the stock and gives the income return to the purchaser of the stock at that

price. For example, a 6% stock purchased at 80 provides a flat yield of 6 × 100/80 = 7.5%.

A redemption yield, which is applicable only to dated stocks, includes the flat yield but also takes into the reckoning any capital gain or loss to redemption. If the 6% stock mentioned above was purchased at 80 in 1980 and was redeemable at par in 1990 the 20 points capital appreciation to redemption would be taken into account. An approximate way of doing this is to divide the number of points the price has to rise by the time in which this must be accomplished, i.e. 20/10 = 2. Adding this to the flat yield produces a redemption yield (gross) of 9.5%.

2 Where a stock has two redemption dates the redemption yield will be calculated to the date when it would appear most likely to be redeemed. This depends on interest rates and the state of the fixed interest market generally.

If it is thought that when the first date is reached the borrower would be able to repay the stock and borrow again more cheaply, this is the date which will be taken. On the other hand if fresh borrowing would require to be at a higher rate, then the redemption will be postponed for as long as possible and the later date will be taken.

3 Stocks are issued with alternative dates in order that the borrower will have some room for manoeuvre as regards redemption. If a stock has only one date the borrower must redeem it then, no matter what the state of the market. If there is a period between two dates during which redemption may take place the borrower can choose the time most suitable to it.

Additional questions

1 (a) Why is it necessary to 'clean' the price of a stock before calculating the yield?
   (b) What reservation must be placed on the yield from an equity share?
2 To which investors do gross redemption yields apply? In the case of other investors what further step must be taken to determine if a particular fixed interest stock is suitable for their requirements?
3 On what basis can the return from a fixed interest stock be compared with the yield from an ordinary share?
4 Outline what you understand by the expression 'switching' in the fixed interest market.
5 What is the main difficulty in assessing the merits of index-linked stocks? Indicate a practical approach to this.

12 Assessment of ordinary shares

Despite their disadvantages, with which the reader will now be familiar, gilt-edged stocks and also the debenture and loan stocks of first class companies have at least the merit that the purchaser knows what he/she will get in return for the money spent on them. That is a regular fixed income and, except in the case of the relatively few irredeemables in existence, the right to repayment of the nominal amount of stock acquired at par not later than on a specified date.

With ordinary shares there is no such certainty and this is an important factor which the equity investor must always remember. Needless to say equity shares are purchased when the investor is optimistic regarding a company's prospects. This optimism should, however, not stem merely from a hunch or a newspaper tip. Attention must be paid, among other things, to certain useful statistical data, the source of which is the company's balance sheets and profit and loss accounts. Each year's data is not studied in isolation but must be related to that of previous years.

12.1 The value of assets

A balance sheet is a statement of a company's assets and liabilities on a specific day in its year. This latter point should be borne firmly in mind as it may not in fact be typical of the company's state of affairs. The individual items may fluctuate considerably between one accounting date and the next. An obvious example would be a company with a heavy Christmas trade. In November it might hold large stocks but very little cash. In January the position could well be reversed.

Traditionally assets were always listed on one side and liabilities on the other, these latter including issued capital and reserves. This can be a little unsatisfactory as it does not distinguish what is owed to outsiders from the assets of the company attributable to shareholders. Nowadays the trend is for balance sheets to be prepared in linear form with liabilities being deducted from assets bringing out a figure of net total assets. Thereafter appears details of how these assets are financed. However, whatever the form of the balance sheet it is a simple matter to rearrange the figures in order to obtain the information required.

12.11 Real value

Determining how far the values given to various assets may correspond to their actual value does give rise to difficulty. The notes to the accounts are useful in this respect in that they provide details of the basis of such valuations including the amount of depreciation written off. The investor must draw his/her own conclusions.

For instance, if buildings were last valued ten years ago they are very probably, although not necessarily, worth considerably more at the present time. Most major companies hold investments, both quoted and unquoted. These will usually be entered in the balance sheet at cost, but the notes will provide the market value of the quoted investments and the directors' estimate the value of the unquoted.

The relevance of asset values depends upon circumstances. Certainly should a winding-up be in the offing they are very important, but in this event they might require to be drastically reassessed. The value, for instance, of a factory as a going concern is one thing, but as a building for which no one has any particular use quite another. On the other hand, quoted investments have a known value which should readily be realizable in the event of the company's liquidation.

A watchful eye should be on the look out for intangible assets usually parading under the description of goodwill. These may arise when other businesses have been taken over at above their asset values, the excess payment being on account of business connections acquired, patents, additional management expertise, etc. Although these may have been well worth obtaining, a severe view is taken of them when appraising a company's assets and it is assumed that they could not be disposed of for any realizable value.

12.12 Net assets per ordinary share

This is the most common asset statistic to be calculated and is simply the division of the tangible assets attributable to the ordinary shareholders by the number of ordinary shares issued. Turning to the balance sheet of A.B. plc (Figure 12.1) the calculation would be as follows:

Total net assets			£1,216,000
Deduct intangibles – goodwill			170,000
Total tangible assets			1,046,000
Less liability to			
Debenture stockholders	£150,000*		
Preference share capital	300,000*		450,000
Residue			£596,000

---

* Repayment assumed to be at par.

Net asset value per ordinary share £596,000/500,000 = £1.19.

This is, of course, a book asset value and anyone taking a close interest in the company would be well advised to consider how this might differ from the real asset value. An idea of this could be obtained by a study of the notes to the company's accounts allied to a knowledge of the company and the field of its operations.

A net asset value standing well above the market value of the shares would indicate that the assets were not being used very profitably. This might be the result of poor management and give rise to a takeover bid from another company with a view to putting them to better use. Alternatively the reason might be that the particular industry in which the company was engaged was facing hard times and profits could not easily be made.

A.B. plc
Balance Sheet as at 31 March 19...

Fixed assets

Land and buildings		£200,000
Plant, machinery, and motor vehicles		290,000
Fixtures, fittings, and equipment		27,000
		£517,000
Investments		
Quoted investments	£55,000	
Unquoted investments	28,000	
		83,000
Current assets		
Stock and work-in-progress	410,000	
Debtors	510,000	
Short-term deposits	60,000	
Cash in bank and on hand	78,000	
	1,058,000	
Current liabilities		
Creditors	488,000	
Current taxation	74,000	
Proposed dividends	50,000	
	612,000	
Net current assets		446,000
Goodwill		170,000
		£1,216,000

Financed by

500,000 ordinary £1 shares issued fully paid	£500,000
Share premium account	36,000
Unappropriated profits	230,000
(Ordinary shareholders' interest)	766,000
300,000 4.2%* cumulative preference £1 shares issued fully paid ...	300,000
£150,000 6½% debenture stock 1984/89	150,000
	£1,216,000

Figure 12.1

There are also some industries like shipbuilding and heavy engineering where much capital must be invested and large fixed assets built up before operations can begin. In contrast an entertainment or advertising agency company could be formed with very little backing in the way of tangible assets. The capital is largely comprised of the expertise and personal qualities attaching to the individuals involved, which gives rise to a high rate of earnings.

To appreciate the significance of asset values requires both considerable knowledge of the company concerned and the ability to interpret this correctly.

12.13 Capital priority percentages

Another exercise which may be carried out from an asset point of view is to calculate the capital priority percentages. This sets out in order of priority the percentage of the net tangible assets available to cover the different types of capital with which the company is financed. With A.B. plc this would be:

Net tangible assets (or stockholders' funds) £1,046,000

Represented by			%	*Priority %* *for capital*	*Overall* *cover*
6½% Debenture stock	...	£150,000†	14.3	0–14.3	7.0 times
6% Cum. pref. shares	...	300,000†	28.7	14.3–43	2.3 times
Ordinary shares	...	500,000⎱	57.0	43–100	
Reserves less goodwill	...	96,000⎰			
		£1,046,000	100		

---

* Formerly 6%.
† Assuming that repayments would be at par.

This calculation has, of course, much relevance for the holders of prior charge capital. The first 14.3% of the assets would be required to repay the debenture stockholders and the reciprocal of the priority percentage, i.e. 100/14.3 tells them that their capital is covered seven times. The preference shareholders would take the next 28.7% of the assets and their overall cover is 2.3 times. It is important when working out the cover for the preference shareholders to take into consideration the proportion of net assets required to repay prior ranking capital. There is sometimes the danger of ignoring this and resting in a degree of false security should, for instance, the calculation be done in the following manner:

Net tangible assets	£1,046,000
Less required to repay debenture stockholders	150,000
	£896,000

$$\text{Cover for preference shareholders} = \frac{\text{Net assets available}}{\text{Net assets required to repay}}$$

$$= \frac{£896,000}{300,000}$$

The answer to this is almost three times and might lead to the fallacy that the value of net assets could fall by two-thirds before the preference share capital would be uncovered by assets. If, however, net tangible assets fell in value to one-third and the debenture stockholders were repaid there would not be sufficient to repay the preference shareholders in full.

$\dfrac{£1,046,000}{3}$	£348,667
Required for debenture stockholders	150,000
	£198,667

There is a shortfall of over £100,000. It is therefore much wiser and safer to rely on the overall cover, in this case 2.3 times, which is made apparent by the priority percentage calculation.

So far as the ordinary shareholders are concerned it tells them that after repaying the prior ranking capital there is still 57% of the net assets available.

This, of course, corresponds to a net asset value of £1.19 per ordinary share.

12.14 The current position

When studying a balance sheet the relationship between current assets and current liabilities must be examined. Current assets are cash, invested cash, trade debtors, and assets held by a company with the intention of turning them into cash. Current liabilities are those claims against the company which it must meet in the near future, i.e. trade creditors, taxation, etc.

When there is an excess of current assets over liabilities, or in other words there are net current assets, this measures the net resources (or working capital) which the company has available to finance its day-to-day operations. Should, however, current liabilities exceed current assets it is evident that the company is using short-term borrowing or credit from its suppliers to finance its fixed assets. This is not a satisfactory situation, particularly if it persists for any length of time, and may mean that to remain in business the company will require to raise additional funds by the issue of further shares or debentures.

The working capital of a company is something indicated by a ratio of the current assets to current liabilities. In A.B. plc it would be

$$\frac{£1,058,000}{612,000} = 1.7$$

It will be noted that some current assets are more liquid than others. For example, short-term deposits can be turned into cash much more readily and with more certainty than stock, work-in-progress, and debtors. Thus a subdivision of current assets can be made to bring out the 'quick assets' or 'liquid assets'. In A.B. plc they would be represented by cash and short-term deposits. Against these would have to be weighed short-term liabilities. For instance, the dividend payments would be due very soon and current taxation would require to be met in the not too distant future.

12.15 Investments

A company's investments are sometimes acquired purely for the purpose of earning income on surplus funds. If so, they would be included with current assets. More frequently they represent holdings in associated companies and are retained because of the value of the trade connection. In this event it is appropriate to treat them as fixed assets as they have a part to play in the continuing success of the business.

12.2 Earnings

Note: The calculations in this chapter are based on corporation tax rate of 50% and basic/ACT rate of 30%.

Necessary though it is to examine a company's asset position the really vital factor is its earning power. It is unusual for quoted companies to fare so badly that they are forced into liquidation, but not nearly so uncommon to find a company with a disappointing profit record over a period of years. The equity shareholders of such a company, instead of receiving regular increases in dividends, may have their dividends cut or even passed altogether. The capital value of their shares will show at best a depressing lack of growth and a fixed interest investment might have proved a much more satisfactory holding.

It is therefore essential to select an equity with prospects of earnings growth, all the more so if the dividend yield on the initial purchase is appreciably below that obtainable from a fixed interest stock.

Although it is the future performance of a company which matters and this is often subject to influences which it is difficult to foresee, there is undoubtedly much useful guidance to be obtained from the study of its past results.

12.21 Dividend cover and earnings yield

One of the questions which an investor will naturally ask when contemplating a purchase of shares will be as to the income yield. Having established this the next step will be to find out what protection is indicated by the last profit figures of the company for the maintenance of the yield, or what hopes he can justifiably entertain for an early increase. For the profit figures he can of course refer to the profit and loss account.

Let it be assumed that the most recent results of A.B. plc showed pre-tax profits of £170,000, and a dividend of 8.4p per share* was paid on the ordinary shares which are priced at 225p.

It is now necessary to determine the maximum amount which the company could pay out from its year's profits by way of dividend.

Profits before taxation	...	...	...	...	... ...	£170,000
Corporation tax at 50%	...	...	...	...	£85,000	
Less ACT preference dividend			£5,400			
ACT ordinary dividend			31,029		36,429	48,571
						£121,429
Preference dividend	...	...	...	...	£12,600	
ACT	...	...	...	...	...	5,400	18,000
						£103,429
Maximum ordinary dividend		...	...	...	£72,400	
ACT	...	...	...	...	...	31,029	103,429

$$\text{Cover for ordinary dividend} = \frac{\text{Profits available}}{\text{Cost of ordinary dividend}}$$
$$= \frac{£72,400}{42,000}$$
$$= 1.724 \text{ times}$$

---

* Gross equivalent 12p per share.

This cover figure could, however, be misleading as is illustrated below under priority percentages.

The profits retained by the company on paying the dividend of 8.4p per share would be £72,400 − £42,000 = £30,400.

Closely associated with cover for the ordinary dividend is the earnings yield. Here the question arises as to what 'earnings' are to be taken. Should they be the maximum amount the company could retain if no dividend is paid (nil distribution method), the equivalent of the maximum gross dividend which the company could pay if nothing were retained (full distribution method), or perhaps some other amount altogether such as pre-tax profits? In view of the fact that earnings yield is normally used to compare the potential return with the dividend yield the full distribution method is generally regarded as the most appropriate.

$$\text{Earnings yield} = \frac{\text{Earned for each ordinary share}}{\text{Price of each ordinary share}} \times 100$$

$$= \frac{£103,429/500,000}{2.25} \times 100$$

$$= 9.19\%$$

Another method of obtaining the earnings yield is to multiply the dividend yield by the cover.

Dividend yield = 8.4 × 100/70 ÷ 225 × 100 = 5.33%
Earnings yield = 5.33 × 1.724 = 9.19%

These calculations are based on the premise that all the profits were earned in the United Kingdom and that there was no unrelieved ACT. The position would not be straightforward if, say, 70% of the company's pre-tax profits was earned overseas and overseas corporation tax was paid on these profits at the rate of 50%.

Profits before taxation:							
Overseas	...	...	...	...	...	...	£119,000
United Kingdom	...	...	...	...	...	...	51,000
							£170,000
Overseas corporation tax at 50%		...	...	...	...		59,500
							£110,500
UK corporation tax on UK income		...	...		£25,500		
Less ACT preference dividend			£5,400				
ordinary dividend			9,900		15,300		10,200*
UK corporation tax on overseas income					£59,500		

Less ACT not relievable against UK income					14,790*	
					£44,710	
Double taxation relief	...	...	...	...	44,710	
						£100,300
Preference dividend	...	...	...	...	£12,600	
ACT	...	...	...	...	...	5,400	18,000
						£82,300
Maximum ordinary dividend	...	...	...	£57,610	
ACT	...	...	...	...	...	24,690	82,300

$$\text{Cover for ordinary dividend} = \frac{\text{Profits available}}{\text{Cost of ordinary dividend}}$$

$$= \frac{£57,610}{42,000}$$

$$= 1.372$$

In this instance the profits retained by the company on paying the dividend of 9.4p per share would be £30,400 less unrelieved ACT £8,100 = £22,300 (see Section 12.22).

The earnings yield would be $\dfrac{£82,300/500,000}{2.25} \times 100 = 7.32\%$.

12.22 Earnings per share and PE ratio

Many investors are more interested in the rate of growth of a company's earnings than they are in the actual dividends paid, such growth of course having a powerful influence on the market price of the shares. Accordingly, they calculate what has been earned per share and as part of the value of such an exercise is the comparison of one company's performance with that of another, irrespective of the differing dividend policies of the companies concerned, it is the 'nil basis' of calculating earnings which is normally used. In other words it is assumed that no dividend is paid on the ordinary shares.

Profits before taxation	...	...	...	...	...	...£170,000
Corporation tax at 50%	...	...	...	...	...	... 85,000
						£85,000
Less Preference dividend	...	...	...	...	...	... 12,600
Earned for ordinary shareholders	...	...	...	...	... £72,400

See Sections 9.2 and 9.21.

Earnings per ordinary share = £72,400/500,000 = 14.5p

It will be observed that the earnings calculated in this way are in fact the actual ordinary dividend payment (£42,000) plus profits retained (£30,400).

An investment 'tool' which came into popular use when corporation tax was separated from personal tax in 1965 is the price/earnings ratio. Although the imputation system has ended this tax separation the PE ratio continues to be widely used. It is a calculation of the number of years which it would take the company to earn for each ordinary share the equivalent of the present market price of the share. Nil earnings per share are normally taken and are, of course, based on the latest figures available.

$$\text{PE ratio} = \frac{\text{Market price of share}}{\text{Earned per share}}$$
$$= \frac{225}{14.5}$$
$$= 15.5$$

The main use of PE ratios is for comparative purposes and this is of particular value when weighing up the merits of companies in the same line of business. However, if international comparisons are involved allowance may require to be made for differing tax systems.

The calculation of earnings per share and the PE ratio on a nil earnings basis is generally regarded as satisfactory for the great majority of companies which have sufficient United Kingdom profits to cover the ACT on their dividends. However, a few very important British companies earn most of their profits overseas as the result of which the payment of dividends means that some overseas tax goes unrelieved.

The earnings of such companies is frequently computed on a 'net basis' by deducting this unrelieved overseas tax from earnings computed on a nil basis. In cases where companies can cover ACT with United Kingdom income the net basis and nil basis do, of course, produce the same answer.

Assume again that of A.B. plc's pre-tax profits 70% was derived from overseas on which overseas corporation tax at the rate of 50% was paid. In order to calculate net earnings it must be established how much extra tax is payable when a dividend of 8.4p per share is being paid on the ordinary shares.

Profits before taxation:

Overseas	...	...	...	...	...	...	£119,000
United Kingdom	...	...	...	...	...	...	51,000
							£170,000
Overseas corporation tax at 50%			...	...	...	...	59,500
							£110,500

UK corporation tax on UK income		£25,500	
Less ACT preference dividend	£5,400		
ordinary dividend	9,900	15,300	10,200*
UK corporation tax on overseas income		£59,500	
Less ACT not relievable against UK income		8,100*	
		£51,400	
Double taxation relief		51,400	
			£100,300
Preference dividend		£12,600	
ACT		5,400	18,000
			£82,300
Ordinary dividend		£42,000	
ACT		18,000	60,000
Profits retained			£22,300

The extra tax payable is the £8,100 ACT which cannot be relieved against United Kingdom income. The earnings calculated on a net basis are:

Earnings on nil basis	£72,400
Less unrelieved ACT	8,100
	£64,300

Earnings per ordinary share = £64,300/500,000 = 12.86p
PE ratio = 225/12.86 = 17.5

The net basis calculation does depart from the 'pure' assessment of earnings divorced entirely from dividend payment considerations. It has the merit of realism in that companies pay dividends and the payment of a given amount by way of dividend can be more expensive for an overseas trading company than for a company with all its operations based in the United Kingdom.

12.23 Income priority percentages

It has already been indicated that the cover for the ordinary dividend as normally calculated can sometimes be misleading. If the company is financed solely by ordinary share capital the cover figure gives the true position. In such a company, for instance, a twice covered dividend means that the profits

---

* See Sections 9.2 and 9.21.

could be halved but would still be sufficient to pay the current rate of dividend. However, if there was also prior charge capital this would not be so, and the way to obtain a clear picture of the effective cover is by the method of priority percentages, this time as far as rights to profits are concerned.

Once again reference is made to A.B. plc, but before setting out the proportion of the company's profits required to pay the interest and dividends it is necessary to make an adjustment because of the way in which corporation tax is charged. The tax, it will be remembered, is levied on the company's profits after they have been reduced by the interest payments on loan capital. This tax saving must therefore be taken into account when measuring the slice of the company's profits required to service the loan capital.

A.B. plc has £150,000 6½% debenture stock on which the gross annual interest is £9,750. Corporation tax on this at 50% is £4,875 so that paying this interest only takes up £9,750 − £4,875 = £4,875 of the company's profits.

Profits after debenture interest and corporation tax	£85,000
Add back net cost of debenture interest	4,875
Adjusted profits available for interest and dividends	£89,875

Income priority percentages

	Cost of interest or dividend	Priority %	Overall cover
£150,000 6½% debenture stock 1984/89	£4,875	0–5.42	18.45 times
300,000 4.2% cumulative preference £1 shares ...	12,600	5.42–19.44	5.14 times
500,000 ordinary £1 shares (dividend of 8.4p per share paid)	42,000	19.44–66.17	1.51 times
Retained	30,400		
	£89,875		

Thus the first 5.42% of profits is required for the debenture interest, the next 14.02% for preference dividend, and the next 46.73% for the ordinary dividend. Altogether they take up 66.17% of the profits leaving 33.83% retained by the company.

Another way of looking at it would be to say that the profits could fall by 33.83% before the ordinary dividend would be uncovered. This is a lower percentage fall than that which might be assumed from the normal dividend cover figure which in this case was 1.724 times. From it the impression might

e gained that profits could drop by 42% (0.724/1.724 × 100) before the
rdinary dividend would be uncovered.

The reason for this discrepancy is the existence of the prior charge capital
which takes a fixed amount of the company's profits before the ordinary
shareholders get anything. In assessing the safety of the ordinary dividend it is
ssential, therefore, to look also at the proportion of the profits required to
ervice the loan and preference capital as set out by priority percentages.

2.24 Gearing

he impact which the prior charge capital has on a company's profits is
nown as gearing owing to the resultant effect that any fall or rise in profits
as for the ordinary shareholders. This can be illustrated very simply.

Suppose that a company has preference capital which must receive £2,500
y way of dividend before anything can be paid on the ordinary. If the
ompany has profits of £5,000 it would be possible to pay £2,500 to the
rdinary shareholders. If profits were halved the preference dividend could be
aid but there would be nothing for the ordinary shareholders. On the other
and if profits doubled to £10,000 then £7,500, three times as much could be
aid to the ordinary shareholders.

In contrast consider a similar company but having only ordinary share
apital. Profits of £2,500, £5,000, or £10,000 mean that these amounts could
e paid to the ordinary shareholders, but as there is no gearing the amounts
which could be paid to them vary in direct proportion to the changes in the
ompany's profits.

Gearing is beneficial to the ordinary shareholders in a company when
rofits are increasing as the whole benefit of the increase goes to them, always
ssuming that the interest and dividends on the prior charge capital have
lready been met. The position is, of course, the opposite should profits drop
s the effect of gearing is to cause the fall to bear disproportionately heavily
n the ordinary shareholders.

It should be noted, however, that gearing losses its effectiveness as the
roportion of the profits taken by the prior charge capital falls. For instance,
uppose that the adjusted profits of A.B. plc. increase by 100% to £179,750
hen by a further 100% to £359,500, and then by a further 100% to
719,000. As the result of the first increase the profits available for the
rdinary shareholders will rise by 124%, of the second by 111%, and of the
hird 105%.

When considering a company's gearing, reference should not be made to
he nominal amount of issued capital but to the fraction of the company's
rofits required to pay the interest and dividends. The method of doing this is
o set out the priority percentages. Alternatively, the equity gearing can be
measured by expressing the cost of paying the interest and dividends on the
rior charge capital as a percentage of the profits available. For A.B. plc, this
ould be £17,475/89,875 × 100 = 19.444%.

When the percentage gearing is known this can be applied to any new profits figure to calculate the effect on what is available for the ordinary. In the event of profits doubling the amount available for the ordinary would be £72,400 × 2 + 19.444% of £89,875 = £162,275.

Where it is preferred to think of gearing in terms of a multiple rather than as a percentage the appropriate figure can easily be obtained.

i.e. $\dfrac{100}{100 - 19.444} = 1.2414$

This multiple is applied to what would have been the proportionate increase or decrease for the ordinary and then added to or subtracted from what was originally available for the ordinary.

i.e. £72,400 + £72,400 × 1.2414 = £162,275.

Although emphasis has been given to the value of priority percentages as regards the ordinary shareholders, they are also of value to the holders of prior charge capital in assessing the safety of their interest or dividend payments. This is particularly so where the prior charge capital absorbs a large proportion of a company's profits.

12.25 Earnings on capital employed

While an investor may feel pleased with the performance of a particular company when earnings for the ordinary shares show a steady upward trend over a period of years he/she should look still further before being fully satisfied. The increase of earnings may have arisen as the result of more capital being employed in the business either through profits having been ploughed back or by fresh loan capital having been raised. So long as new loan capital employed by the company earns more than the cost of servicing it, the increased earnings derived from both these sources of capital will accrue to the benefit of the ordinary shareholder.

It is, however, important to examine the earnings rate of the company, not just as regards the nominal capital but in the light of the total resources being used by the company. A further statistic is required – earnings on asset employed – which is pre-tax profits plus loan stock interest expressed as a percentage of the issued capital, reserves, and loan capital after deducting therefrom any intangibles. For A.B. Company this would be

$\dfrac{£179,750}{1,046,000} \times 100 = 17.2\%$

If this percentage rises or remains steady the investor can remain satisfied and justifiably so. However, should it show a consistently downward trend he/she must be wary even though earnings for the ordinary shares are still increasing. The company is making less profitable use of the total asset employed, and should adverse factors arise as they may well do in the form of, say, a go-ahead competitor, or a credit squeeze, there may not be so very much to spare before a further drop in overall profitability bites severely into the ordinary earnings.

12.26 Profit margins

Since the Companies Act 1967 companies are required to publish their turnover which means that it is now possible to appraise their actual trading experience. Profit margins can be worked out by taking trading profits as a percentage of turnover. The ideal situation is, of course, that both turnover and profit margins should rise. Where turnover increases but profit margins fall the company is running faster only to stand still. Where both fall there are grounds for disquiet.

12.27 Cash flow

Companies can expand either by raising further capital by the various methods open to them or by ploughing back profits. They must also set aside from their profits each year a sufficient sum as depreciation in order that their fixed assets may be replaced when they wear out or become outdated.

It is therefore important to examine a company's internal capacity to generate money. This is described as its 'cash flow' and is normally taken to be the depreciation plus undistributed profits, although sometimes distributed profits may also be included. It is, however, the combination of the former two items which will indicate whether or not a company is likely to have to avail itself in the near future of the new capital market.*

12.3 Reserves

In most company balance sheets it will be found that after deducting liabilities from assets what is left over is greater than the issued capital. The difference is accounted for by the reserves, which together with the issued capital represent the stockholders' funds.

Reserves chiefly arise from the appropriation of profits for the purpose of expanding the business, replacing assets as they become worn out, equalizing dividends in bad years, and meeting various requirements of the business as they fall due. They may also arise from the issue of shares at a premium, from capital profits, or by the revaluation of fixed assets, for example writing up the value of buildings.

It is usual for companies to have both capital and revenue reserves although the obligation to distinguish between them has been abolished by the Companies Act 1967. This is a change only in what must be disclosed and

---

*Further information regarding a company's cash position is now available from the statement of sources and application of funds which accompanies its annual accounts.

does not affect what is legally distributable. Accordingly, capital reserves still cannot be distributed through the profit and loss account, for example in the payment of dividends.

In theory all revenue reserves could be available for the payment of dividends in future years. However, they may have been utilized years ago in the acquisition of assets required for the business and are therefore no longer in liquid form. A guide as to whether reserves may be drawn on to meet dividends in a profitless year may be obtained by noting the extent to which the company holds liquid assets, such as cash and investments.

12.4 Inflation accounting

At the beginning of this chapter mention was made of the importance of determining the real value of the assets appearing in a balance sheet as opposed to their book value which is conventionally based on historical cost. With a high rate of inflation these values appearing in a company's accounts do not give anything like a proper reflection of its position.

For instance, a company may appear to be making adequate profits but the amount which it is setting aside each year for depreciation of assets is related more to historical than replacement value. When these assets require to be renewed the company could be faced with liquidity problems. The increase in stock value between the beginning and end of an acccounting year may increase profit figures but stock can only be replaced at a higher cost. On the other hand, the value of real property may be very much understated, and the cost of borrowing falls in real terms as the years go by.

Much study and discussion as how best to cope with this problem has taken place but so far it has been found impossible for agreement to be reached on any system that would completely replace historical cost accounting. Following the acceptance of the Statement of Standard Accounting Practice No. 16 (SSAP 16) it is now for a trial period a requirement for all quoted companies (with a few exceptions such as insurance companies, property companies and investment trusts) and also for large unquoted companies, that alongside the historic accounts there is, as a supplement, current cost accounts consisting of a profit and loss account and a balance sheet together with explanatory notes.*

The adjustments in the supplementary figures include depreciation based on the current value to a company of its fixed assets, the replacement of the historic cost of stock sold during the period by its up-to-date value, and a monetary working capital adjustment (broadly, debtors less creditors) reflecting the higher cost of sales and purchases over the year. Normally these three items will reduce a company's profits as computed on the historic cost

---

* The period during which this was a requirement ended on 31 December 1984 and, so far, no replacement inflation accounting standard has been agreed. Meanwhile, some companies are continuing to produce the SSAP 16 supplementary form of accounts.

basis. However where a proportion of the net operating assets is financed by net borrowings, a gearing adjustment is made which adds back to profits that part of these deductions deemed not to be financed by shareholders.

A company will therefore have two sets of figures with the current cost accounts providing a more realistic assessment of the state of its affairs and usually indicating a lower level of profitability. In appraising these accounts it should however be kept in mind that companies have considerable discretion as to the valuation of assets and also in the choice of indices used for the calculation of operating adjustments.

12.5 Management

There is no doubt that first class people at the top make a vital difference to a company, no matter whether it is on the crest of a wave of expanding demand for its products, or whether it is striving to adapt itself in the face of adverse economic conditions. In times of ever-increasing change it is more important that the directors and senior executives of a company should be of the highest calibre than it is for there to be a good historical record. There is in business no guarantee that the past will repeat itself.

Certainly to a large extent results speak for themselves, but a progressive performance in the past may have been due to a driving personality who has left the company or to a board of directors which is now ageing. On the other hand, a mundane unspectacular company may spring to life as the result of the infusion of new blood. Assessing the effect of management changes or how the present management will cope with the challenges of the future is no easy matter. However, some indication of the capabilities of the personalities involved may sometimes be gleaned by perceptive reading of the financial press.

12.6 Sources of information

The basic information which a potential investor may require about a company is contained in its annual report and accounts together with the chairman's statement, supplemented nowadays by interim reports. It is not necessary for him to go to the trouble of obtaining the original documents as there are various sources from which he can get hold of all the essential details over a considerable period of years in summarized form.

Chief among these are the cards published for each individual company – and frequently updated – by the Exchange Telegraph Company. As well as producing much statistical data all the recent official company statements are also recorded. Most brokers subscribe to this service and are willing to make it available for the use of clients.

For the history of a company's business activities, details of capital issued, its subsidiaries, and practical matters such as the address of its registered office or transfer office, reference may be made to the *Stock Exchange*

Official Year Book. This volume also contains full information as regards the terms of issue of gilt-edged securities.

   The most up-to-date source of a company's activities is the financial press from which, as well as the factual reports, much enlightened comment can also be obtained. The leading journals in this connection are the specialist *Financial Times* published daily and the weekly *Investors Chronicle*. Nowadays most national newspapers provide valuable, although necessarily less comprehensive, information in their financial columns.

Typical question

The issued share capital of X.Y. plc consists solely of £20 million ordinary stock, the current price of a £1 stock unit being 220p. The pre-tax profits all earned in the United Kingdom were £4 million and a dividend of 7.35p per stock unit was paid. Corporation tax was at the rate of 50% and basic rate/ACT 30%. Calculate 1 dividend yield; 2 earnings yield; 3 PE ratio; 4 cover for dividend.

Suggested answer

1   Dividend yield $= \dfrac{\text{Dividend per stock unit (gross)}}{\text{Price of stock unit}} \times 100$

$= 7.35 \times 10/7 \div 220 \times 100$

$= 4.8\%$

2   Earnings yield $= \dfrac{\text{'Full earnings' for each ordinary £1 stock unit}}{\text{Price of each £1 stock unit}} \times 100$

$= \dfrac{£2,857,143/20,000,000}{2.20} \times 100$

$= 6.5\%$

'Full earnings' arrived at as follows:

Pre-tax profits	...	...	...	...	...	£4,000,000
Corporation tax at 50%	...	...	...	£2,000,000	
Less ACT	...	...	...	...	...	857,143	1,142,857

Largest possible distribution from current year's earnings plus related ACT (£2,000,000 × 10/7)   £2,857,143

3   The PE ratio is the number of years which it would take the company to earn (earnings being calculated on a 'nil distribution' basis) for each ordinary stock unit the present market price of the unit.

Pre-tax profits	...	...	...	...	...	£4,000,000
Corporation tax at 50%	...	...	...	...	...	2,000,000
Earnings if no distribution made	...	...	...	£2,000,000

$$\text{PE ratio} = \frac{\text{Price of each £1 stock unit}}{\text{Earned for each £1 stock unit}}$$

$$= \frac{£2.20}{2,000,000/20,000,000} = 22$$

4   Cover for dividend $= \dfrac{\text{Profits available for dividend}}{\text{Cost of dividend}}$

$$= \frac{£2,000,000}{1,470,000} = 1.36 \text{ times}$$

Additional questions

1   A company's report and accounts are important to an investor, but what items in those accounts have particular significance to him/her? Give reasons fully.

(The Institute of Bankers, *Investment*)

2   (a)   State what is meant by 'gearing', and illustrate your answer by means of examples.

    (b)   Explain the general proposition that high gearing is advantageous in good times, and low gearing safest when trading conditions are unfavourable.

(The Institute of Bankers in Scotland, *Theory and Practice of Investment*)

3   What reservations must be borne in mind in assessing the information contained in a company's balance sheet?

4   A company has the following capital structure:

£300,000 7% unsecured loan stock 1980/85.

£250,000 4.2% (formerly 6%) cumulative preference stock.

200,000 ordinary shares of £1 each fully paid.

Profits after corporation tax at the rate of 50% are £95,000.

A dividend of 10.5p per share is paid on the ordinary shares. Calculate the priority percentages. Explain the advantages of doing so, particularly from the point of view of the safety of the ordinary dividend.

5   What statistical data would persuade you that a company's shares could be regarded as being in the 'growth' category?

6   Where, apart from a company's accounts, can the information relevant to its past record and present development be found?

13 Spreading the risk

The purchase of ordinary shares frequently turns out to be a profitable venture, but unfortunately it can also at times result in substantial or complete loss of capital. There is always the danger of a company meeting with unexpected difficulties and accordingly an investor is ill-advised to put all his/her eggs in one basket. The investor's equity stake should not consist entirely of the shares of one company but should be spread among first class companies engaged in various spheres of activity.

One snag as far as the small investor is concerned is that his funds may be so limited that he could only acquire a diversified list of investments if he were to purchase them in extremely trivial quantities. This would be expensive commissionwise and he would not make himself popular with his stockbroker.

There are also many people of not so moderate means who are generally aware of the attractions of owning ordinary shares but have neither the time nor the inclination to make a close study of the factors involved. For such individuals investment and unit trusts provide an ideal medium for participation in the advantages of equity investment.

In many important ways investment and unit trusts are similar. The principal of both is that by the purchase of a single holding the investor acquires an interest in a large number of companies, perhaps even hundreds. The investor also gets the benefit of the management of experts of the trust portfolios. As well as containing a wide selection of stocks of companies in this country, such portfolios may also include a substantial proportion of overseas holdings, the supervision of which is much more difficult for the individual investor owing to the additional problems caused by their distant location, such as the obtaining and appreciation of information, not to mention the added complication of currency fluctuations.

Although by investing through trusts an individual safeguards himself against disastrous loss of capital arising from the misfortunes of one or two companies, the prices of shares and units move up and down in concert with the general trend of equity markets. A purchaser certainly cannot assume that his holding will increase steadily in value from the date he acquires it. If he had made his purchase at the top of a bull market the position may be quite the reverse and many months, if not years, may elapse before his holding recovers to the value at which it was bought. As in all investment the importance of good timing cannot be over-emphasized.

There are several technical differences between investment and unit trusts, and as these are not without practical significance each category must be considered individually.

13.1 Investment trusts

An investment trust is not legally a trust at all but a joint stock limited liability company. Its issued share capital, as with all such companies, is of a fixed amount and for this reason investment trusts are sometimes referred to as 'closed end trusts'. Additional capital can, of course, be issued from time to time subject to the normal company procedures for so doing.

13.11 Capital gearing

As well as equity capital, investment trusts almost invariably have preference and debenture stocks which provide an element of gearing to the benefit of the ordinary shareholders in times of rising market prices. The way in which income can be affected was illustrated in Chapter 12, but as one of the prime objectives of investment trusts is to increase the capital value of the ordinary share holdings it is also important to appreciate the relevancy of gearing in this connection. It must be borne in mind, however, that the effect of gearing will be reduced should the investment trust itself invest in fixed interest stocks.

Example
An investment trust has the following capital:

£5 million in debenture stock
£10 million in ordinary shares

It is invested as to £2.5 million in fixed interest stocks and £12.5 million in equities.
  Suppose the value of the equities rises by 20%.

Value of funds invested in equities would then be...	£15m
Add value of fixed interest holdings	2.5*
Total value of portfolio	17.5
Deduct value attributable to debenture stockholders	5.0
Value of assets attributable to ordinary shareholders	£12.5m

---

* For illustration purposes assumed to have remained constant although in practice it will also vary in value but normally to a more limited extent than equities.

Thus an increase in the value of the equities to the extent of 20% has increased the assets attributable to the ordinary shareholders by 25%. Similarly, if in the first place all the funds had been placed in equities the benefit of the rise to the ordinary shareholders would have been 30%. On the other hand, if £5 million of the funds had been placed in fixed interest stocks the capital gearing would have been neutralized and an increase in assets attributable to the ordinary would be directly proportionate to the increase in value of the equities.

Less frequently investment trusts may have negative gearing as the result of their fixed interest investment exceeding the amount of prior charge capital raised. The effect of this is to reduce the benefit to the ordinary shareholders of any given rise in the value of the equity content of the portfolio.

Example
An investment trust has the following capital:

£2.5 million in debenture stock
£10 million in ordinary shares

It is invested as to £5 million in fixed interest stocks and £7.5 million in equities.

Suppose the value of the equities rise by 20%.

Value of funds invested in equities would then be...	...	...			£9m
Add value of fixed interest holdings	...	...	...	...	5.0*
Total value of portfolio	...	...	...	...	...	£14.0
Deduct value attributable to debenture stockholders		...	...	2.5
Value of assets attributable to ordinary shareholders		...	...	£11.5m

Here a rise of 20% in value of the equities has been geared down to an increase of 15% in the assets attributable to the ordinary shareholders.

When equity shares fall gearing has the opposite effect on the value of the assets attributable to the ordinary shareholders, i.e. positive gearing is a disadvantage and negative gearing an advantage.

13.12 Asset values

The preceding paragraphs have been concerned with the assets attributable to the ordinary shareholders. This is but one step away from asset value – sometimes known as the break-up value – per ordinary share which is

---

* Again assumed constant.

obtained by dividing the total attributable assets by the number of issued ordinary shares.

While the asset value of each ordinary share has a significant influence on the market price of the share, the actual price is governed by the normal market forces of supply and demand. When there are more buyers than sellers about the price rises and when sellers are in preponderance the price falls.

If the market price is above the break-up value, the shares are said to be at a premium; if less, at a discount. Usually the shares of most trusts are at a discount on their asset value, the extent of which depends on the swings of stock market opinion. For example, a share with a net asset value of £1.20 may be priced around £1.08, i.e. at a discount of 10%.†

When calculating the net asset value per ordinary share there is the alternative method of deducting the prior charge capital at its market value as opposed to its nominal value. As the market value may be well below the nominal value this practice inflates the asset value.

Investment trusts do not distribute the whole of their income but retain a proportion, now restricted by the capital gains tax provisions, as a reserve and also for investment for the ultimate benefit of shareholders. This retention of income is sometimes given as one of the reasons for the 'area of undervaluation' in the market price of investment trust shares.

The considerable divergence in the discounts or premiums on the asset values in individual trusts is based on the market rating of their future prospects. Here the degree of expertise with which the management looks after the portfolio is of paramount importance. Management is not always easy to assess but when it is of the highest calibre it is an 'intangible' well worth more than a little extra in the way of cost. Calculations to measure the skill of management based on past record are in fact made by brokers and others closely concerned with the investment trust market.

13.13 Marketability

A problem with some of the smaller trusts is to acquire a holding as most of the shares are tightly held and the market is narrow. With the larger trusts, of which there is a considerable number, no such difficulty arises and the shares can be purchased at any time. Another feature of the investment trust market is that its rises and falls tend to lag behind those of ordinary share markets as a whole.

---

† While at many times in the past this might have been a typical discount, in recent years there have been considerable fluctuations and occasionally discounts have been as much as 30–40%.

13.14 The spread

The majority of investment trusts conform to the conventional pattern of being very largely committed to equities and having a wide spread of investment throughout commerce and industry in this country together with a stake in overseas companies, principally in the United States of America.

There are a few specialized trusts whose funds are invested mainly in a particular sector of industry, such as electronics or oil or in a specific geographical area, for example, the Far East. Usually the name should indicate when a trust of this nature is involved, but it is always a sound idea to study the analysis of holdings in order to ensure that the desired diversification of investment is being provided.

13.15 Split capital trusts

There are some variations from the traditional investment trust pattern, arising mainly from the all too familiar burden of heavy taxation. One such innovation is the split capital trust which is a trust with two classes of nominal capital – income shares and capital shares. The income shares receive all income earned by the whole trust capital whereas the capital shares, which consequently receive no income, get all the appreciation. This type of trust has a fixed life, perhaps twenty years, after which the income shares are repaid at par and the whole of the residual assets are divided among the capital shareholders.

The splitting of the capital provides the capital shares with a high measure of gearing as far as entitlement to the division of assets is concerned. The price of the capital shares tends, therefore, to fluctuate more violently than the value of the shares in the underlying portfolio. The moral is to be cautious as regards buying such shares when markets are high as there is an inherent loss potential of considerably magnitude, but when markets are low they offer the prospect of more than average capital growth. Owing to the swing in prices there is scope for successful 'trading' in the shares as opposed to holding them as long-term investments.

The income shares provide holders with a good starting income, at least as far as equity investment is concerned, together with the prospects of increasing dividends throughout the period of the trust. They are not so risky as the capital shares but the drawback, of course, is that when repayment at par takes place the value of money will almost certainly have depreciated. If purchased above par there will also be loss of capital in money terms.

There are further variations of this theme such as the introduction of a third type of capital in the form of debenture stock. This is an additional source of gearing from which the income shares can eventually also derive benefit once the income earned on the capital provided by the debenture stockholders exceeds the net cost of meeting the interest on it.

13.16 'B' Shares

Another development has been the issue by investment trusts of 'B' shares which rank in all respects with the ordinary shares except that instead of receiving cash dividends they receive an annual scrip issue, also in 'B' shares. Originally the amount of the scrip issue was equivalent at ruling prices to the gross amount of dividend paid on the income ranking ordinary shares. However, following the introduction of imputation tax the majority of trusts with 'B' shares after some initial hesitation accepted that the scrip issue should be equivalent to the actual cash dividend paid on the ordinary without taking into account the related tax credit. To compensate 'B' shareholders for this reduction in the amount of their annual entitlement a once and for all small additional scrip issue was made to them.

'B' shares with the annual scrip issue equal to the actual cash dividend offer no particular attraction to the basic rate taxpayer and they are positively disadvantageous to the non-taxpayer. Since the Finance Act (No. 2) 1975 made the recipient liable to higher rate tax on the appropriate amount of cash (i.e. the equivalent net dividend) grossed up at basic rate they have ceased to have their obvious appeal for high rate taxpayers.

Most of the 'B' shares on issue may be converted into the ordinary at a certain date after the close of each annual accounting year.

13.17 Taxation

Investment trusts are liable to pay tax at the ruling corporation tax rate on their income. However, as dividends received from United Kingdom companies are already 'franked' no further impost arises on income derived from this source.

The position is different as far as overseas income is concerned as although double taxation relief is allowed for the withholding tax deducted abroad it is not allowed in respect of the corporation tax paid in the overseas country. Investment trusts must therefore pay United Kingdom corporation tax on this income, although any interest paid by the trust on its loan capital together with its own administration expenses may be offset against this overseas income before the amount chargeable to corporation tax is computed. Taxation thus bears heavily on trusts with a sizeable proportion of their funds invested outside the United Kingdom. Such trusts are accordingly more attractive for those seeking capital growth rather than current income.

So long as they comply with certain conditions trusts are exempt from capital gains tax (see Section 10.131). These conditions are:

(a)   The trust's revenue must be derived wholly or mainly from shares and securities.

(b)   The trust must not have more than a certain proportion of its assets in one holding. This proportion is usually 15% but there are exceptions.

(c)   The trust's shares must be quoted on a United Kingdom stock exchange and it must not be a 'close' company.

(d)   All the realized capital gains must be retained by the trust.
(e)   The trust must not retain more than 15% of the income which it
      receives on its underlying holdings. (This condition has been relaxed
      during a period of dividend restraint.)

13.2 Unit trusts

The legal status of unit trusts is quite different from that of investment
trusts as they are constituted by a deed of trust which, in the case of all
authorized unit trusts, must be approved by the Department of Trade.

13.21 Trustees and managers

The deed of trust appoints a trustee which is invariably a bank or an
insurance company. The functions of the trustee are to hold the securities
and cash belonging to the trust, to maintain a register of unit holders, to
issue share certificates, and to pay the dividends. The trustee also keeps a
general watching brief over the other party to the arrangement, the
management company. As laid down in the Prevention of Fraud (Investments) Act 1958 all advertisements must be approved by the trustee,
particularly from the point of view that no statements are made which
might be misleading to the investor. The trustee and the management
company must be completely independent of each other.

   The managers are responsible for the investment policy of the trust, the
trustee only being concerned to the extent that no investments are acquired
of a type not authorized by the trust deed or in excess of the permitted
proportion of the total portfolio. The trust deed may lay down, for instance,
that not more than 5% of the total funds may be invested in one company.

   The managers attend to the general administration of the trust and have
the important function of selling units to the public. Although application
can be made for a Stock Exchange quotation nearly all the buying or selling
of units by the public is done through the managers, either directly or by
utilizing the services of an intermediary such as a bank or a stockbroker.

13.22 The managers' prices

The prices at which the managers will buy or sell units (the bid and offer
prices) are computed according to a formula laid down by the Department
of Trade and Industry. These prices are based on a valuation of the
underlying securities after taking into account such items as dealing costs,
dividends due since the last ex dividend date, and in the case of the offer
price the managers' initial charge. There is usually a spread of around $6\frac{1}{2}$–
$7\frac{1}{2}$% between the managers' bid and offer prices, although still keeping
within the formula it would still be possible for it to be in the region of 12–
13%.

   When a fund is expanding, i.e. more units are being issued than are being
sold back to the managers, the prices are based on the offer price of the

underlying securities. When a fund is contracting they are based on the bid prices unless the managers are prepared to take a loss. It is therefore in the interests of existing holders that a fund should be expanding as they then get a higher price for their units when they wish to realize them.

Apart from this technicality the prices of units are not, as in the case of investment trusts, governed by the supply and demand for them. When there are more investors buying units than there are holders wishing to sell them back to the managers further units are created. On the other hand, when there are more sellers than buyers the managers liquidate some of the underlying holdings and reduce the number of units on issue. Because of this flexibility in the number of units in existence unit trusts are sometimes described as 'open end trusts'.

Most managers are willing to deal in the units of their trusts on any business day, in which event daily valuations of the underlying securities are made. In a few trusts, however, dealing only takes place at longer intervals, say, fortnightly or once a month. This reduces administration costs as does also the higher minimum subscription which some trusts impose in order to avoid having a large number of small uneconomic holdings on their books.

13.23 Block offers

Managers are keen to expand their funds and one method of doing this is by block offers of a certain number of units to the public at a price which remains fixed for a few days. The block offers are attended by a lot of publicity in the form of newspaper advertisement, which media also contains a form of application for units. A few years ago probably most holders acquired their initial units as the result of such offers, but price wise it may not necessarily be the best time for purchasing them.

13.24 Income

While there is no legal compulsion on unit trusts to pay away all their available income to unit holders it is the usual practice to do so. The reason for this is that whether such income is distributed or not the tax authorities treat it as being the unit holders' taxable income for the year in which it is received by the trust. A few trusts with 'accumulating' units, however, do plough back all their income, and most have schemes whereby net dividends can be retained and used to purchase further units on unit holders' behalf.

Generally the provisions for corporation tax and capital gains tax as outlined in Section 13.17 apply also to unit trusts, although owing to the difference in capital structure some of the conditions are not applicable to unit trusts.

Since 31 March 1980 authorized unit trusts investing only in British Government or other UK public authority stocks have been liable to tax at basic rate on their income instead of corporation tax.

13.25 Management charges

The charges which management companies may levy on unit holders were until December 1979 restricted by law. Over a twenty year period of a trust the maximum charge permitted was a total of $13\frac{1}{4}$%. Since this legal restriction was lifted most groups have increased their charges although the pattern remains the same with an initial charge of, say, 5% included in the offer price and an annual levy in the region of $\frac{3}{4}$–1% on the value of the trust portfolio deducted from income.

Another source of income to the managers can arise from dealing in the units, i.e. buying them back from investors and subsequently selling them on to new holders at a profit.

13.26 Wide choice

Most management companies have several unit trusts under their wing as the result of which the companies benefit from the spread of costs of administration. Each unit trust in such a group has a completely separate identity but to a certain extent they are complementary to each other in that they cater for different requirements.

Some go all out for capital growth, others place high current income as their prime objective, and there are middle of the road trusts which endeavour to strike a happy medium between both. The investor must decide what best suits his own personal circumstances. He should, however, be careful not to choose a specialist trust such as one investing entirely in, say, commodity, insurance, or overseas shares if what he really requires is a wide diversification of investment. Following the changed tax charge in 1980 (see Section 13.24) a spate of gilt-edged unit trusts have come into being, making available managed funds in this type of investment to individual investors.

In 1985 a new type of unit trust, known officially as a 'unit portfolio managed fund', became available from some companies with several trusts under their management thus providing a double layer of investment supervision. These 'funds of funds', promoted under varying descriptive titles, are subject to certain conditions among which are that the top fund can buy units only in its own sub funds and must spread its investments over at least four sub funds with none accounting for more than half the total. Only one initial charge is allowed but two sets of annual charges are permissible. An advantage of this type of managed fund is that switches can be made among the underlying funds without incurring capital gains tax as could arise if an individual investor switched funds at a profit himself and his annual exemption was exceeded.

With the large number of unit trusts in existence the investor may understandably have difficulty in knowing which to choose. To aid him the financial press and other specialist journals from time to time publish performance tables covering past periods and pick out their versions of the 'top twenty'. While these are obviously not conclusive as to what the future may bring, other things being equal it would be difficult to argue against the selection of a trust with a consistently good record in the past.

As between investment trusts and unit trusts professional opinion tends to favour investment trusts for the long term in view of their gearing and lower administrative costs. In terms of ease of purchase, however, there is no doubt that the unit trusts cater for the small investor.

13.3 Offshore funds

Offshore funds are funds constituted and located outside the United Kingdom, such location normally having been chosen in order that favourable tax treatment may thereby be obtained. While the underlying holdings of many of these funds are spread internationally (including the United Kingdom) some are of a more specialist nature. The majority of the funds are of the unit trust type in that they are open-ended although a few operate on investment trust principles.

It is important to remember that while tax advantages may accrue through investing in overseas funds these funds are not subject, like United Kingdom authorized unit trusts, to DoT supervision and they may in some cases be situated in countries where there is very little jurisdiction protecting the investor against exploitation by those to whom he has entrusted his money and about whom he might find difficulty in obtaining sufficient reliable information in order to form a proper assessment. This problem can, however, be largely overcome by sticking to funds which are backed by substantial United Kingdom institutions.

The tax consequences of investing in offshore funds require careful scrutiny by purchasers in the light of their particular residence and domicile. The chief attraction until recently for United Kingdom investors was the exemption of offshore funds from capital gains tax which means that the portfolio can be actively managed unhindered by capital gains tax considerations. On the sale of his holding the United Kingdom investor is liable to tax on his gains but during the period of his investment the money which would have been required to meet the tax on the gains of a United Kingdom liable fund is still working for his benefit. However this attraction has been eliminated by the capital gains tax exemptions according to United Kingdom investment and unit trusts.

As authorized United Kingdom unit trusts and investment trusts providing world-wide spread of investment are readily available to the United Kingdom resident there is under present tax and legislation, and with Exchange Control having been removed, no great incentive for his utilizing offshore funds for this purpose. They do provide certain tax advantages for non-residents and also capital transfer tax benefits to the non-domiciled investor who wishes his wealth or at least part of it to be in effect looked after by

United Kingdom investment managers operating through the medium of an offshore fund, say in the Channel Islands. Offshore gilt-edged funds have the attraction that dividends are paid without the deduction of tax although for the United Kingdom investor this may mean that his tax liability has been deferred.

13.4 Equity linked life assurance

The difficulty of timing a purchase is one which confronts all investors. The managers of unit trust have long been aware of this problem and have encouraged investors to join schemes whereby a regular fixed monthly sum is invested in units. This prevents an investor from buying a large number of units at the wrong time. It has the advantage that more units are bought when prices are low than when they are high and is known as pound averaging.

This idea was the forerunner of unit trust linked life assurance which expanded at a tremendous pace during the 1960s. In order to promote this several unit trust managements formed subsidiary assurance companies. However legislation was introduced in 1984 denying life assurance relief for premiums paid under life assurance policies in respect of contracts made after 13 March 1984 and this important factor must be kept in mind when reading the remainder of this chapter. Contracts made prior to this date are not affected and there is accordingly an added incentive to keep open ended policies, where the relief continues to be available, in force for as long as is reasonably possible.

This removal of life assurance relief makes direct investment in unit trust savings schemes more attractive for most investors as, apart from their greater flexibility, the tax factor has tilted in favour of unit trusts. The reason for this is that unit linked insurance funds are liable for capital gains tax whereas unit trusts are exempt as is also the individual investor provided his gains when realized are covered by his annual exemption. Qualifying unit trust linked policies still have some attraction for higher rate taxpayers who would be paying this additional tax on unit trust income received by them direct but who can collect the policy proceeds in due course free of tax, the insurance company in the meantime having paid tax on its income at around the basic rate.

13.41 The premium

There are two types of scheme, one lasting for a fixed period of years and the other being open ended in that it can go on indefinitely until such time as the investor or to be more technically accurate the policy holder decides to surrender the policy. A fixed premium is paid under banker's or other standing orders usually monthly but sometimes at quarterly, half-yearly, or yearly intervals. This premium is split into two parts, by far the largest of which is used to purchase units in the fund selected by the investor and these units are then allocated to him. The income of the fund is normally automatically reinvested for the benefit of policy holders.

Premiums paid at less frequent intervals attract slightly better terms than those paid monthly. At the beginning of a plan a charge in some form – perhaps the non-investment of the first two monthly premiums – is invariably made to meet the costs of setting it up.

The proportion of the premium invested in units, usually in the region of 90–95%, depends upon the investor's age at commencement and also where fixed period plans are concerned on the length of the period for which they are to run. The smaller part of the premium goes to the fund which has to provide the assurance cover when participants die during the currency of their plan.

13.42 Benefits

On the maturity of a fixed term plan the holder receives the units allocated to him or alternatively their cash value at the prevailing bid price. The open ended plan continues until the holder decides to surrender the policy whereupon he receives the bid value of the units. In both types of plan there will be some provision for a minimum sum payable, for instance, that on maturity or surrender after fifteen years no loss can accrue to the holder in that he cannot receive less than the amount of the total premiums paid.

On the death of the holder during the currency of the fixed term plan his heirs normally receive all the units bought so far plus cash equal to the remaining premiums he would have paid under the policy had he survived. With the open ended plan the death benefit may also be based on the bid value of the units but in both types of plan there is a guaranteed death payment which frequently is in excess of the minimum requirement in order to obtain life assurance tax relief (see Section 13.43).

It should be noted, however, that before all benefits related to the value of the units are paid out a deduction may be made therefrom by the assurance company to cover the tax on its realized capital gains. Otherwise so long as the policy remains within the qualifying category no other tax is payable.

13.43 Life assurance relief (pre 14 March 1984 policies)

An advantage of unit trust linked life assurance is that if the policy is a qualifying one the premiums are eligible for normal life assurance relief.

The qualifying requirements for policies taken out after 1 April 1976 are basically that the premiums must be payable annually or more frequently for a period of at least ten years and must be fairly evenly spread over the period. In the case of endowment policies (fixed term plans) the sum assured must not be less than 75% of the premiums payable throughout the whole term of the policy. However, where the life assured's age exceeds fifty-five years at the date of commencement of the policy this percentage is reduced by 2% for each year above fifty-five. For whole life policies with surrender values (open ended plans) the requirement is that the sum payable on death is not less than 75% of total premiums on the assumption that death occurs at age seventy-five.

The relief is 15% of gross premiums up to a total of £1,500 or one-sixth of an individual's income for tax purposes for the fiscal year, whichever is the greater. It is obtained by the life assured paying a net premium to the assurance company and the latter recovering the balance from the Inland Revenue.

Assume that a man, aged 41, takes out a fifteen year qualifying policy with monthly premiums of £10 and $93\frac{1}{2}$% of the premiums are invested in units.

Total annual premium of £120 of which $93\frac{1}{2}$% invested   ... £112.20
Net premium paid by life assured to company £102.00
(Tax relief 15% of £120 = £18)

Therefore for a net outlay of £102 the man is allocated units costing £112.20 together with 'free' life assurance.

13.44 Discontinuance

At any time during the currency of a fixed term plan the holder may normally discontinue it and withdraw the units accumulated on his behalf subject to the deduction of capital gains tax. He may, however, find himself with a higher rate tax liability on the excess of the value of the units over the contributions paid if he does this within the first ten years. A similar liability may arise from the early surrender of an open ended plan.

Early discontinuance will also bring the plans within the Inland Revenue 'claw back' tax relief provisions for pre 14 March 1984 policies surrendered or made 'paid up' within four years. In this event the proceeds payable to the holder will be reduced* by tax relief previously obtained.

13.45 Priority – assurance or investment?

A disadvantages of equity linked policies is that despite the guaranteed sum payable at death, the actual sum paid should this contingency occur might prove disappointing if stock markets were at a low ebb at the vital time. At maturity or surrender, also, markets may be low and the plan holder may find himself receiving less than he had anticipated. He may, of course, be able to retain the units for a recovery in price, but it is possible that at this particular juncture in his life – perhaps retirement – he requires cash. It could be most disappointing if the units a year or two before the maturity of the policy had been standing at a much higher level.

---

* This reduction is subject to a ceiling as follows:

Time of surrender	Claw-back	'Ceiling'
In first two years	15%	Surrender value less 85%
In third year	10%	Surrender value less 90%
In fourth year	5%	Surrender value less 95%

A point worth bearing in mind is that with a conventional with profits endowment policy the benefit of gains during its currency would have been periodically consolidated, by means of bonuses, with the nominal amount payable on death or maturity.

A would-be participant in unit trust linked life assurance should be clear as to his objectives. If his main purpose is to obtain the maximum protection for his dependants in the event of his premature decease he should consult with an insurance broker to obtain particular requirements on the most favourable terms by means of conventional life assurance. Should this first priority be largely catered for, or its necessity not arise, unit trust linked life assurance is a worry free method of building up a stake in equities with the extra of life assurance thrown in.

In conclusion it must be mentioned that following the surge in demand for unit trust linked life assurance many life assurance companies have felt compelled to introduce, as an addition to their wares, a wholly equity linked life policy.

13.5 Single premium policies or bonds

Unit trust management groups and assurance companies also provide facilities for the investment of lump sums linked to life assurance through single premium policies. In this case usually the whole premium is used to purchase units on behalf of the participant although an initial charge of around 5% may be included in the price of the units. Usually nowadays, the units are of the accumulating type whose value is increased by income accruing from the underlying investments.

The units may be in an equity fund (frequently a unit trust), a property fund, a fixed interest fund, a money fund (taking advantage of the best deposit rates), an international fund or what is variously described as a managed fund, flexible fund, three-way fund, etc. However, whatever name is given to the last type of fund the point is that the underlying investments are a mixture of equities, property, and fixed interest stocks. The investor therefore at a stroke obtains an interest in a very diversified range of holdings. The managers of the fund endeavour to readjust the amount committed to the three sectors from time to time according to what they judge to be the market outlook. However, practical considerations frequently preclude dramatic changes in the proportions held being effected in the short term.

The insurance benefit under these policies is of limited value. For example, at age twenty-one a single premium of £1,000 may provide basic guaranteed cover of only £2,500 (although it is frequently somewhat higher) and by age sixty this may have fallen to the amount of the premium, £1,000. It is, of course, to be hoped that if death occurs during the currency of a policy which has been in existence for a reasonable period of time the value of the units will be more than the basic sum assured, in which case they determine the value of the benefit under the policy.

The policy can be surrendered at any time (although see Section 13.62) whereupon the holder receives the equivalent cash value in his units subject to a deduction made by the assurance company in respect of capital gains tax. This deduction may also be made when payment arises on death.

The question will normally arise in the potential investor's mind as to whether he should purchase bonds or unit trusts. As well as assessing his investment requirements he will take into account his own tax position and that of the underlying funds. For the basic rate taxpayer the unit trust will usually be more tax efficient than the insurance (bond) fund.

13.51 Higher rate tax liability

If the holder is a higher rate taxpayer he or his executor, may be liable to pay tax on the whole of the excess of the proceeds over the premium paid. However, although the whole of the excess is liable to tax, in order to determine the rate payable it is the excess of the proceeds divided by the number of complete years during which the policy was in force which is added to the taxpayer's income for the year in which the proceeds are received. This is known as top-slicing.

For example, suppose a single premium of £2,000 is paid and after ten years the policy is surrendered for £3,000. The whole gain is £1,000 but the annual portion is £100 and it is this £100 which is added to the policy holder's income to determine his rate of tax. Should this put him into the range where he is liable to tax at, say, 60% then his tax bill in respect of the policy proceeds will be £1,000 at 30% (60% − basic rate of 30%) = £300. However, if his other income is, say, £5,000 the addition of another £100 will not bring him into a rate of tax higher than the basic 30%, so he has nothing to pay.

13.52 Use in special situations

Although they have been stripped of the tax advantages accruing to qualifying policies nevertheless single premium bonds still have uses in meeting special situations.

For example, a high rate taxpayer may find them useful as a means of accumulating capital during his working life. Throughout the currency of the policy no higher tax rate will be payable as the income belongs to the assurance company (paying tax at 30% on dividends and 37½% on interest and rents) so, therefore, more income will be available for the purchase of additional units or for reinvestment in the fund than if the investor himself was receiving income in respect of a straight purchase of the same number of units. He may arrange for the surrender of the policy when his income drops on retirement and thus avoid, or at any rate effect a reduction in, the amount of higher rate tax which would otherwise be payable but for the existence of the policy.

Single premium bonds are attractive where an individual's income fluctuates substantially between one year and another. They can be cashed in a poor year. Also, the wife of a high rate taxpayer might buy bonds but not cash them until her income has dropped following the death of her husband, or it may be desirable to make a settlement on the minor children of a high rate taxpayer. Someone with a lump sum to invest might find it beneficial to purchase a single premium bond, probably a managed bond, and utilize the annual withdrawal facilities to pay the premiums of a qualifying policy. They are from time to time used in capital transfer tax avoidance schemes such as inheritance trusts.

This is a province of frequently changing legislation as well as technical complication. A specialist in these matters, such as an accountant, solicitor, or insurance broker should be consulted before action is taken.

13.53 'Income' from capital

With the intention mainly of catering for the smaller investor, there are bond withdrawal schemes for the purpose of providing him with an 'income'. The amount withdrawn each year may be, say, 6% of the value of the bond and if the bond increases in value by a greater percentage than the amount taken out by this method there will still be some appreciation in his capital remaining invested in the bond.

No basic rate tax liability arises in respect of these withdrawals but should the investor be liable to tax at higher rates he may find himself faced with an assessment.

New rules apply for each policy year falling wholly after 13 March 1975. A bondholder is allowed to set off against his withdrawal a 'premium allowance' equal to 5% per annum of the single premium. This allowance is cumulative up to a total of twenty years but withdrawals made before the policy anniversary after 13 March 1975 are ignored and the premium allowance excludes the percentages appropriate to the previous policy years.

Every year the excess value of withdrawals over the accumulated premium allowance is subject to higher rate tax. When a bond is finally cashed the chargeable gain (if any) is calculated by deducting the original premium plus the 'excess values' already taxed from the surrender value plus all previous withdrawals.

Example
Bond for £1,000 purchased 1 April 1975.
Annual withdrawals £60.
Final surrender 1 April 1985 for £650.
Each year for nine years there will be excess value of £10 (£60 − £50) liable to tax.
On final surrender the liability will be:
Surrender value £650

Add previous withdrawals	...	...	...	...	...	...	540
							£1,190
Less premium paid		...	...	...	...	£1,000	
Plus excess value	...	...	...	...	...	90	£1,090
							£100

If in fact a negative gain arises in the terminal calculation there is a provision of offsetting it against income for higher rate tax.

Top slicing relief (see Section 13.51) is applicable with the relevant number of years being:

1 On the first chargeable event – from the purchase of the bond.
2 On subsequent chargeable events, excluding final encashment of the bond – from the previous chargeable event.
3 On final encashment – from the purchase of the bond.

13.6 Property bonds

Perhaps the most striking feature in the field of single premium bonds has been the spectacular development of property bonds which has made investment in property readily available to the person in the street. While technically the bonds are single premium life assurance policies and are for legal purposes subject to the Insurance Companies Acts, they are in effect property unit trusts.

Authorized unit trusts are not permitted to invest directly in property as distinct from the shares in property companies. It should, however, be mentioned that there are unit trusts investing directly in property available to pension funds and other bodies with exempt tax status. Where all the owners of the units in such a trust are not liable for tax the trust itself is exempt from United Kingdom capital gains tax, and the unit holders themselves are able to recover the income tax paid by the trust on its income, net of property management expenses, when the income is distributed to them. The trusts are not liable for corporation tax. All literature issued by the trusts requires DoT approval and they are organized on much the same lines as other unit trusts.

13.61 Valuation

A distinction arises between unit trusts and property bonds as regards the valuation of the underlying holdings. With unit trusts the matter is relatively straightforward as the stocks and shares held have known market values. It is quite a different story with real property as the value is not really known until the propery is sold. What normally happens is that at least once a year the properties are subject to a full independent professional valuation and each month these values are adjusted by experts in order that current offer and bid prices can be published. However, no matter how experienced the valuer or how scientific his approach the valuations are largely a matter of opinion and it must be recognized that there could be considerable divergences in this respect between one expert valuer and another.

13.62 Liquidity

This could be a problem for companies issuing property bonds as properties are not so readily saleable as stocks and shares. The managers of the funds must, therefore, maintain a reasonable liquidity ratio to guard against the situation arising from a net redemption of bonds. Should this develop on any scale some of the managers reserve the right to defer encashment for six months. The provision may also apply to the property sector of a managed fund. Some bond funds do have substantial backing from major city institutions and where safety of investment is important purchasers should stick to bonds in this category.

13.63 Shares or bonds?

Investment in bricks and mortar has traditionally been an effective hedge against inflation. An investor is now offered the alternative of investing either in the shares of property companies or in property bonds. Although sophisticated city opinion tends generally to favour property shares the choice is not all that clear cut for the ordinary investor.

One of the attractions of the property company is its gearing which should, unless misfortune hits the company, redound in due course to the benefit of the ordinary shareholder. Property companies are also freer to plan their purchases and developments when they consider the time to be opportune whereas the bond funds must be influenced to a large extent by the rate of inflow of their funds. While some of the bond funds are entering the field of property development, in addition to the purchasing of established properties as investments, it is reckoned that the companies have the edge over them in this at times very profitable, albeit speculative, form of enterprise. With the companies, too, there is always the possible windfall of an unexpected takeover bid.

An important factor to be kept in mind is that the shares of property companies fluctuate much more violently in price than do the units of a property fund. While this obviously could be a source of quick profit it also means that a shareholder might be forced to sell at a substantial loss if he/she required his cash back when stock markets are low. For the small investor particularly there is more safety in a soundly backed property bond. The value of the units are unlikely to fall by 25% in the course of a fortnight as is by no means unheard of in the case of a share.

The comparative tax positions are worth considering although the imputation system does not bear so hard on the company as was the case when corporation tax was first introduced. Property companies pay corporation tax on income and 30% on capital gains. The shareholder's basic rate tax on dividends is discharged by the company's ACT but he may be liable to higher rates of tax and also capital gains tax if he sells his shares at a profit. Property bond funds are taxed as life assurance funds −37½% on income and 30% on realized capital profits. The bond holder pays neither tax on income nor on capital gains unless he is liable for higher rates of tax in the year when his bonds are cashed in which event he will be assessed as described in Section 13.51.

13.7 Friendly societies

Friendly societies issue insurance policies which have special advantages in that their insurance funds are completely exempt from tax and when policies mature the proceeds are free of all tax in the hands of the policy holder. Policies are available to anyone aged 18 to 70 but the main snag is that the amount which can be invested is restricted by law to £100 per annum this being paid over a period of ten years. In order that the policies have qualifying status, thus allowing the proceeds to be tax free, the sum assured is £750.

As in the investment of these funds the societies are subject to the Trustee Investments Act 1961 (see Section 15.23) at least half the amounts received must be invested in narrower range securities. The investment approach of the societies varies and this is something the potential policy holder will wish to investigate. Some societies invest 50% in equities either directly or through the medium of unit trusts while others commit their funds wholly to building societies. Here again is an unusual feature in that the friendly societies are able to receive building society interest on a gross basis by making a tax reclaim to the Inland Revenue.

If the investor surrenders a policy before the ten year period has been completed he suffers the disadvantage of not receiving the surrender value of the policy, only the premiums paid being returned. A point to note is that the friendly societies do not come within the Policyholders' Protection Act 1975 (see note to Section 1.6) and a factor which could influence the choice of society is the difference in their fee charging levels which in some instances seem rather high. However clearly their tax exempt status gives the societies a head start to outperform other funds providing a similar spread of underlying investment.

Societies are also prepared to accept lump sums of up to £1,000 the bulk of which they will temporarily hold on behalf of the investor in a building society or in the form of a single premium investment bond withdrawing sufficient of this each year to meet the annual premium. Alternatively they may purchase a temporary annuity. The normal rules of taxation apply to this lump sum investment whatever the arrangement.

Typical question

As manager of a growing pension fund which is completely free of restrictions on its investment policy, you are asked to report to the trustees on the possibility of investing in property:

1 By way of shares in property companies.
2 By way of units in a tax free property unit trust.
3 Direct in property.
Outline the memorandum which you would prepare.

(The Institute of Bankers, *Principles and Practice of Investment*)

Suggested answers

Investment in real property has in the past been effective as a hedge against inflation. There would appear to be no reason to suggest that it will not be likewise in the future.

When deciding how a stake in property should be acquired the pension fund's tax exempt status should be kept firmly in mind.

1 *Shares in property companies*
   A property company pays corporation tax (assumed at 50%) on its income, and tax at 30% on its capital gains. Shareholders not liable to tax can claim the basic rate tax credit in respect of income distributions paid to them. However, the company must pay mainstream corporation tax of at least 20% (with corporation tax at 50%), depending upon the amount of its distributions, on its taxable profits and this is not recoverable by tax exempt shareholders. Neither is the capital gains tax paid by the company. Investment by the fund in property company shares is, therefore, unattractive in view of the tax burden involved.

2 *Tax free property unit trusts*
   These trusts have been set up to cater for tax exempt funds wishing to invest in property and are exempt from capital gains tax. The trusts are liable for income tax on their income, net of property management expenses, but when the income is distributed the exempt funds are able to reclaim all the tax paid.

   The managers of the unit trusts are responsible for the selection of suitable properties and thereafter for the factoring. A good spread of property investment is obtained from the underlying portfolio.

   The unit trusts provide a simple and satisfactory method of investing in property.

3 *Direct investment in property*
   Such investment tax wise would be no different from 2. The pension fund would, however, require to obtain the services of experts to select suitable properties and advise on them from time to time. It would also require either to appoint factors to attend to the routine administrative matters connected with the properties or attend to them itself. These would include the letting of the property, rent collecting, insurance, attending to landlord's repairs, etc., and would involve a considerable amount of work.

   Investment by way of property unit trust or trusts would appear to be the most suitable course, although if the fund became really large, direct investment in property might be considered a feasible proposition.

Additional questions

1 What are the main differences between investment trusts and unit trusts. Discuss their advantages and disadvantages as an alternative to an individual portfolio.

   (The Savings Bank Institute, *Personal Savings and Investment*

2 Explain what is meant by split capital investment trusts. For what category of investor do they cater? Might they have any disadvantages?

3 Outline the tax position of investment and unit trusts.

4 Distinguish between the respective functions of the trustees and managers of unit trusts.

5 What is unit-linked insurance, and what are the advantages and disadvantages of such schemes?

   (The Institute of Bankers in Scotland, *Theory and Practice of Investment*

6 Property bonds have made a rapid advance in popularity over the past few years. What are property bonds, and what are the advantages and disadvantages of investing in them?

   (The Institute of Bankers, *Principles and Practice of Investment*

7 What are the tax implications of:
   (a) Cashing a single premium policy or bond;
   (b) Withdrawing an 'income' from a bond?

14 Market movements

The prices of stocks and shares are constantly varying and anyone with only a nodding acquaintance of the Stock Exchange will soon have realized that they may move quite widely over relatively short periods of time. Although long term the trend of ordinary shares as a whole may be upwards, this is by no means straight line appreciation but is the overall result of fluctuations of substantial dimension in both directions.

When the main way in which prices are moving is upwards this is known as a bull market and when the main movement is downwards, a bear market. Within these primary movements there are secondary reactions in the opposite direction lasting for a matter of weeks, or perhaps even months. The point is that in a bull market the falls peter out before making any great impact and in a bear market the rises are relatively not of great consequence. The secondary movements are themselves made up of a jagged pattern of the ups and downs of day-to-day prices.

Figure 14.1

Figure 14.1 illustrates how the shares constituting the *Financial Tim* Ordinary Share Index (see Section 14.21) behaved, day-to-day moveme being ignored, from the beginning of 1981 to the end of 1985.

Generally there is the tendency for all ordinary shares to be moving in same direction although individual sectors of the market may be affected special factors, for example tobacco shares as the result of a cancer scare mining shares following new ore discoveries. An individual price reaction a company's performance is frequently very much influenced by the gene trend. Excellent profit figures in a bull market would probably cause share price positively to race ahead, whereas the same figures during a be market might produce an indifferent response.

14.1 Factors affecting prices

The reasons for market movements are at times clear and logical. On oth occasions they may be a little obscure and can only be understood by discerning appreciation of the interplay of various influences involved. point to keep in mind is that active investors are always looking to future and endeavouring, often successfully, to anticipate events. As result of this, for example, a severe package of monetary and fiscal measur to contain inflation may not cause any fluctuation in gilt-edged stocks, the announcement of bumper profits and a dividend increase may have lit effect on a company's share price. The reason is not that these basic fact have been ignored but that they have been discounted in advance and t appropriate price adjustments already made.

14.11 Political

It is no secret that some governments are by their philosophy fundamenta unfavourably disposed towards private enterprise. Although for practi considerations they may be prepared to allow a mixed economy consisti of both nationalized industry and private enterprise to exist there is, to s the least of it, a lack of sympathy towards the interests of shareholders.

The measures which such governments can be expected to take increases in company taxation, particularly when profits rise, together wi restrictions on the raising of dividend payments. There will also be tendency towards more government control over industry coupled with gradual process of outright nationalization. The perpetuation indefinitely office of such a government would not augur brightly for ordina shareholders.

The political risks in some countries are greater than in others. Investme overseas has in some cases additional risks in that foreign governmen spurred by nationalistic as well as doctrinaire impulses, may legislate agai non-resident investors. This may be by fiscal means, or perhaps exchan rates will be manipulated to their disadvantage. These possibilities must borne in mind both as regards overseas companies and British compan ith substantial overseas operations. There is always the danger of ationalization of assets without payment of fair compensation.

4.12 Economic

rofits are the foundation on which a company's prosperity rests and ccordingly share prices are closely tied to the economic climate, both in this ountry and beyond. In times of recession when business is slack it is hard for ompanies to make profits and the converse is the case when trade is xpanding.

In this country since the Second World War successive governments have ll regarded it as their duty not to let the economy run unbridled the full cycle etween boom and depression, with all the hardship attendant on the latter. nstead they have endeavoured to maintain it on the even keel of steady xpansion. In this, unfortunately, they have frequently been hindered by alance of payments problems when it has become imperative to damp down usiness activity in order to overcome the immediate crisis.

The sort of action they have required to take has been to raise interest rates, npose credit restrictions on banks, increase down payments for hire urchase and reduce repayment periods, increase taxes in the purchase of oods, impose wage freezes, and a variety of other restrictive measures most f which are not good for company profits and therefore share prices. The pposite is, of course, true when such measures are relaxed.*

It must also be mentioned that the economies of industrialized countries ffect each other, and in particular the state of business activity in the USA as a profound influence on the economy of Great Britain and many other ountries.

Another compelling factor since the Second World War has been the march f inflation and with it the distrust of fixed interest stocks. This has resulted a a weight of money which formerly would have been committed to fixed iterest stocks now finding its way to ordinary shares, thus supporting them t higher levels. Inflationary conditions generally, but not always, enable igher profits to be earned. Dividends can, therefore, be increased and this to ome extent at least compensates for the falling value of money.

The changed relationship between fixed interest stocks and ordinary shares ; exemplified by what is known as the 'reverse yield gap'. Until 1959 the ield on undated gilt-edged as represented by 2½% Consols was less than the verage yield of the stocks constituting the *Financial Times* Ordinary Share ndex. The reason for this was that ordinary shares were regarded as being iskier investments than gilt-edged stocks. The amount by which the *inancial Times* Ordinary yield exceeded that on 2½% Consols was referred

---

Since 1979 an over-riding objective of the Government has been the reduction of what had ecome an alarmingly high rate of inflation principally by control of the money supply.

to as the 'yield gap'. Inflation has so altered investors' assessment of the ris
involved that for example, on 31 January 1986 2½% Consols were yieldi
10.13% and the *Financial Times* Ordinary Shares 4.45%, a reverse yield g
of 5.68%.*

14.13 Emotional

The main price movements both upwards and downwards tend to
overdone. The reason for this is that investors, whether they are priv
individuals or the professional managers of institutional funds, are r
calculating machines but human beings. They are, therefore, influenced
the market atmosphere which they in turn have themselves helped to crea

When prices are rising in a bull market a mood of optimism prevails, a
clouds on the horizon are easily shrugged aside as being of little consequen
Of course, so long as the general body of opinion thinks prices are going
rise they will rise. Everyone wants to be 'in the market' and not miss out
the capital profits which are there for the taking. As the result of this a b
market has a momentum which takes it above the levels which t
fundamental facts of the situation would otherwise dictate.

The opposite state of affairs applies in a bear market. Prices which a
falling, initially as the result of sound reasoning, sink to unduly depress
levels as pessimism gets the upper hand.

14.2 The indices

As well as knowing the prices of individual shares, investors and
concerned with these matters find it useful to have a method of measuri
over a period of time both the relative position of the market as a whole ar
to a lesser extent, the various sections of which it is comprised. For tl
purpose various indices are compiled and published daily.

14.21 FT Ordinary Share Index

The best known index is the *Financial Times* Ordinary Share Index calculat
as an unweighted geometric mean of the prices of its constituents, these bei
twenty eight leading industrial ordinary shares selected to give a f
representation of the main industries in the United Kingdom and tv
financial shares (introduced recently in place of two industrial shares). T
index commenced on 1 July 1935 on which date the combined prices of t
underlying shares were accorded the number 100. At various times on ea
business day the prices of these shares (or shares substituted for the origin
for compelling reasons such as the latter no longer being representative

---

* The reverse yield gap may also be established by comparing the average gross redemption yi
on the 25 years high coupon British Government Stocks with that on the FT Actuaries All Sh
Index. On 31 January 1986 the gap as so measured was 6.37%.

heir particular industry) are taken in order to calculate the appropriate umber.

The lowest and highest index numbers recorded up to February 1986 were 9.4 on 26 June 1940 and 1281.5 on 27 February 1986. Also of interest as vell as the actual number are the average income and earnings yields, and the /E ratio published each day for the underlying shares.

A criticism commonly levelled at the FT Ordinary Index is that it is ompiled from a handful of shares compared with the vast number of equities juoted on the Stock Exchange and that accordingly it is not sufficiently epresentative. Also special circumstances affecting one of the constituents of uch a thinly spread Index, such as a takeover bid, could give an inaccurate eflection of price changes of the market as a whole.

However, a perhaps more important inadequacy of the Index lies in its alculation as a geometric mean which imposes a continuing downward drift n its values if compared with the values calculated by arithmetic means. Accordingly it is not suitable for long-term portfolio comparisons although in practice it is sometimes used for this purpose. It should be confined to omparing short-term fluctuations in the prices of ordinary shares.

4.22 FT Actuaries Share Indices

he Actuaries Shares Indices are arithmetic averages of prices weighted ccording to the equity capitalizations of the companies concerned. They are much more comprehensive group and are published for every business day n the *Financial Times*, the base date for the majority being 10 April 1962. he main groupings are the 500 Share Index and the All Share Index which is he 500 Index plus the Financial Group, Investment Trust, Mining Finance nd Overseas Traders. Within these are individual indices covering around orty constituent sections and subsections. There are also indices for Fixed nterest Stocks and the British Government stocks being subdivided into their our basic categories. This new format introduced in 1977 includes an 'x d dj. 19... to date' column which represents the gross interest received since he beginning of the calendar year and this is provided in order that the performance of a gilt fund rolling up interest can be measured. A subsequent ddition has been a section for index-linked stocks similarly provided with he 'x d adj' as is also the Debenture and Loan Stock Index and the Preference hare Index.

The All Share Index, which covers a wide range of commercial and ndustrial shares, oils, financials, etc. reached a high of 752.86 on 27 ebruary 1986, having fallen to a low of 61.92 on 13 December 1974.

As well as being suitable for comparison with actual portfolio performance he Actuaries Indices also provide a valuable means of comparing the relative novements of the various sectors of the market. For example, on 28 February 986 the index for motors was 273.77, chemicals 875.53 and oil and gas 119.64.

14.23 *Financial Times Stock Exchange 100 Share Index*

This further index of share prices known as FT-SE 100 Index or mo colloquially as 'Footsie' came into being to accommodate the Londc International Futures Exchange's introduction of a futures contract on t movement of equity share prices and the Stock Exchange's own traded optic contract (see Section 6.43) on such movement. A new up to the minute guic to Stock Exchange prices was required, the FT Ordinary Share Index n being sufficiently representative of the whole market and the FT Actuaries A Share Index being too complicated in its calculation to produce the frequenc of information required.

The FT-SE 100 Index is a weighted arithmetic average of 100 listed U companies being generally those with the largest market capitalizations. T constituent companies are dropped from the Index and replaced when becomes apparent from their market price movements that such action justified.

For the convenience of its users the Index was set at 1000 rather than t conventional 100 on 1 January 1984. It has to date had highs and lows 1549.5 on 27 February 1986 and 986.9 on 23 July 1984.

14.3 Timing

Obviously, the ideal way of making money on the Stock Exchange is to buy the bottom of the market and sell at the top. The great drawback to th otherwise excellent plan of campaign is that no one can be sure when t crucial times arrive until they have become part of history. However, just in days of old man sought to discover a process of manufacturing gold, so modern times there have been attempts to devise systems which w automatically tell an investor when profitably to buy or sell his/her share

Such systems as have been developed do not claim to give the appropria signal right at the top or the bottom. Rather they are designed to indicate major change in the direction of price movements while still in the initi stages. Two original examples of this approach are the Dow system and t Hatch system. Much controversy surrounds the value of the use of syster but it must be recorded that among the protagonists are many who opinions are certainly deserving of respect.

14.31 *The Dow theory*

This theory depends on the plotting of daily price indices on charts. originated from the United States and in its pure form is related to tv indices, industrials, and rails. Before any conclusions may be established t one index must confirm the other. In this country there is, of course, now rails index but advocates of the theory claim that it can be usefully applied other indices.

In essence it is maintained that there is a primary movement in the mark at all times for, say, a year or years together with secondary movements usually lasting either for a few weeks or months. The day-to-day movements of which the secondaries are comprised are ignored.

14.311 *Change of primary*

The principal objective is to discover when there has been a change in the primary movement and it is the behaviour of the secondaries which are vital in determining when this has taken place. Three secondary movements are involved before such a conclusion is reached. In a primary bull market the first of these is a reaction, then a rally which, however, fails to reach a new high level, and then another reaction which drops below that of the previous one.

In Figure 14.2 which for the purposes of simplicity is highly artificial, A–B is a primary bull market in which there are three clear cut secondary reactions.

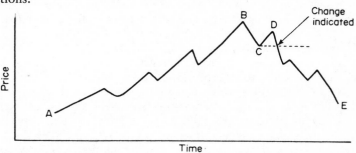

Figure 14.2

The suggestion of a change came when after what appeared to be the fourth secondary reaction B–C the ensuing recovery C–D fell short of B. Once the drop from D went below the level of C the chartist would conclude that the primary bull market had changed to the primary bear market B–E.

The change from a primary bear to a primary bull market is indicated by the opposite movements. In Figure 14.3 the point is where after the fall H–I had failed to establish a new low the rally I–J passed the level of the previous rally G–H.

Difficulty sometimes arises in practice by confusing secondary and minor movements. The distinguishing feature is time. Where each phase lasts only a few days it is of no significance so far as the theory is concerned. A secondary movement must last for at least a few weeks.

The volume of business being done at certain stages in the cycle is also used to interpret the state of the market. Basically it is maintained that if volume increases along with rising prices the signs are bullish and if volume decreases with falling prices they are bearish. At the top of a bull market there may,

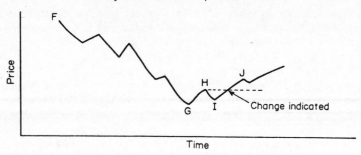

Figure 14.3

however, be a great flurry of activity as shrewd investors liquidate the
holdings, while at the bottom of a bear market business may be very qui
owing to a general state of apathy. Some of the tenets are at times apparent
contradictory and require to be treated with reserve by the uninitiated.

14.312 'Lines' and 'triangles'
Various other patterns emerge from charts out of which, mysteriously c
occasion, theorists claim to deduce future trends. Perhaps the simplest is
'line' shown in Figure 14.4 which is a sideways movement within a pri
range of around 5%. This indicates that buyers and sellers at this level are, fc
various reasons, evenly matched and there is doubt for some time as to wh
will gain the ascendancy. When either buying or selling within this ran;
peters out a substantial movement one way or another is anticipated.
Figure 14.4 buyers have triumphed over sellers and the price level has move

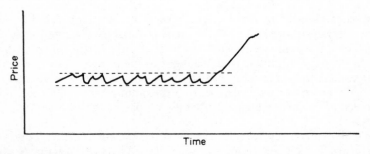

Figure 14.4

up sharply from its former confines. The time to buy is as soon as the brea
away occurs. The theory also maintains that the longer the line persists t
greater will be the extent of the ultimate rise or fall.
   Triangles (Figure 14.5) have similar applications, the difference being th

as the formation progresses the resistance prices of buyers and sellers come closer together. Eventually one or other of the opposing forces gives way and there is a strong movement against them. In Figure 14.5 buying at a particular level within the triangle has fizzled out so prices have fallen away sharply.

Charts may, of course, be constructed either for a share index or for individual shares.

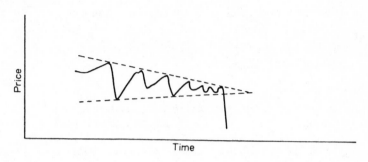

Figure 14.5

14.32 The Hatch system

This is an automatic system based on the premise that if an investor sells at 10% below the top of the market and buys at 10% above the bottom he is doing as well as can reasonably be expected. It can be applied to an index, a group of shares, or an individual share, and there are some variations in the working of the system. However, once the method to be used is decided upon it must be adhered to and all automatic signals obeyed. For simplicity in illustration the following example applies the system to a single share.

An investor, say, in March buys a share for £1.70 and immediately deducts 10%, giving him a sale price of £1.53 (£1.70–0.17). If at any time the price falls to £1.53 he immediately sells the share.

On a fixed date each month, in this case let us say the first of the month, he takes the price of the share and if this price is above his purchasing price or the previous month's price he deducts 10% from this price, thus establishing a higher selling price. Otherwise the selling price remains the same.

During the rest of March the price of the share at no time falls to £1.53 and the 1 April price is £1.69. As this is lower than the purchase price no change is made to the selling price.

During April the price again does not fall to to £1.53 but the 1 May price £1.84. As this is higher than the purchase price a new selling price must b established: £1.8

Deduct 10% 0.1

Selling price (replacing £1.53) £1.6

In May the price does not fall to £1.66 and the 1 June price is: £1.9

Deduct 10% 0.1

Selling price (replacing £1.66) £1.7

In June the price does not fall to £1.76 and the 1 July price is £1.93. As th is lower than the 1 June price of £1.95 no adjustment is made to the sellir price.

During a bull market this process may go on over a long period with tl selling price being adjusted upwards. However in this example the price fa to £1.76 in July and the share is sold.

The Hatch operator then works out a purchase price of £1.76 + 10% £1.94, which would be adjusted downwards if the subsequent prices on tl first days of the months which followed were below £1.76. Whenever h automatic purchase price was reached he would buy.

A refinement of the system would be that to calculate his/her control sellir or buying prices he would work out the average price for the previous mont rather than use the single price on a fixed date.

Although for illustrative purposes an individual share price has been us investors are advised to apply the system to a representative group of leadir shares, called the 'operating portfolio', which may be expected to move harmony with the market and thus obtain the benefits of averaging. Th theory can then be operated by reference to an index which does n necessarily require to reflect exactly the portfolio held. More correctly sellir and buying prices can be worked out based on the shares in the portfolio

In this latter event, when the operator is in the market selling prices are aga worked out monthly for each share. Also on this particular date each mont the whole operating portfolio will be valued and an overall sale value (movin calculated by taking 10% off this value. Should the total portfolio fall to th overall control value on any subsequent valuation date, all the shares n already sold on the indication of their individual control prices will be sol

When out of the market the Hatch investor will continue to value the shar in his operating portfolio, working out both entry prices for individual shar and an overall entry valuation when all individual shares not so far purchas as the result of their own price movements will be acquired.

The system is not meant for short-term speculation but for the long term, and operators should be prepared to stay with it for a considerable run of years. A point to notice is that potential losses are limited to 10% of the amount invested on each occasion whereas potential gains are restricted by the extent of the upward fluctuations of the market.

Another advantage of the system is that it prevents selling too soon in a long bull market or buying too early in a bear market. It does, however, have the drawback that if markets move narrowly for a prolonged period, as they sometimes do, the investor can be put in and out with a succession of small losses. In order that a profit may arise when the system is in operation the market must rise by over 22.2%. For example, suppose that the bottom of the market is given the value 100, the Hatch operator will buy at 110. If the maximum rise is to 122.2 the selling price is $122.2 - 12.2 = 110$.

Typical question

Factors governing movement of share prices may be either special or general. Discuss this fully and quote a few examples of each category.
(The Institute of Bankers in Scotland, *Theory and Practice of Investment*)

Suggested answer

Broadly speaking, share prices as a whole tend during any given period to be moving in the same direction. However, although all shares are in some degree affected by this overall trend, individual shares or sectors of the market are specially influenced by their own particular circumstances.

The general factors causing movements of share prices usually stem from political or economic sources. For instance, if a government hostile to private enterprise is elected, share prices are likely to fall. Should it be apparent, however, that government actions are going to cause inflation then ordinary shares may rise as they give investors more protection against the fall in value of money than do fixed interest stocks. Severe measures of restraint on the economy, necessary because of balance of payments crises, such as high interest rates, credit restrictions, and increased taxation have a depressing influence on markets, while their removal has the opposite effect. Overseas stock markets, particularly Wall Street in the United States, have repercussions in the prices of shares in this country.

Groups of shares can be vulnerable to special situations. For instance, oil shares might be depressed by wars or social unrest in those parts of the world where the companies operate. On the other hand the discovery of a rich new source of oil would move the shares upwards. Similar factors could also play an important role in the price levels of mining shares.

Some industries may be dependent on exporting their products to overseas countries. Shareholders of such companies carry the inherent risk of the overseas countries starting to manufacture the goods themselves and drying

up the companies' outlets. The textile industry in this country has had to fac
this problem.

Changes in taxation may bear down more heavily on some sectors tha
others. For example, property companies which distribute nearly all the
income were badly hit by the introduction of corporation tax. Selectiv
employment tax also discriminated against industries such as store
hoteliers, etc.

As far as individual shares are concerned the price will be influenced by th
profits of the company. If these drop and there is no likelihood of earl
recovery the share price will, at best, be in the doldrums even although a bu
market is in full swing. A takeover bid either rumoured or actual is also
powerful force as regards the price of a company's shares.

It is recognized as a fact that most share price movements, once established
are inclined to be overdone, either rising too high or falling too low. This
caused by the added impetus of the human emotions of optimism an
pessimism.

Additional questions

1 Discuss the importance of 'good timing' in dealing in Stock Exchang
   securities. Illustrate your answer, if possible, by reference to the *Financi*
   Times index of ordinary share prices.
   (The Institute of Bankers in Scotland, *Theory and Practice of Investmen*
2 A company may announce excellent profit figures but the price of i
   shares in the market may not rise. Suggest possible reasons for this.
3 How has inflation affected the respective attractions of fixed intere
   stocks and ordinary shares? What do you understand by 'the reverse yiel
   gap'.
4 Describe the main features of the *Financial Times* Ordinary Share Inde
   and compare it with the *Financial Times*-Actuaries 500 Share Index.
                (The Savings Bank Institute, *Personal Savings and Investmen*
5 (a) What movements are necessary to indicate a change from a primar
        bull to a primary bear market according to the Dow theory?
   (b) What are 'lines' and 'triangles'? Explain how they may help a
        investor to time his/her purchases and sales.
6 Briefly outline the Hatch system.

15 Portfolio planning

The objective of a private investor is to make his capital produce the greatest possible net sum for him. It is of little consequence whether this is achieved by means of income received or by capital growth. If the latter there is no bar on him realizing some of his profits and using them to meet his current requirements. Other things being equal it is, of course, simpler to finance needs from income rather than to be continually selling small amounts of stock.

15.1 General principles

15.11 Preliminary assessments

Before setting about the task of selecting investments for himself an individual must make a rational assessment of his personal position. He must be clear in his mind as to the financial responsibilities resting on his shoulders and also give serious thought as to what future commitments he might possibly be called upon to discharge. In particular the relevance of the following points should be weighed up one against the other in order that the pattern of his investment requirements might emerge.

1 Age

A young person can look a long way ahead in his/her planning while as the years go by the rewards of investment must be more immediate.

2 Responsibilities

A married man with dependants has a duty to see that they are properly provided for in the event of his early decease. Sufficient life assurance is the prime requirement.

3 Commitments

Is cash likely to be needed in the foreseeable future for, say, house purchase or helping a member of the family? If so liquidity must be provided for to avoid sales being forced when markets are low.

4 Pension arrangements

If these are adequate a greater proportion of the total sum to be invested can be placed in equity shares as the pension provision can broadly be likened to fixed interest investment.

5 Rate of tax
For the high tax payer capital appreciation is more valuable than current income.

6 Total amount available
The person with very limited funds can ill afford to risk losing part of them.

7 Temperament
It is necessary to keep calm and not rush into buying or selling shares without having given proper thought to such action. Some people are unable to do this in which event their equity investment should be limited to unit or investment trusts with a view to holding for the long term and letting the managers do the worrying.

8 Personal feelings
Are there any sectors of the market, such as tobaccos or breweries, where the holding of the type of shares are unacceptable on other than purely investment grounds?

It is not always easy for the individual investor to be objective about all this. An impartial investment adviser can often make a better job of it, if he/she can prise out all the relevant information without too much difficulty.

15.12 Liquidity
Mention has already been made of the need to make provision for expected commitments. If some time may elapse before they will materialize appropriately dated gilt-edged stocks may be a suitable haven for the fund meantime. Good class debentures (dated) would also suffice. However, if the commitments are just round the corner, banks, buildings societies, or short term deposits with soundly backed finance companies will fill the bill.

As well as making provision for known commitments it is wise always to hold a proportion of one's capital in a form which can, if necessary, be turned into a definite cash sum with the minimum delay. No one knows just what the future has in store and the necessity of not being caught in the position of having to realize marketable securities when they happen to be temporarily at a low ebb is one of the canons of successful investment. The small investor is particularly vulnerable to this danger. Before exposing himself to the risks inherent in equity investment he should have a reasonable sum tucked away in the bank, building society, or national savings certificates, etc.

15.13 Diversification

Some investors these days are completely equity minded and will have no truck with fixed interest stocks whatsoever. While this is a point of view which can be expounded convincingly during the course of an equity bull market it ignores the fact that there are hazards in equity markets as a whole from which fixed interest stocks, in particular gilt-edged, are immune.

A soundly based portfolio should, therefore, contain a fixed interest content and it is the size of this which should first of all be decided upon. Here the personal factors are all-important. There are various permutations of these, but as a general proposition the smaller the portfolio and the older the investor the higher should be the proportion of fixed interest stocks.

Once this allocation has been made the question of equity selection can be considered keeping in mind that sound investment, as opposed to speculation, demands that there should be a reasonably wide diversification of interest, both industrially and geographically. An overseas interest can be obtained by investing in British companies which carry out many of their activities abroad, by direct investment in foreign* companies, or through overseas orientated investment or unit trusts. A stake overseas assumes added attraction at times when the pound sterling comes under pressure and the possibility of further devaluation looms on the horizon.

Although diversification is necessary for prudent investment it should not be indiscriminate or simply used as a substitute for making a reasoned decision. There will, inevitably at all times, be certain industries facing particular difficulties and until signs of recovery are apparent they should be avoided.

Different industries have their own characteristics. Generally capital goods industries are more cyclical than consumer industries and accordingly their profits fluctuate to a greater extent over the years. The more stable industries are therefore to be found in the consumer section, for example breweries, food, stores, and tobacco where the customers come along year in year out. Bank shares make very sound although normally unexciting holdings. On the other hand mining and plantation shares are of a speculative nature. Each industry requires careful study and it takes time and experience to become familiar with its many facets which may, of course, be continually undergoing a process of change. A point which must always be remembered, however, is that money can be lost, particularly in the short term, even in what are regarded as the soundest of shares – frequently referred to as 'blue chips' – if they are purchased at the wrong time.

---

* While the removal of Exchange Control regulations in October 1979, with the consequent disappearance of the dollar premium, simplified and increased the scope of overseas investment, it must be kept in mind that currency risks still remain and choosing the right currency is as important as choosing the right share.

15.14 Supervision of holdings

The question often arises as to the size of individual holdings in a portfolio. Again, there are no hard and fast rules and the total value of the portfolio is relevant. The private investor, however, should be on his guard against taking on too great a burden by purchasing a very large number of holdings. Probably thirty is about as many as he can look after properly unless he is a great enthusiast with an abundance of spare time on his hands. Professional investors are in a different category and are able to supervise a vastly greater number of shares.

Each holding does not necessarily need to be of the same size. As a general rule larger sums can be invested in established, well proven, companies with lesser amounts in smaller promising companies which have still to prove themselves over a period of time.

A well-chosen selection of shares should not require frequent changes to be made. However, the investor should keep in daily touch with the market in order to get the feel of what is going on. Occasionally something may happen which will call for immediate action by way of sale or purchase.

Once or twice during the year an investor should make a thorough review of his portfolio and decide whether any share should be discarded in favour of better prospects elsewhere. He may also have one or two shares which show substantial gains and he must take the difficult decision as to whether they are now too high and should be sold, or whether the respective companies' performances in the future will result in them going from strength to strength. Often a compromise by the selling of part of a holding and diversifying elsewhere is the safest solution in the circumstances.

There are various headings under which investment experts group ordinary shares. A private investor in the administration of his portfolio could well employ those used for the FT-Actuaries Share Indices which are published daily in the *Financial Times*.

15.15 Portfolio problems

Some consideration will now be given to the planning of two portfolios and the indication of the lines along which they should be set up. There is unfortunately, no perfect solution, and what seems sensible at one period of time – in this case January 1986 – can in retrospect appear to be somewhat misguided. In practice, of course, changes in emphasis can be made as the months and years go by.

Example

A young widow with two small children has the sum of £20,000 to invest being the proceeds of her late husband's insurance policies. She has no other sources of income other than the Department of Health and Social Security.

The urgent requirement here is to produce right away a steady income in order to assist the widow in the immediate future. As a secondary measure some thought should be given to try and do something to maintain the value of this income over the next few years. There is unfortunately a considerable conflict between these two objectives particularly if there should be another acceleration in the rate of inflation.

A suggested allocation of funds is as follows:

			Income produced	
(a)	Building society account	£3,000	£270	(f.o.t.)
(b)	Guaranteed income bond for five years ...	£3,000	£300	(f.o.t.)
(c)	Guaranteed income bond for ten years ...	£3,000	£270	(f.o.t.)
(d)	Equally between two long dated high coupon debenture stocks of good class companies at a little under par	£4,000	£460	(gross)
(e)	Medium dated British Government stock just under par maturing in thirteen to fourteen years time	£3,000	£330	(gross)
(f)	Income unit trust	£4,000	£240	(gross)

(a) To provide easy access to cash for any emergency which may arise. In order to obtain this current rate of interest, 9% along with immediate withdrawal facilities, it would be necessary to shop around the building societies. If the balance falls below £500 the interest rate would drop to 7%. The choice of a building society instead of an investment account with the National Savings Bank was made in the first place because the widow would be liable for basic rate tax on the top slice of her income and secondly because of the easier withdrawal facilities.

(b) and (c) To provide a useful high income with capital being returned in full after five and ten years respectively. Although a lower rate of interest would be obtained from the ten year bond it would be prudent to spread the maturity dates as in five years time interest rates may have fallen and it might not be possible to reinvest the proceeds so advantageously. Two different insurance companies would be used.

(d) The long dated debenture stocks would produce flat yields of around 11.5% over a long number of years.

(e) To provide a high and safe income and to be redeemed after the ten year income bond and before the debenture stocks.

(f) Immediate income is being sacrificed here in the hope that in the coming years there will be progressive increases in the amounts distributed. Any such increases will also be reflected in the capital value of the units.

Note: Higher yields than those obtained from the debenture and British Government stocks could have been obtained from National Savings products such as Income Bonds but as the interest rates on these can be reduced on six weeks' notice it was decided to secure the slightly lower yields which were certain to continue for fixed periods.

Example

As the result of the maturing of an insurance policy taken out many years ago by a wealthy businessman £100,000 is received by his son who is in his mid-twenties and is already earning £20,000 per annum.

As the son will be liable for high rates of tax on the top layer of his income should his portfolio become income orientated the policy will be to aim for capital growth. This points in the direction of a substantial equity stake, probably in the region of 70–80%, with the balance committed to low coupon fixed interest stocks.

Dealing with the fixed interest section first of all, £5,000 would be regarded as a reserve for contingencies and would be invested in British Transport 3% Stock 1978/88 standing at 87 and thus offering thirteen points of tax free gain to redemption in just over two years time. Should a quick sale be required to meet some cash requirement it is unlikely that any loss of capital will be involved.

A question relating to the remaining £15,000 to be committed directly to fixed interest stocks is the future rate of inflation. While there are hopes that it will continue to fall these may prove ill founded particularly should there be a change of Government with different priorities. Accordingly it is decided to compromise by investing £7,500 in $2\frac{1}{2}$% Exchequer Stock 1990 at 77 giving twenty three points of capital appreciation to redemption in the not too distant future and £7,500 in Treasury 2% Index-Linked Stock 1996 at 111. Applying the increase in the RPI from the issue of this latter Stock to date would indicate a 'current par value' of 141.43.

An alternative would be to utilize £5,000 of the funds earmarked for the $2\frac{1}{2}$% Exchequer Stock 1990 in the purchase of National Savings Certificates 31st Issue yielding 7.85% free of all tax after five years. Over the five year period the National Savings Certificates would probably provide a slightly better return but this would have to be weighed against the necessity of holding them for the full term thus sacrificing flexibility.

Timing is of utmost importance in equity investment and at the beginning of 1986 the market is at a high level, there having been a bull market for several years. Optimism still abounds as it usually does at this stage in a bull market and this of itself may take prices further together with the rampant takeover fever from which even mammoth companies are no longer immune. Factors to be taken into account apart from the probability that shares in general are fully valued in relation to earnings are the conflicting consequences of both falling oil prices and weakness in sterling, the possibility of the return to even higher interest rates, and looming up before long the unsettling prospect of a General Election. However, although it would be unwise to risk serious mistiming by investing immediately all the funds available for the equity section of the portfolio, uncertainty being concomitant with equity investment it could also prove to be a mistake to commit no funds to the market which could remain strong.

With the current freedom from Exchange Control regulations, investment can be made in overseas markets and it might be rewarding to set aside £25,000 for this purpose keeping in mind that overseas stock markets fluctuate too, some showing much more volatility than the United Kingdom Stock Exchange. £70,000 would be regarded as being available for direct equity investment (£45,000 in the United Kingdom and £25,000 overseas) and of this £40,000 would in the meantime be withheld for further phased purchases over the coming months on market setbacks possibly in sectors not represented such as banks, oils, buildings, and chemicals. It would as a temporary measure be held on easily accessible terms with a bank or a building society.

It is suggested that the initial equity portfolio be constructed by investing in shares in the following sectors:

United Kingdom

Electricals	£2,500
Breweries	2,500
Entertainments and catering	2,500
Food retailing	2,500
Food manufacturing	2,500
Insurance (composite)	2,500
Property	2,500

United States

Energy	2,500
Consumer	2,500
Technology	2,500

Far East

Unit or investment trust specialising in his area	2,500

Europe

Unit or investment trust specialising in this area	2,500

With regard to the investment in the United States it might be that in view of the relatively small amount involved it would be preferable to use the vehicle of a unit or investment trust (or a United States 'mutual fund') thus obtaining wider diversification and obviating the more onerous task of monitoring individual overseas holdings.

£10,000 is so far unaccounted for. It is proposed that this be invested in a single premium bond with underlying investments of fixed interest, equities and property. Each year the son would withdraw 5%, i.e. £500, and use this to pay the premiums to the extent of £100 on a friendly society policy and £400 on a qualifying with profits life assurance policy. Although life assurance relief is no longer available there would still be some tax advantage to the higher rate taxpayer in the qualifying policy.

15.2 Special position of trustees

In many ways a trustee applies the same principles as does the private investor in the managing of a portfolio. There are, however, two important differences.

15.21 The beneficiaries

In the first place more than one party may be interested in the trust funds an
their respective interests must be given due weight by the trustees. Sometime
these interests may conflict. One party may be entitled to all the trust incom
during his/her lifetime after which the capital may be paid over to anothe
party or parties. The first party would benefit by the trustees investing for a
high an income as possible, whereas the second party's interests would bes
be served by an all out growth policy. In these circumstances it is the trustees
duty to endeavour to strike a fair compromise.

There are various types of trusts most of which fall into recognize
patterns. For example, by his will a husband may set up a trust whereby o
his death his widow receives the whole income from his estate during he
lifetime after which the capital is paid to his children. A rich man in order t
reduce the family tax bill may have placed capital in trust for his youn
children, the income to be accumulated on their behalf until they attai
majority and thereafter to be paid to them, with the capital perhaps bein
made over at a later date. A trust may be formed to 'protect' a daughter wh
is unable to look after money so that she gets all the income during he
lifetime but is unable to squander the capital. The trustees adapt thei
investment policy according to the requirements of the beneficiaries.

15.22 Investment powers

The second important point is the trustees' investment powers. In the dee
setting up the trust the trustees may be given completely unfettered powers o
investment in which case there is more or less no restriction on th
investments they may hold. On the other hand the deed may set out certai
limited categories of investments which may be retained or purchased, or i
may be altogether silent as to the trustees' investment powers.

Until 1961 trustees, unless empowered by the deed to do so, were no
permitted to hold any securities other than those prescribed by the Truste
Act 1925 or the Trusts (Scotland) Act 1921. Broadly these consisted of gilt
edged stocks and as the result of this the value of many trust funds suffere
severe erosion owing to inflation. In order to stop the continuance of thi
unfortunate state of affairs the Trustee Investments Act 1961 was passed.

15.23 Trustee Investments Act 1961

Under the Act the trust fund may be divided into two equal parts –
narrower range fund and a wider range fund. If made, it is prudent that th
division should be on the basis of a valuation by a person reasonably believe
by the trustees to be qualified to make it. The narrower range fund mus
consist exclusively of narrower range investments but the wider range fun
may contain either narrower range or wider range investments. These may b
summarized as follows:

Narrower range investments

Not requiring advice

1 National Savings Income Bonds, National Savings Deposit Bonds, National Savings Certificates, and Ulster Savings Certificates.
2 Deposits in the National Savings Bank.

Requiring advice

1 Fixed interest securities issued by the United Kingdom, Northern Ireland, or Isle of Man Governments and registered in the United Kingdom or the Isle of Man, and Treasury Bills.
2 Securities on which interest is guaranteed by the United Kingdom or Northern Ireland Governments.
3 Fixed interest securities issued in the United Kingdom by public authorities or nationalized undertakings.
4 Fixed interest securities issued and registered in the United Kingdom by any Commonwealth government or local authority.
5 Fixed interest securities issued and registered in the United Kingdom by the International Bank.
6 Debentures registered in the United Kingdom of a company incorporated in the United Kingdom.
7 Bank of Ireland Stock.
8 Debentures of the Agricultural Mortgage Corporation Limited or the Scottish Agricultural Securities Corporation Limited.
9 Fixed interest loans of local authorities in the United Kingdom and Belfast City and District Water Commissioners.
10 Debenture, guaranteed or preference stocks of British water companies.
11 Gilt-edged and fixed interest unit trusts authorised by the DTI.
12 Building society deposit accounts.
13 Mortgages on heritable property in Scotland and on freeholds or leaseholds of sixty years or more in England and Wales or Northern Ireland.
14 Perpetual rent charges on land in England and Wales or Northern Ireland and fee farm rents, and in feu-duties or ground annuals in Scotland.
15 Fixed interest securities issued in the United Kingdom by the European Investment Bank or by the European Coal and Steel Community.
16 Certificates of Tax Deposit.

Wider range investments

1 Fully paid up share capital issued and registered in the United Kingdom by a company incorporated in the United Kingdom.
2 Building society shares.
3 Units of unit trusts authorized by the Department of Trade.

Note: The securities of companies incorporated in the United Kingdom to qualify under the Act must be quoted on a recognized United Kingdom Stock Exchange. Shares or debentures must be fully paid up except for new issues to be paid up within nine months. No funds may be invested under the Act in the shares or debentures of a company unless its total paid up capital is at least £1 million and a dividend has been paid on all its share capital in each of the five years preceding the investment. The expression 'debenture' in the Act includes debenture stock and bonds, whether constituting a charge on assets or not, and loan stock or notes.

Under section 7 of the Trustee Act 1925, trustees in England have power to retain or invest in securities payable to bearer which, if not so payable, would have been authorized investments.

The division once made is final and the equality of value between the funds will soon disappear. No property may be transferred from one fund to another unless a compensating transfer is made at the same time. Any additions to the trust after the division has been made are added 50–50 to each fund. Withdrawals from the trust may, rather surprisingly, be made from either fund at the trustees' discretion.

15.231 Advice

Except in the case of one or two narrower range investments, before exercising his/her powers under the Act the trustee is obliged to take advice from a person who is reasonably believed by the trustee to be qualified by his/her ability in the practical experience of financial matters. However, the necessity to obtain advice does not apply where the trustee is himself an investment expert, or, where there are two or more trustees, one of them is so qualified.

When the powers have been exercised the trustees must also have the portfolio reviewed at appropriate intervals by an expert. In order to give his/her advice the expert must be made fully aware of the objectives of the trust and, when given, the advice must be in writing or subsequently confirmed in writing.

15.232 Special range fund

The powers conferred under the Act are in addition to those already available to the trustees. As mentioned above the deed of trust itself may contain authority to hold certain investments. These may, for example, be shares in a family company, a certain category of quoted shares, or land and buildings. When a division is made such assets must be excluded therefrom and held separate in a special range fund. Should realizations be made in the special range fund and no reinvestment made in special range investments, the proceeds must be allocated 50–50 to the narrower and wider range funds.

15.233 Gradual process

Although legally the wider range fund may be wholly invested in equities, in practice it may still be desirable for it to contain a proportion of fixed interest stocks. The reason for this is that a complete switch to equities all at once would mean a substantial drop in revenue and severe hardship to the income beneficiary. The trustees may consider it their duty to make the change over gradually.

15.24 Charities

Charitable funds are also administered by trustees and again, if the investment powers conferred by the deed of trust are not adequate, advantage may be taken of the Trustee Investments Act. There are one or two special features to be kept in mind.

Charities are completely exempt from all United Kingdom taxes and a high income is usually required to meet the needs of causes which they serve. Charities may also go on indefinitely, not like personal trusts which must eventually come to an end. However, although investment advisers might wish to introduce a substantial growth element to the portfolio in the long term interests of the charity they may be precluded from doing so by the pressing demands of the present.

15.25 Pension funds

Approved pensions fund trusts are wholly exempt from all United Kingdom taxes.

A distinctive feature of pension trusts is that there is no great need to distinguish between capital and income as both are held for the same parties –pensioners and prospective pensioners. When a pension fund is set up an actuary calculates the contributions required to provide the proposed scale of pensions. For this he/she uses a rate of interest, say, $4\frac{1}{2}\%$ compound. It is the aim of those responsible for the investment policy of the fund to better this rate thus establishing reserves which will become available to augment pensions. Most funds have wide investment powers but where these do not exist the powers under the Trustee Investments Act are available.

Many pension funds are steadily increasing in size as the income from contributions and investments is in excess of the pension payments. Such funds must, therefore, be continuous investors and are constantly on the look out for suitable repositories for these cash accumulations.

Most of the large pension funds have large gilt-edged portfolios as the result of which profitable switching can be carried out as opportunities arise. The fixed interest section will be balanced both as regards the types of fixed interest stocks and the maturity dates. It would not be prudent to have too much of a fund maturing at around the same time as there is always the risk that this might be during a period when it would be difficult to reinvest the redemption monies on similarly attractive terms.

There will be a tendency to shorten or lengthen the average life of the portfolio as interest rates rise or fall. If interest rates are rising new money is better committed, temporarily at least, to the short end of the market where there is more protection against loss of capital value. When rates look like falling the move to the longer dates can be made. In assessing the relative merits of fixed interest stocks it is, of course, the redemption yields which are vital.

As with other portfolios diversification is important with the equities. Owing to the size of the bigger funds it is necessary to invest in a large number of companies in order to avoid too high a proportion of the equity of any one single company being held. Against this must be weighed the problems of administering a vast number of shares.

Direct investment in overseas companies will from time to time have some attraction from the growth point of view. When deciding upon this it must be borne in mind that a withholding tax may be deducted from dividends in respect of which a tax exempt pension fund has no way of obtaining relief.

Typical question

'X', who died on 1 April 1968, bequeathed his estate to pay the income to his wife for life with the remainder to his children. No investment powers are contained in the will.

You are not concerned with the investment merits of the particular holdings which are as follows:

	Price	Value £
£2,000 6% Funding Stock 1993...	81	1,620
£5,000 3% Redemption Stock 1986/96	50½	2,525
£2,000 Australia 6% Stock 1981/83	84	1,680
A$ 2,000 Commonwealth of Australia 4½% Inscribed Stock 1972 ... ...A$ 100.10		928
£1,000 3½% Conversion Stock 1969	98	980
£1,000 South Africa 5½% Stock 1974/76	85	850
£2,000 Canadian Pacific Railway Co. 4% perpetual debenture	49	980
£1,000 Whitbread & Co. Ltd 7¾% debenture 1989/94	98	980
£1,000 Watney Mann Ltd. 8% unsecured loan stock 1990/95	98	980
500 Economic Insurance Co. Ltd £1 shares (25p paid)	£1.80	900
400 Allied Breweries Ltd ordinary 25p shares ...	£1.00	400
£500 Halifax Building Society on share account ...		500
100 Rio Tinto Zinc Corp. ordinary 50p shares	£7.50	750
50 De Beers Consd. Mines Ltd 50 cent shares ...	£31.00	1,550
100 XYZ. Co. Ltd ordinary shares (a private company)	£2.00	200
500 Richardsons Westgarth & Co. Ltd ordinary 50p shares	£0.31¼	156

(Dividends paid for the year to 31 March 1964 5%
Dividends paid for the year to 31 March 1965 5%
Dividends paid for the year to 31 March 1966 Nil
Dividends paid for the year to 31 March 1967 Nil
Dividends paid for the year to 31 March 1968 5%)

1000 Harland & Wolff Ltd ordinary £1 stock units ...	£0.90	900

(Dividends paid for the year to 31 December 1963 2½%
Dividends paid for the year to 31 December 1964 2½%
Dividends paid for the year to 31 December 1965, 1966, 1967 nil)

200 Shell Transport & Trading Co. Ltd ordinary 25p shares (bearer)	£4.60	920
300 Imperial Chemical Industries Ltd ordinary £1 shares	£3.50	1,050
2000 Save and prosper income units	£0.392	784
		£19,633

Having completed the administration of the estate you are required to divide the investments for the purposes of the Trustee Investments Act 1961.

Would your division have been the same if the will contained a power to retain stocks and shares of any brewery company?

(The Institute of Bankers, *Principles and Practice of Investment*)

Suggested answer

The following holdings will require to be sold as their retention is not authorized under the Trustee Investments Act 1961.

	Value
A$ 2,000 Commonwealth of Australia 4½% Inscribed Stock 1972 (not issued in UK)	£928
£1,000 South Africa 5½% Stock 1974/76 (not issued by a Commonwealth government)	850
£2,000 Canadian Pacific Railway Co. 4% perpetual debenture (company not incorporated in UK)	980
500 Economic Insurance Co. Ltd £1 shares (25p paid) (not fully paid)	900
50 De Beers Consd. Mines Ltd 50 cent shares (company not incorporated in UK)	1,550
100 X.Y.Z. Co. Ltd ordinary shares (a private company) ...	200
500 Richardsons Westgarth & Co. Ltd ordinary 50p shares (dividends not paid in each of the last five years)	156
1,000 Harland & Wolff Ltd ordinary £1 stock units (dividends not paid in each of the last five years)	900

200 Shell Transport & Trading Co. Ltd ordinary 25p shares
(bearer) (shares must be registered) 920*
                                                                  _____

For the purpose of the answer to the question assumed to have been
acutally sold for the value £7,384
                                                                  _____

Narrower range fund   Value
£2,000 6% Funding Stock 1993   ...   .   £1,620
£5,000 3% Redemption Stock 1986/96   2,525
£2,000 Australia 6% Stock 1981/83   1,680
£1,000 3½% Conversion Stock 1969   980
£1,000 Whitbread & Co. Ltd 7¾% debenture 1989/94   980
£1,000 Watney Mann Ltd 8% unsecured loan stock 1990/95   ...   980
Cash from sales   1,051
                                                                  _____
                                                                 £9,816
                                                                  _____

Wider range fund   Value
400 Allied Breweries Ltd ordinary 25p shares £400
£500 Halifax Building Society on share account   500
100 Rio Tinto Zinc Corp. Ltd ordinary 50p shares   750
300 Imperial Chemical Industries Ltd ordinary £1 shares   ...   1,050
2000 Save and Prosper income units   784
Cash from sales   6,333
                                                                  _____
                                                                 £9,817
                                                                  _____

If the will contained power to retain stocks and shares of any brewery company
the undernoted three holdings would have been placed in a special range fund
before the remainder and the cash proceeds of the sales were divided 50–50
into the narrower range fund and the wider range fund:

£1,000 Whitbread & Co. Ltd 7¾% debenture 1989/94
£1,000 Watney Mann Ltd 8% unsecured loan stock 1990/95
400 Allied Breweries Ltd ordinary 25p shares

Additional questions

1   What do you understand by portfolio planning? Discuss fully.
                                    (The Institute of Bankers, *Investment*

---

* This sale of the 'Shell' bearer shares would be necessary under the law of Scotland. However in
England their retention would appear to be authorized under section 7 of the Trustee Act 1925
Accordingly in an English trust they could be held in the Wider Range Fund with the consequent
transfer of £460 cash from the Wider Range Fund to the Narrower Range Fund in equalization

2 You are the manager of a growing pension fund, wholly invested in equities. Discuss the reasons why you would or would not consider investment in gilt-edged securities at the present time.

(The Institute of Bankers, *Principles and Practice of Investment*)

3 'Three hundred equities, if they are rightly chosen, are sufficient as a selection ground for most portfolios. I feel that increasing the number of shares under consideration to an unmanageable number is no way of diversifying.'

William G. Nursaw

Having regard to the foregoing, advise your chairman on the investment policy of your organization.

(The Chartered Institute of Secretaries, *Secretarial and Administrative Practice-II*)

4 An investor who is a high rate payer has a portfolio consisting of £8,000, divided equally among shares in gold mines, electronics, insurances, and oils. His intention is that in fifteen years time when his two children have reached the age of twenty-one, he will divide the investments between them. He has no need to touch his capital or the income from his investments until then. Suggest any possible changes so that a maximum sum may be available to his children when they reach their majority.*

(The Institute of Bankers in Scotland, *Theory and Practice of Investment*)

5 If you are requested to advise a client on the investment of a certain sum of money what questions would you wish to ask him/her before coming to your conclusion.

(The Savings Bank Institute, *Personal Savings and Investment*)

6 In what ways may a United Kingdom investor obtain an overseas interest in his/her portfolio? Why might such an interest be desirable?

Although the age of majority has been reduced to eighteen it is suggested that age twenty-one is taken for the question.

16 Protecting the unwary

Throughout financial history there have been all too many occasions when ordinary people have lost their money as the result of reckless and fraudulent statements inducing them to invest it in what were, in effect, dubious enterprises right from the start. Sometimes they should have been put well and truly on their guard by the extremely high returns they were encouraged to expect, but apparently where the prospects of sudden riches are offered gullibility knows no bounds. Be that as it may, the authorities try to protect the innocent from those who would exploit them.

The Companies Acts lay down what must appear in prospectuses when shares are offered to the public. They also regulate the running of a company and insist on the regular dissemination of information relevant to the conduct of its affairs. However, this has not yet been sufficiently all-embracing to safeguard the unwary, particularly as far as non-stock exchange investment is concerned, and it has been necessary to embody further legislation in the form of two statutes – The Prevention of Fraud (Investments) Act 1958, and The Protection of Depositors Act 1963.

In the first half of the 1980s as the result of certain malpractices which had occurred particularly in the areas of investment advice and dealing outside the recognized Exchanges a concensus of feeling grew that more comprehensive investor protection legislation was required. This was reinforced by the forthcoming ending of single capacity on the Stock Exchange and the building up of conglomerates where institutions, many of which were international in character, would have an arm operating in well nigh every aspect of financial activity in the City. After wide discussion of possible courses of action a Financial Services Bill, subjecting all forms of investment including insurance and commodity linked investments to regulation, is being processed through Parliament in 1986. It is intended that this will become operational by the end of the year.

In anticipation of the new legislation two regulatory bodies were created – the Securities and Investments Board (SIB) and the Marketing of Investments Board (MIB) – but it would appear likely that they will merge initially as SIB which will subsequently be re-named. In the meantime SIB whose members must be approved by the Government and Bank of England is in course of assuming the functions of the Council for the Securities Industry (see Section 16.5) which will disappear.

Underneath the SIB will be self regulatory organizations (SROs) projected as being seven in number representing various sections of the investment services, for example, the Stock Exchange and the Investment Brokers, Managers and Dealers (IBMD) being a combination of the National Association of Securities Dealers and Investment Managers and the Life Assurance and Unit Trust Regulatory Organization. Before being recognized as SROs these bodies will have to satisfy the SIB as to the standards required of their members and that they are able to control the activities of such members. A strong point claimed for this system is that the office bearers of the SROs, themselves being practitioners in their particular spheres, will be well equipped to lay down appropriate codes of behaviour and make sure that they are being adhered to. Nevertheless despite the precautions being taken to obviate misconduct it will be necessary for reasonable compensation arrangements to be put in place either individually by an SRO or through the SIB to cover a client's loss through misbehaviour or negligence by an authorized business or member thereof.

In order to achieve a prime aim of the new legislation of ensuring more effectively than hitherto that dishonest or unprincipled investment businesses will not exist all investment businesses will require either to satisfy the SIB direct as to their fitness and so obtain authorization (thereafter being subject to SIB rules) or belong to an SRO. Authorization can also be obtained through membership of a recognized professional body. Carrying on business without proper authorization will be a criminal offence.

Of particular value to the private individual is the new rule which will make it clear that on being consulted by a client as to a type of transaction a firm must seek out and recommend the most suitable transaction of that type for the client and not be influenced by what will be to its own advantage. This has heightened relevance with the proliferation of conglomerates where the advancing of the overall interests of the group must not be to the detriment of a client.

While the basis of control will still rest on self regulation it is the intention that the SIB, backed by the new legislation, will be in a stronger position where necessary to deal with offenders and will where appropriate have a close association with the fraud squad. As will be apparent the Financial Services Bill when it reaches the Statute Book will consolidate and strengthen many of the protective measures detailed in this chapter.

16.1 The Prevention of Fraud (Investments) Act 1958

This Act has wider ramifications than those purely directed against the perpetration of fraud. There is, however, an important section entitled 'Penalty for fraudulently inducing persons to invest money' under which anyone found guilty of such an offence may be liable for a term of imprisonment not exceeding seven years. This fate may befall anyone who 'by any statement, promise, or forecast which he knows to be misleading, false or deceptive, or by any dishonest concealment of material facts, or by the reckless making (dishonestly or otherwise*) of any statement, promise or forecast which is misleading, false or deceptive induces or attempts to induce another person' to enter into an agreement to acquire or secure a profit from securities or to take part in† any scheme under which such persons participate in profits arising from property other than securities. Further, anyone who conspires to commit such an offence will be similarly liable for such punishment.

An affiliated section places restrictions on the distribution of circulars inviting people to invest money under threat of imprisonment for up to two years or a fine of up to £500, or both. Prospectives issued under the Companies Acts, authorized unit trust literature, members of organizations such as the Stock Exchange, and exempted and licensed dealers are among various categories outside the orbit of this section.

16.11 Licensed dealers

The Act which consolidates previous legislation provides for the compulsory licensing of all dealers in securities, and any unlicensed person carrying on such business is liable for imprisonment for up to two years or a fine of up to £500, or both. In order to ensure solvency of dealers before licences are granted deposits or appropriate guarantees are required.

The Department of Trade must be kept in touch by holders of licences with any changes in their addresses and the Department has power to make rules as to the conduct of business of such dealers. Licensed dealers' names are published and the general purpose is to prevent unscrupulous or irresponsible persons from selling shares to the public. Exempted from these provisions are members of the recognized stock exchanges, the Bank of England, any statutory corporation or municipal corporation, any exempted dealer industrial and provident societies, building societies, and any person acting in the capacity of trustee or manager of an authorized unit trust. Not less than once a year the Department of Trade publishes a list of exempted dealers which among others includes the names of all the well-known joint stock banks, merchant banks, trustee savings banks, and insurance companies.

16.12 Building societies and unit trusts

There are also provisions for the control and investigation of building societies and the Department of Trade is empowered to appoint inspectors to investigate the administration of a unit trust scheme if it is in the interests of unit holders so to do and the matter is one of public concern.

In 1982 the building societies established a scheme which will secure up to 90% of investors' capital if a society collapses or suffers severe loss. In

---

* Incorporates amendments in Protection of Depositors Act 1963 now superseded but re-enacted by Banking Act 1979.
† *Ibid.*

practice the main building societies maintain adequate free reserves and liquid funds to provide against unexpected contingencies and accordingly have been granted trustee status by the Chief Registrar of Building Societies.

16.13 Licensed Dealers (Conduct of Business) Rules 1960

As empowered in the Prevention of Fraud (Investments) Act 1958 the Department of Trade has made and published Rules to which licensed dealers must conform. These include the information which a licensed dealer must provide when offering to dispose of or acquire securities, the particulars which must appear on contract notes, and the books, accounts, and documents which must be kept. They also forbid a licensed dealer to make calls on a person with a view to dealing unless requested by the person concerned to make the call or unless that person has done security business with the licensed dealer at least three times during the preceding seven years.

A licensee is precluded from entering into contangos and options unless he/she acts as an agent and the transaction is supported by a corresponding transaction with a member of a recognized stock exchange. He/she must not hold him/herself out in any advertisement or business letter, etc., as dealing in securities under the authority of the Department of Trade or any government department and in all communications and contracts must describe him/herself by the term 'licensed dealer in securities'.

A considerable part of the Rules is also devoted to the requirements which must be met by a licensed dealer when making a takeover offer.

16.2 Protection of depositors

Legislation to protect depositors was incorporated in the Protection of Depositors Act 1963 but this has now been superseded by the more comprehensive Banking Act 1979 which stemmed from the 1973/74 fringe bank crisis and the EEC harmonization of banking law.

16.21 Recognized banks and licensed deposit-takers

In order to be able to accept deposits from the public, institutions must now be licensed to do so by the Bank of England either by being accorded the status of recognized banks or that of licensed deposit-takers. The distinction between the two categories is not intended to reflect judgements as to their credit-worthiness but rather their function, although it is required that a recognized bank must for a reasonable period of time have enjoyed the somewhat indefinable qualities of a high reputation and standing in the financial community. Essentially it must also provide in some depth a wide range of banking services in this country.

16.22 Bank of England supervision and powers

Both recognized banks and licensed deposit taking institutions are subject to the continuing approval, monitoring and supervision of the Bank of England.

Should they be in breach of the standards required the Bank has power to revoke the recognition or licence of such institutions, either immediately or following notice of intention to take such action. In certain circumstances when revocation takes place the Bank may grant the institution a conditional licence lasting for not longer than twelve months, the conditions being such as the Bank considers to be necessary to protect the interests of depositors, for example by restricting the granting of credit or the making of investments by the institution. When giving notice to an institution with regard to proposed action to terminate its deposit-taking authority the Bank may also protect the interests of depositors by making directions to the institution prohibiting it as to disposal of assets and from entering into certain types of transaction etc.

Bodies exempt from the prohibitions of the Act include the National Savings Bank, The Post Office, Building Societies, Friendly Societies, and also members of the Stock Exchange in the course of business as a broker or a jobber.

In the execution of its monitoring role the Bank may require a licensed institution to provide it with information as to the conduct of its business and to produce books and documents. Also, if it appears desirable to do so in the interests of depositors, the Bank may appoint 'one or more competent persons' to investigate and report to it on the affairs of any recognized bank or licensed deposit-taker. An area where the Bank maintains a close watching brief is over a wide field of advertising with particular attention being given to any material which could be regarded in any way as being misleading as a result either of what it contains or what it omits to reveal. Powers are available to the Bank to prohibit the issue of certain types of advertisement.

16.23 Deposit Protection Scheme

The 1979 Banking Act provides for the setting up of a Deposit Protection Scheme which will guarantee depositors repayment of 75% of the amount deposited with recognized banks and licensed deposit-takers up to a maximum of £10,000 in the event of a default. This is clearly aimed at the protection of smaller investors but should not be used as an excuse for lack of discernment as regards to whom one's money should be entrusted. Currency deposits are not included within this protection.

The Scheme will be supported by a Fund based on contributions levied on the recognized banks and licensed deposit-takers on a pro rata basis subject to a minimum and a maximum.

16.3 Insurance Companies Amendment Act 1973

So far as straight sales of units or unit trusts are concerned the investor is protected from misleading advertisement by the Prevention of Fraud (Investments) Act 1958 already referred to, and the door to door selling of units by sales people is strictly forbidden. However, until the passing of the Insurance

Companies Amendment Act 1973 no such inhibition attached to what was in effect the selling of units under the cover of life assurance policies.

Under this Act the Department of Trade has wide powers to make regulations governing the form and contents of advertisements of life assurance policies. It specifically makes the giving of reckless statements, forecasts, etc., which are misleading a punishable offence.

A further safeguard against high pressure selling was the introduction in January 1980, under powers made available by the Insurance Companies Act 1974, of a 'cooling off' period of ten days after the decision to take out unit-linked and other types of long-term policies. All life assurance companies must issue a Statutory Notice to new policy-holders, included in which their attention is drawn to their right to cancel the policy within this period without loss.*

16.4 The City Code on Takeovers and Mergers

The occasion of a takeover bid has at times proved a happy hunting ground for those in a privileged position to enrich themselves, while at the same time less than fair treatment has been meted out to the smaller and weaker shareholder. The City itself has been aware of this and for some time its leading institutions have been trying to lay down a voluntary set of rules in order that justice might be served. From this has evolved *The City Code on Takeovers and Mergers*, which is subject to frequent revision to counter such unacceptable practices as may develop. In an attempt to ensure that the rules are adhered to a Takeover Panel has also been appointed.

16.41 Behaviour of directors

The behaviour of directors is naturally one of the main targets of the Code. Directors are in a position of trust and must always put the interests of shareholders as a whole, together with those of employees and creditors, before those of themselves and their associates. For example, they must not buy shares of a company on the strength of inside knowledge (now a criminal offence under the 1980 Companies Act) that a bid is in the offing. In this context the term associates has a wide meaning and includes, among others, close relatives and financial advisers.

A temptation open to directors in a company making a bid, or while a bid is in contemplation, is to come to a special arrangement at above the bid price with one or two substantial holders of the offeree company in order that victory may be won. The Code now insists that all shareholders of the offeree company shall be treated similarly by the offeror company and no favoured treatment accorded to any influential individual or group.

Another danger to the interests of the rank and file shareholders could be

---

* See Section 1.6 regarding the Policyholders Protection Act 1975.

that the directors of the offeree company might do their utmost to defeat a bid, not because it is not in the best interests of the company but because their own jobs might be in jeopardy. Shareholders, the Code insists, must always be given sufficient evidence, facts, and opinions upon which an adequate judgment may be reached, and any action to frustrate the bid should be approved by shareholders at a properly constituted general meeting.

There must be no recklessness or unwarranted optimism by the directors of either the offeror or the offeree company in making forecasts of profits. Both the company's accountants and its advisers, where these exist, must report on the forecasts in the same document in which they are made. A close watch on forecasts is being kept by the Takeover Panel and should they be missed the parties concerned may be invited to provide the Panel with an explanation.

All documentation addressed to shareholders must be subject to the same standards of care as is required by a prospectus within the meaning of the Companies Act 1985. A further requirement is that all takeover documents or announcements must be lodged with the Panel secretariat at the same time as they are dispatched or made.

16.42 Procedure

The Code has much to say regarding the procedure of the company making the bid which in the first instance should be put to the Board of the offeree company or its advisers. For example, when an offer is made for the whole of the equity share capital of a company or such part of it which if accepted in full would result in voting control, it must not become unconditional unless the offeror company has acquired or agreed to acquire more than 50% of all the votes exercisable at a General Meeting of the offeree company. Offers which are unconditional from the start are not now permitted. Accordingly shareholders who accept what may be an unsatisfactory offer are protected by the refusal of the majority so to accept.

An offer must initially be open for at least twenty-one days after the posting of the offer and, if revised, must be kept open for at least fourteen days from the date of posting written notification of the revision to shareholders. Unless the offer has been declared unconditional an acceptor is entitled to withdraw acceptance even after the expiry of twenty-one days until such time as the offer is declared unconditional. Offers which have become unconditional must be extended for not less than a further fourteen days unless not less than fourteen days prior notice to the contrary has been given by the offeror. However, such notice is not capable of being enforced in a competitive bid situation.

Other than when a competing offer has been declared or has become unconditional, a formal offer may not be withdrawn during its currency except with the permission of the Panel. Another important rule is that should an offeror who has announced his intention to make an offer not proceed with the formal offer within a reasonable time he must be prepared to justify his failure to do so to the Panel. The announcement must not merely have been a ruse to enable shareholdings to have been disposed of at an inflated price. However, an announced offeror need not proceed with his formal offer if a competitor has already posted a higher offer.

When an offer is announced all conditions (including those relating to acceptances, quotations, and any required increase in capital) to which it may be subject must be clearly indicated. In particular where an offer comes within the statutory provisions for possible reference to the Monopolies and Mergers Commission a condition that the offer will be withdrawn if there is a reference must be included. All conditions must be fulfilled or the offer must lapse within twenty-one days of the first closing date or the date the offer becomes or is declared unconditional as to acceptances, whichever is the later.

There are further specific rules to ensure that all shareholders of the offeree company are treated similarly by the offeror company. If the offeror company or any person 'acting in concert'* with the offeror purchases shares in the market or otherwise during the offer period at above the offer price it is required to offer an increased price to all acceptors, such price being not less than the highest price of the shares so acquired during the offer period. Also where the offeror and anyone acting in concert has purchased through the market or otherwise more than 15% of any class of the offeree company's shares during the offer period and within one year prior to its commencement the offer for the shares of that class must, subject to any dispensation granted by the Panel, be made in cash or with a cash alternative at not less than the highest cash price paid for the shares during the offer period and within one year prior to its commencement.

Although technically more than 50% of the votes must be held in order to control a company the Panel regards 30% as conferring effective control. Practical difficulties arise in marshalling the votes of a heterogeneous and sometimes lethargic 70% to oppose a compactly held 30%.) It is accordingly laid down, again subject to any dispensation granted by the Panel, that where 30% of the shares conferring voting rights has been acquired by anyone or by parties acting in concert, by whatever means and over whatever period, an offer must thereupon be made to the remaining shareholders in cash or be accompanied by a cash alternative at the highest cash price paid within the preceding year.

A similar offer must be made where anyone together with parties acting in concert holds not less than 30% but not more than 50% of the voting rights

---

* 'Persons acting in concert' comprise individuals or companies who pursuant to an agreement or understanding (whether formal or informal) actively co-operate through the acquisition by any of them of shares in a company to obtain or consolidate control of that company.

and such person together with parties acting in concert acquires in any perio
of twelve months additional shares in the offeree increasing such percentag
of the voting rights by more than 2%. The Code forbids the acquisition of
30% stake, or where applicable the increase by 2%, if the compulsory offe
then required could only be implemented if such offer would or might c
necessity be dependent on the passing of a resolution at any meeting c
shareholders of the offeror or upon other conditions, consents or arrange
ments.

Where more than one class of equity capital exists an offer must b
extended to all classes on comparable terms. This has particular applicatio
to 'A' ordinary or non-voting shares.

After a bid has been announced the parties to it and their associates are fre
to deal in the market or otherwise at arm's length subject to daily disclosur
to the Panel, the Stock Exchange, and the Press, not later than twelve noon o
the next dealing day of the sales and purchases in the shares of the offeror an
offeree companies. Should the Stock Exchange consider that any 'unusua
dealings' have taken place the matter must be referred to the Panel fc
investigation.

16.43 Panel's power

A weakness of the Code is that it does not carry the force of law. The Panel i:
however, not completely powerless and if it appears that the Code has bee
breached the offenders will be summoned before it to justify their action
Should the Panel find them guilty there is a right to appeal to a separat
Appeals Committee of the Panel. In this event of the original findings bein
upheld the Panel can resort to the following courses of action:

(a) Issue a public reprimand.
(b) Ask the particular association of which the offender is a member to tak
    disciplinary action. The Stock Exchange has agreed to do this followin
    the Panel's findings and also, if necessary, to withhold quotation fro
    any new securities involved in a bid thus strengthening the Panel's han
    against offeror companies unless they are bidding wholly in cash. Th
    Issuing Houses Association has amended its regulations so as to ensur
    that the Panel's findings are accepted as binding on its members.
(c) Refer the matter to the Department of Trade which would examine th
    case under the terms of the Prevention of Fraud (Investments) Act 195
    by which it might revoke either the exemption or licence of a dealer an
    thereby close his/her business.

16.44 Self-discipline

The City institutions maintain that the interests of both companies an
shareholders are best served by this system which is basically one of sel
discipline. They claim that it can be operated by the Panel with great

flexibility and speed in action than could be achieved by Government officials backed by statutory authority. While not everyone agrees with such a view the extension of this principle to broader fields could not unreasonably be regarded as recognizing at least a certain degree of success by the Panel in accomplishing its objectives.

16.5 Council for the Securities Industry

In order to provide a fully comprehensive surveillance of all aspects of security trading and maintain proper standards of behaviour the Bank of England set up the Council for the Securities Industry in the spring of 1978. The Council which is a self-regulatory body relies, like the Takeover Panel, for its authority on the willingness of the various groups, of which the city is comprised, to support it.

The chairman, deputy chairman, and three lay members of the Council are appointed by the Bank of England. Other members include the Takeover Panel's chairman nominees or chairmen representing the clearing banks, accepting and issuing houses, investment and unit trusts, insurance, accounting bodies, the Confederation of British Industry, pension funds, and the Stock Exchange. Assuming the commitment of all these interests to back up the Council's rulings it would appear that life should be difficult if not impossible for any party found guilty of flouting accepted financial ethical standards.

The Takeover Panel, initially at least, constitutes one of the main effective arms of the Council whose role is not intended to bring about dramatic changes overnight. Instead its powers are expected to evolve and grow in areas where the need for varying degrees of supervision and control become evident.

Such an occasion arose in 1980 when the Council responded with considerable alacrity to the notorious 'dawn raids' which took place on the Stock Exchange, whereby substantial holdings were purchased in a number of companies mainly from institutional holders at a price well above the normal market price at that time. The objection to these deals was that they took place very quickly without giving the small investor the opportunity to participate as he was unaware of what was happening until the transactions were completed, and thus the temporarily inflated price was not available to him.

To counter such activity the Council introduced rules* which broadly lay down that if a purchaser wishes to acquire shares carrying more than 5% of the voting rights in a company resulting in his stake being over 15% (but less than 30% when an offer would require to be made to shareholders in terms of the City Code on Takeovers) he must do so by making a partial

---

* These are varied from time to time to counter any undesirable practices which may develop.

offer to each shareholder, which procedure is governed by the City Code o
Takeovers, or alternatively allow time for all shareholders to tender shares t
him. In the latter event the intending purchaser states the number of shares h
wishes to acquire and the maximum price he is prepared to pay. At least seve
days notice must be given *inter alia* in two national newspapers before the da
on which the tender offer closes.

Guidelines have also been issued by the Council as regards the persona
dealings of professional investment managers to ensure that conflict of interes
does not arise or that information obtained in a professional capacity is no
abused. For example, a fund manager might be tempted to buy shares on his
her personal account knowing that the price is likely to be boosted by a larg
purchase on account of his fund. One specific guideline requires the reportin
of all dealings to managers' employers on condition that they are treated i
confidence.

16.6 Bad advice

Many investments are purchased as the result of advice received from stock
brokers, bank managers, and investment counsellors. Inevitably some of thes
purchases will on occasion result in irrecoverable loss and the question may b
asked if the investor has any right of action against such professional advisers

By giving such advice stockbrokers, etc., impliedly promise to take prope
care in so doing. The fact, however, that an investment turns out to be a ba
one does not mean that proper care was not taken in the giving of the advic
There may well have been reasonable grounds for it at that particular time. I
order to obtain compensation an investor must prove negligence on the part c
the adviser, and in practice this can often be very difficult.

As far as bank managers are concerned the case of Woods *v* Martin's Ban
and Another 1958 is of some interest. The Bank was sued *inter alia* on th
grounds of negligent investment advice given by one of its managers. Negli
gence was actually proved in this case. In his findings the judge stated tha
although the manager need not have given the advice, as the result of his s
doing the law imposed on him an obligation to advise with reasonable care an
skill. He continued 'Clearly it (the advice) was not negligent because it turne
out to be wrong. Nor could the manager be negligent because he failed t
exercise some extraordinary skill or care. His only obligation was to exercis
ordinary care and skill which the ordinary bank manager in his position migh
reasonably be expected to possess'. None of the manager's advice 'came withi
measurable distance of being reasonably careful or skilful' and so judgmer
was awarded to the plaintiff.

Typical question

Write short notes on the Prevention of Fraud (Investments) Act 1958 and th
Licensed Dealers (Conduct of Business) Rules 1960.

(The Institute of Bankers, *Principles and Practice of Investmen*

Suggested answer

The Act is aimed directly against those who would attempt to obtain investors' money by unfair means. It provides for the imposition of a prison sentence not exceeding seven years on anyone who consciously or recklessly makes misleading, false, or deceptive statements, promises, or forecasts, or dishonestly conceals material facts in order to induce another person to agree to acquire securities or participate in any other scheme with a view to sharing in profits. It also places a general restriction, again with penalties for transgressors, on the distribution of circulars inviting people to invest money.

A considerable part of the Act is concerned with the licensing of dealers in securities. Apart from various exempted categories, such as members of recognized Stock Exchanges and specifically exempted dealers among which are most of the joint stock banks, merchant banks, and trustee savings banks, no one is allowed to deal in securities without a Department of Trade licence.

The Act also has provisions for the control and investigation of building societies, and the Department of Trade is empowered, where circumstances justify such action, to appoint inspectors to investigate the administration of a unit trust scheme.

In the Act the Department of Trade is given power to make rules as to the conduct of licensed dealers. These are set out in the Licensed Dealers (Conduct of Business) Rules 1960. Among other things the rules are concerned with the information which a licensed dealer must provide when offering to dispose of or acquire securities, impose restrictions on the calling on people with a view to dealing in securities, detail the information which must appear in contract notes, and stipulate the books, accounts, and documents which must be kept. They also lay down certain requirements to be met by licensed dealers when making a takeover offer.

As regards licensed dealers, the Act and Rules were largely concerned to prevent 'share pushing'. However by 1981 many dealers had developed the business of managing small investors' portfolios and, under pressure from the City, the Department of Trade agreed to review the position in order that legislation protecting the small investor against certain malpractices might be introduced.

Additional questions

1 How does the Banking Act 1979 protect the public against being invited to deposit money with unsound financial institutions?
2 Discuss whether or not you consider that a banker could be held liable for negligence if shares bought on his/her advice suffer a substantial fall in price.
   (The Institute of Bankers in Scotland, *Theory and Practice of Investment*)
3 What is the reason for the issuing of 'The City Code on Takeovers and Mergers'? Outline the main rules regarding the behaviour of directors.

4 (a) In what way must forecasts by directors of a company involved in a takeover bid be supported?
   (b) What restrictions are there on takeover offers becoming unconditional?

5 The weakness of the Code is that it does not carry the force of law. Describe the sort of action which may be taken by the Takeover Panel against a party who breaks its rules.

6 Outline the system by means of which it is intended that investment business will be regulated by the end of 1986.

17 The creation of wealth

If any community is to improve its future standard of living it must set aside part of its current income in order to increase its capital resources. It must build up assets such as machines, factories, roads, harbours, airports, etc. These, once completed, will increase income, but during the period of their construction while investment in the economic sense is taking place they necessitate some sacrifice in the form of reduced consumption.

In order that these income-producing assets may be constructed labour is required, and to remunerate this labour and also obtain the necessary materials capital must be provided. The source of this may be the State, which in effect means that the members of the community are being compulsorily required to meet the cost. Alternatively, it may be put up voluntarily by individual members of the community out of their cash surpluses. In a socialist society the former method is employed and in a capitalist society the latter, while in a mixed economy capital is provided from both sources.

17.1 The facilities of the market

For some time now the United Kingdom has had a mixed economy, but there is still a vast amount of industry and commerce which depends largely on private sources for the obtaining of capital with which to finance its development. That these sources can be so readily tapped is due to the joint stock company and to the existence of the Stock Exchange.

17.11 Profitability the measure

It is, of course, far from being the case that any company can ask these non-governmental sources for capital and automatically expect to receive it. New companies when formed are usually of no great size and the shares are owned by a small circle of holders, perhaps all in one family, but all of whom must be convinced that the company is going to be successful before they will subscribe for their shares. So far as existing companies are concerned they will be judged largely on their record and can expect to receive the required cash, if at all, only on terms commensurate with their past performance.

If a company has shown high efficiency and profitability investors will be only too eager to subscribe funds for it in the form of equity capital. Should its performance have been more pedestrian it may be unable to raise fresh equity capital but may be able to obtain the amount required by means of a debenture or loan stock at whatever its market rating may be. However, should its record be dismal, shareholders and others who have already seen money committed to the company turned to poor account are not likely to be willing to subscribe more, probably to go the same way.

There is also, of course, a demand for shares already in existence of those companies which are prospering, and a lack of it for companies which are struggling. The price of the former rise and the latter fall. This in itself aids or restricts the opportunities for raising further cash.

Thus the efficient get money to expand while the inefficient find their businesses contracting and withering away. The market place is where the decision – based on a general consensus of opinion – is taken as to who merits funds being made available to them in order to increase the future wealth of the community.

Naturally mistakes are sometimes made and the inefficient get hold of capital which they dissipate by their ineptitude, or perhaps unforeseeable misfortune strikes at what appeared to be a promising enterprise. Be that as it may it is, by and large, the people who made the mistake in the allocation of these funds who suffer. There is very clearly a strong incentive for 'the market' to make the right allocation.

17.12 Prospect of reward

In order that individuals may be persuaded voluntarily to make their cash surpluses available to others they must be satisfied that it is in their own interests to do so. When providing equity capital for a company it is not sufficient for the subscriber only to be of the opinion that the company will use it profitably. He must also feel confident that the benefits of this profitability will find their way back to him in the not too distant future, probably by way of increasing dividends and an enhanced value for his shares. If there is not a reasonable chance of this happening he will ask himself what point there is of taking the risk which the acquisition of equity shares inevitably entails.

Likewise, an individual will not be enthusiastic about lending money to the Government at a fixed rate of interest if the value of money is rapidly falling owing to inflation. When inflationary conditions exist high rates of interest will be demanded by lenders of money, a proportion of this interest being regarded purely as compensation for the drop in money value.

17.13 Power to the institutions

Much of industry and also the Government itself are to a large extent financed as the result of these voluntary decisions. Private individuals are, of course, one source of these funds. However, owing to high rates of taxes on income, capital gains tax, and capital transfer tax, it is becoming increasingly difficult for individuals to be the owners of huge personal fortunes. At the same time a considerable redistribution of wealth is taking place in favour of the working and lower middle classes. Thus, while there are fewer people with enormous cash surpluses there are more with moderate amounts of cash available over and above what is required for the immediate necessities of life.

One result of this is that the ownership of share capital is swinging away from private individuals to the institutions* such as the insurance companies, pension funds, investment and unit trusts, which together now control huge funds and can if they wish exert considerable influence over a company's affairs.

Through the expansion of the unit trust movement a large number of small investors are helping to swell the pool of capital available for equity investment. There are, however, many more individuals who pay life assurance premiums or make pension fund contributions but who in no way see themselves as providing finance for industry. They are most certainly doing so. The value of their pensions and the sums payable under 'with profits' policies will accordingly be affected by the prosperity or otherwise of the companies in which they have indirectly acquired a stake.

17.2 Government participation

17.21 The need to supervise

Since the Second World War it has been common ground between both major political parties in this country that the economy cannot be left solely to the decision-taking of the private sector. The price of allowing economic forces alone to have the say entailed a cycle between boom and depression, in the latter causing much hardship, particularly in the form of unemployment.

The reason for this cycle was attributed to the relationship between savings and investment, the meaning of the latter in this context being, of course, the creation of capital assets. The ideal situation is where the amount invested, say, in any one year is balanced by an equal amount saved. This absolute state of equilibrium cannot easily be achieved as, for one thing, in a free economic society people act independently and on their own initiative. When an industrialist decides to build a factory his primary financial concern is where he can obtain the necessary funds to do so. His problems are largely limited to his own particular business and his interest in the economy as a whole may be of a very restricted nature. When private individuals save money it is not normally because they wish to provide funds for someone else to invest but because they themselves wish to be better off in future.

Should investment exceed savings this brings about an inflationary state of affairs because the wages, etc., paid to the workers employed on capital projects are not immediately reflected in an increase of consumer goods

---

* The Conservative Government is endeavouring to correct this in the course of privatizing the nationalized industries and also by the proposed introduction of a Personal Equity Plan on 1 January 1987 whereby income tax and capital gains tax concessions will be granted to individuals investing up to £200 a month or £2,400 a year in ordinary shares.

available in the market. There is therefore, temporarily at least, a situation where more money is chasing the same amount of goods, the natural result of which is a rise in prices. This rise in prices usually means that profits are easier to earn and thus there is the incentive for industrialists to keep expanding their activities, with the result that investment keeps ahead of savings during this phase and there is a continual process of inflation feeding on itself.

On the other hand, where savings exceed investment there will be a falling off in the demand for consumer goods that are already being produced and these will therefore accumulate. This, of course, acts as a severe check to industrialists' plans for expansion; investment is curtailed, and many factories will close down and companies go into liquidation as the process of deflation, which also feeds on itself, runs its course.

17.22 Corrective measures

The Government now accepts the responsibility of exerting the appropriate pressures on the economy to avert the two extremes. This it does either by monetary or fiscal means. The former includes the interest rate weapon, for example an increase in interest rates encourages saving and discourages investment, most investment being made with borrowed money. It also involves credit restrictions on banks and hire purchase companies, wage and dividend limitations, etc.

The fiscal powers of the Government are operated through the budget. If there is a budget surplus, i.e. the Government takes in more from the public than it spends, this is deflationary. Such a situation can be created either by increases in taxation or by reduction by the Government of its own expenditure. To stimulate the economy the Government may budget for a deficit and spend more than it collects by way of revenue. Again this may be achieved by the Government easing its demands on the taxpayer or by increasing its own expenditure, for example by expanding its own works programmes.

Taking everything into consideration it can be said that successive governments have been reasonably successful in their control over the economy. There were tremendous advances in the general national prosperity during the period 1945/1970, and poverty on the scale hitherto known has been largely eliminated. Unfortunately the 1970s and the early 1980s with the high prevailing rates of inflation together with increased unemployment, has seen some erosion in living standards.

17.23 More direct involvement

As well as exercising a control over the general economic climate the Government involves itself more directly in industrial affairs. This is not just confined to the nationalized industries such as coal and steel. It also has a considerable direct influence over the private sector.

Subject to frequently changing rules companies have for many years been able to write off their capital investment against their profits before taxation the amount so allowed often showing considerable divergence from the depreciation charged in their annual accounts.

The system until recently widely in force was that of capital allowances which were comprised of two constituents, first year allowances and annual writing-down allowances. In order to encourage investment by easing the financial position around the time of purchase high first year allowances were granted. However first year allowances have largely been phased out, being reduced to nil for expenditure incurred after 31 March 1986, although they are still available in certain regions designated as Enterprise Zones.

Investment incentives are from time to time available in the form of direct cash grants or rates exemption to those regions where it is particularly desired to encourage industry. While the aim of both tax allowances and investment grants is to encourage capital investment there is a vital distinction as to the way in which their respective benefits are bestowed. A tax allowance being a charge against profits reduces a company's tax bill and is of value only to a company which makes profits. It is of no help to a company which is unable to do so. On the other hand an investment grant is a cash payment and benefits the profitable and profitless alike.

In past years Governments have temporarily introduced such measures as a selective employment tax to encourage the transfer of labour from the service to the manufacturing industries or paid a regional employment premium as an incentive to employers to take on labour in the less favoured areas. More recently, tax reliefs have been given to endeavour to stimulate the growth of new trading ventures.

Under the current Business Expansion Scheme an individual may obtain full tax relief by investing up to £40,000 per annum in the shares of new companies or in established companies satisfying certain conditions among which is that they must not be quoted on the Stock Exchange or the USM. Also in order to be eligible the company must carry on a qualifying trade which broadly must come within the ambit of manufacturing, wholesale and retail, and research and development. There are various rules which have to be complied with before the relief can be obtained, an important one being that normally the shares must be held for five years.

Labour Governments have more enthusiasm for direct intervention in industry than do Conservative. In 1975 the Labour administration set up the National Enterprise Board (a successor to the Industrial Reorganization Corporation wound up by their opponents when in office) with a view to extending public ownership into profitable sections of industry. More recently its main functions have been stated as being, first, to provide funds for industrial investment alongside the existing sources of finance in the private sector, second, to promote the rationalization or restructuring of companies or groups in particular sectors of industry, and third, to act as a state holding company for shares in companies which the Government or the Board deemed it appropriate to acquire.

A government agency which would appear to meet with some favour from both parties is the Monopolies and Mergers Commission. The Commission is charged as one of its duties to examine certain proposed company mergers to make sure that they are in the interests of the industry concerned, the country as a whole, and that the consumer does not suffer by too much power being concentrated in a few dominant groups.

Much argument abounds as to the extent to which the Government should concern itself with industrial affairs with some advocating steady progress towards complete control. To enter into debate as to the ideal economic structure is beyond the scope of this book. Suffice to say that in this imperfect world private enterprise, served by the joint stock company and the stock exchanges, has contributed much towards the amazing improvements in the standard of living over the years, not the least of which being those which have accrued since 1945.

Typical question

Since 1945 there have been radical changes in the ownership of the share capital of United Kingdom companies. What have these changes been and what in your view are the reasons for them?

(The Institute of Bankers, *Principles and Practice of Investment*)

Suggested answer

During this period there has been a decrease in the proportion of the share capital of United Kingdom companies owned by private individuals and an increase in that owned by the institutions such as the insurance companies, pension funds, investment and unit trusts. Together these institutions now control enormous funds.

This has been brought about largely by the redistribution of wealth in the country. Owing to high taxation, particularly in the top income brackets, it is difficult for private individuals to accumulate a lot of wealth during their lifetime. Capital gains tax takes its toll and capital transfer tax makes severe inroads into large fortunes either on the occasion of lifetime gifts or on death.

Salaries and wages paid to the lower middle and working classes have greatly increased over this period as the result of which more individuals in this category have been in the position, if they so wished, of being able to allocate part of their income to other than the immediate necessities of life. This has manifested itself in the growth of the unit trust movement. Also more people belong to private pension funds and have taken out life assurance, thus providing these institutions with regular sums to invest.

Owing to tax concessions particularly the life assurance relief available on policies taken out prior to 14 March 1984 many well off people as well as those of more moderate means find it to their advantage to invest part of their surpluses through the medium of life assurance rather than by direct investment in stocks and shares.

Additional questions

1 What part does the Stock Exchange play in providing capital for industry and for the Government? Explain how the market mechanism regulates the demands of government and industry, keeping them within the resources of the common capital pool.
   (The Institute of Bankers in Scotland, *Theory and Practice of Investment*)
2 Why is economic investment necessary? Are there any dangers in it being left solely to private enterprise?
3 What steps might the Government take either to encourage or discourage economic investment generally throughout the country?
4 Outline the function of capital allowances. How do they differ in their application from investment cash grants?

Appendix A

Department for National Savings

Commission charges on purchase or sale of British Government stocks

Purchases
Where the purchase price
(a)   does not exceed £250   £1
(b)   exceeds £250   £1 and a further 50p for every £125 (or part)

Sales
Where the proceeds
(a)   are less than £100   10p for every £10 (or part)
(b)   are £100–£250   £1
(c)   exceed £250   £1 and a further 50p for every £125 (or part)
Value Added Tax is paid by the Department for National Savings.

Appendix B

Ad valorem transfer stamp duty

Consideration	Duty*
Not exceeding £50	...50p
Exceeding £50 but not exceeding £500	...50p for every £50 or part thereof of consideration
Exceeding £500	...£1.00 for every £100 or part thereof of consideration

Ad valorem stamp duty is not payable in the undernoted categories of transfer. A fixed duty of 50p (nominal stamp duty) is payable.

(a) A transfer arising from the appointment of a new trustee of a pre-existing trust, or from the retirement of a trustee.

(b) A transfer as security for a loan, or a re-transfer to the original transferor on repayment of a loan.

(c) A transfer to a beneficiary under a will of a specific legacy of stock, etc.

(d) Transfer of stock, etc., forming part of an intestate's estate to the person entitled to it, not being a transfer in satisfaction or part satisfaction:

    (i) in England and Wales of the sum to which the surviving spouse has a statutory entitlement under an intestacy where the total value of the residuary estate exceeds that sum, or the sum due to the surviving spouse in respect of the value of a life interest which he/she has elected to have redeemed;

    (ii) in Scotland of any of the monetary rights of the surviving spouse under the provisions of Section 8 (1) (a) (ii), Section 8 (1) (b) or Section 9 (1) of the Succession (Scotland) Act, 1964, as amended by the Succession (Scotland) Act 1973, and by Statutory Instrument 1977 No 2110 The Prior Rights of Surviving Spouse (Scotland) Order 1977.

(e) A transfer to a residuary legatee, the stock, etc., forming part of the residue divisible under a will.

(f) A transfer, to a beneficiary under a settlement on distribution of trust funds, of stock, etc., forming the share or part of the share of whatever funds the beneficiary is entitled to under the terms of the settlement.

---

* These rates are to be halved as from 27 October 1986.

(g) A transfer on and in consideration of marriage of stocks, etc., to either party to the marriage or to trustees to be held on the terms of a duly stamped settlement made in consideration of the marriage.

(h) A transfer by the liquidator of a company of stocks, etc., forming part of the assets of the company to the persons who were shareholders, in satisfaction of their rights in a winding-up.

(i) A transfer to a mere nominee of the transferor, where no beneficial interest in the property passes.

Note: Transfers on or after 22 March 1982 in favour of charities are exempt from stamp duty.

Appendix C

Eurobonds

With the lifting of Exchange Control restrictions, United Kingdom residents wishing to broaden their portfolios are free to invest in the Eurobond market which previously was regarded by many investors in this country as shrouded in some degree of mystery. This is a huge international bond market, the borrowers being a vast selection of governments, international institutions, and corporate bodies.

The distinguishing feature of a Eurobond is that it is an issue underwritten by an international syndicate of banks and sold mainly in countries other than the country of the currency in which it is denominated. It differs from a foreign bond which is also international but is primarily underwritten by the institutions in one country, denominated in that country's currency, and largely sold there. A Eurobond could, for example, arise from a Japanese company borrowing in United States dollars or the Australian Government in Deutsch Marks with both bonds being subscribed for on an international basis.

The attraction to the United Kingdom investor of the Eurobond market is that if offers him the opportunity to tie part of his investments to the fortunes of a variety of currencies as opposed to being linked to sterling should he hold, for example, a British Government Stock. The importance of choosing the right currency at the right time is merely stating the obvious.

Eurobonds are all issued in bearer form and the interest coupons are paid without deduction of income or withholding taxes. However, while some bonds known as 'straight bullet' issues are subject to terms similar to United Kingdom gilts in that they have a fixed coupon and a fixed maturity date for the whole issue, there are many carrying a variety of provisions, some of which are unfamiliar to the United Kingdom investor. Ignoring the many individual anomalies which exist, Eurobonds may be in convertible form offering a fixed return together with the option to convert into common stock of the borrowing company; they may have a single or multi-currency option giving investors the right to receive interest or repayment of capital in other than the currency of issue, or the interest rate may be floating with reference to the six months London Inter Bank Offer Rate; they may be issued deeply discounted and paying no interest. A feature of some bonds is that they may be redeemed at any time at a fixed price above par by the borrower while others are redeemable in instalments by annual drawings.

Although many Eurobonds are quoted on the Stock Exchange dealing is largely conducted in the 'secondary market' by telephone call between the market makers, i.e. international banks and brokers in the major financial centres. The market makers do not charge commission but make a profit on the difference between their buying and selling prices.

The private United Kingdom investor is unlikely to be encouraged to approach these market makers direct unless he/she has at least £50,000 to invest and he/she will require to initiate the transactions through a bank or stockbroker who will charge a discretionary commission for their services. Bonds are issued in denominations of, for example, US $1,000 or Dm 1,000 with the minimum transaction expected to be in the region of £5,000 in value.

Interest on a fixed rate bond is usually paid once a year and the price quoted for the capital value of the bond excludes the accrued interest which is calculated separately in establishing the total cost. A United Kingdom investor may arrange for the bonds to be held on his/her behalf by a bank in this country and should this be the case the bank, although receiving the interest gross, will normally deduct tax at basic rate before passing the interest on to him/her.

Investing in Eurobonds demands a more sophisticated approach than is required when purchasing United Kingdom fixed interest securities and the investor daunted by this may prefer to use the medium of a Eurobond fund thus obtaining the benefit of both currency spread and professional management.

Appendix D

The holding company

Frequently in the news for one reason or another are industrial holding companies. These are companies which may do no actual trading on their own account, all or a large part of their activities being carried out through subsidiaries, a subsidiary being a company in which it has a controlling interest. A holding company may also have sub-subsidiaries as the result of a subsidiary in turn itself having a subsidiary. Owing to the diversity of their activities, often in quite unrelated fields, industrial holding companies are sometimes referred to as conglomerates.

This type of organization makes available, when required, top class management, finance, and some of the economies of large scale administration to smaller companies which are unsuitable for complete amalgamation under one management. On the other hand the subsidiaries can be left to carry on much of their day to day business without interference from the parent company. They can, therefore, avoid some of the problems incurred in the control of huge enterprises.

Although the wide interests of holding companies provide the benefits of diversification it is in practice sometimes found that the group's progress may be held back by one or two of its members which get into difficulties. The problem is to get all the subsidiaries operating profitably at the same time.

Subsidiary companies may be wholly or partly owned. If the latter there will be minority shareholders whose rights must be given some consideration. There may be a natural tendency to regard the group as being more important than the subsidiary with the result that the lot of minority shareholders in a subsidiary is not always altogether a happy one. The holding company in its annual report must, of course, under the Companies Act reveal much vital information regarding its subsidiaries (see Section 4.4).

The Government has at times been rather dubious about the desirability of the continued growth of industrial holding companies. In the Board of Trade handbook on mergers published in 1969 it would appear that it regarded them as to some extent impeding efficiency by blocking mergers, horizontal or vertical, between companies in the same line of business. Also, although the holding company structure does not directly affect competition it may do so indirectly by making them unresponsive to it in some of the spheres in which they operate, particularly so far as the big groups are concerned.

Glossary

Amortization Providing for the repayment of debt by the allocation of sums for this purpose, such as by the setting-up of a sinking fund. Alternatively, setting aside a portion of income to replace the loss of capital involved in the holding of a wasting asset.

Arbitrage The practice of transacting in securities quoted in two different markets, buying in one and selling in the other to take advantage of small price anomalies and thereby bringing them into line.

Authorized capital The amount of the nominal capital of a company authorized in the Memorandum of Association and on which capital stamp duty is paid.

Averaging The buying of the same share at different prices thus establishing an average cost of each share in the total holding. Sometimes resorted to when the price of the share has fallen below that of the initial purchase.

Bear In the narrow sense applied to someone who sells shares he does not hold with a view to buying them back at a lower price. More broadly it covers anyone who is pessimistic regarding the movement of share prices.

Bear squeeze Pressure being put on bears to deliver. May have the effect of forcing prices up.

Bed and breakfast The selling of a stock one day and buying it back on the following day, the object of the exercise being to establish an allowable loss for capital gains tax purposes. Such transactions usually take place just before the end of the fiscal year and are relatively inexpensive in terms of commission and price differential.

Best The instruction to a broker to buy or sell a share at the best price obtainable.

Blue chip An equity share of the highest calibre.

Bull In the narrow sense applied to someone who buys shares not with the intention of paying for them but with a view to selling them at a higher price before being required to do so. Broadly it covers anyone who is optimistic regarding the movement of share prices.

Bulldog bonds The name given to bonds denominated in sterling when foreign governments and other foreign borrowers raise money by issuing bonds in the United Kingdom.

Call The further instalment(s) which may require to be paid on shares not fully paid at the time of issue. Often encountered during the first few months in the lives of new issues.

Closing Buying or selling to close a bargain in securities entered into in the same account.

Dealer An alternative name for a jobber.

Drawn bond A bond in respect of which notice has been given that it has been selected for redemption.

Drop-lock stock A loan issued at a floating rate of interest with the protective provision for the lender that if interest rates fall to a certain level the loan then becomes a fixed interest stock, i.e. the rate can fall no further.

Easier Descriptive term applied to the market when prices are lower.

Even The state of a jobber or other operator when he has no position either one way or another in a share.

Ex All Means that share is being dealt in without transactions carrying with them any of the entitlements about to be bestowed on holders of the shares, e.g. dividends, bonus or rights issues.

Firm Term describing market when prices are steady.

Flotation The marketing of a new issue.

Free Market A market in which it is easy to deal in substantial quantities of a stock.

Funding Replacing short-term borrowing by the raising of long-term or permanent capital.

The Funds   British Government and British Government guaranteed stocks.

House   Familiar term to describe the Stock Exchange premises in London.

Issued capital   The amount of the authorized capital of a company which has been issued.

Joint book   The partial merging of the businesses of two jobbers for the purpose of dealing in partnership in a particular share or shares.

Kaffirs   The colloquial name given to the shares of South African mining companies.

Limit   A restriction on an order given to a stockbroker to the effect that he/she should not buy above or sell below a certain price.

Limited market   Description of the market in a particular share where it is difficult to deal in any great quantity of the shares.

Lock up   Term applied to shares which should be purchased and held for the long term rather than with the view to making an early profit.

Market capitalization   The value put on a company by the stockmarket calculated by multiplying the number of shares in issue by their market price.

Mixer   A high yielding stock which is in itself not outstandingly attractive when measured by normal investment standards but which is included in a portfolio in order to increase the average yield. It is sometimes known as a 'yieldsweetener'.

Money stocks   Short dated gilt-edged stocks used as alternatives to deposits.

Money transactions   Those which are transacted for cash as distinct from the account.

Name   An alternative term to describe the ticket issued by the buying broker.

NPV   No par value.

Preferential form   Companies making new issues to the public usually send their own shareholders a special application form often distinguishable by its pink colour in order to give them preferential treatment if they wish to apply for the new stock or shares.

Put through   When a broker receives an order from different clients to buy and sell the same security he is allowed to match one against the other. In order to carry out the transaction fairly to both sides he puts the business through a jobber who in the circumstances limits his turn to a trifling amount.

Rigging the market   The process of causing prices either to rise or fall by artificial means.

Shake out   A sharp market setback as the result of selling by bulls.

Shunters   A name given to brokers who transact business on an arbitrage basis with different exchanges.

Spread   The difference between a market maker's or jobber's buying and selling prices.

Stale bull   A speculator who has bought a stock in anticipation of a rise in price which fails to take place.

Stop loss   The instruction to a broker immediately to sell a share should it drop to a certain price.

Tap stock   Usually applies to a new government stock a large quantity of which in the first place been taken up by government departments. The market is aware that the stock is available at a certain price and absorbs it over a period of time. Tap stocks are used by the authorities to 'manage' the gilt-edged market.

Waiter   The name given to attendants on the Stock Exchange, London originating from the time when business was carried out in a coffee house.

Index